The
Key to
the Kalevala

The Key to the Kalevala

PEKKA ERVAST

Translation by Tapio Joensuu
Edited by John Major Jenkins

BLUE DOLPHIN PUBLISHING

The Key to the Kalevala by Pekka Ervast
English translation © 1996 of
Kalevalan Avain (1916) by Pekka Ervast
Translation / Editing team: Tapio Joensuu, Kempele & Oulu,
Kesarannantie 1, FIM-70420 Kuopio, Finland
John Major Jenkins, Louisville, Colorado

We gratefully acknowledge the great good fortune of being granted permission
by Eino Friberg to use his 1988 English translation of the Kalevala. Friberg's
translation is unparalleled for its poetic beauty and its accurate presentation
of the original meter of ancient Finnish poetry.

Published by Blue Dolphin Publishing, Inc.
P.O. Box 8, Nevada City, CA 95959
Orders: 1-800-643-0765
http://www.bluedolphinpublishing.com

ISBN: 1-57733-021-8

Library of Congress Cataloging-in-Publication Data

Ervast, Pekka.
    [Kalevalan avain. English]
    The key to the Kalevala / Pekka Ervast : translation by Tapio Joensuu :
edited by John Major Jenkins.
        p.   cm.
    Includes bibliographical references.
    ISBN 1-57733-021-8
    1. Kalevala.   2. Mythology, Finno-Ugrian.   I. Jenkins, John Major.
II. Title.
PH325.E713 1998
894'.54111—dc21   98-34846
                                                                        CIP
Cover art: Reo Lintera

The title page illustration is from a decorative band found in East Götaland
(western Sweden). It depicts the events of Kalevala Runo 5, in which
Väinämöinen unknowingly hooks Aino on his fishing line (Haavio 1952:207).

Printed in the United States of America

10   9   8   7   6   5   4   3   2   1

Table of Contents

Introduction   vii

Foreword   xxxi

I. The Kalevala as a Holy Book
1. What is the Kalevala?   3
2. The Kalevala as a Holy Book   8
3. The Key to the Kalevala   12

II. The Mysterious Knowledge of the Kalevala
The Theological, Anthropological, and Soteriological Key
4. Was the Ancient Finnish Religion Animistic?   19
5. Humans or Gods?   24
6. The Holy Trinity   28
7. The Virgin Birth   32
8. The Act of Creation   36
9. The Act of Salvation   45
10. The Lemminkäinen-Forces   50
11. Lemminkäinen-Christ   56
12. The Ilmarinen-Forces   60
13. Ilmarinen, Fire and Iron   65
14. Ilmarinen and the Sampo   74
15. Reincarnation   79
16. In the Cottages of Tuonela   85
17. The Playing of Väinämöinen   93

III. The Kalevala's Inner Ethic
Occult-Psychological or Practical-Soteriological Key

18. The Way of Knowledge	105
19. Joukahainen	110
20. Aino	115
21. Lemminkäinen	121
22. Ilmarinen	126
23. The Works for Wages	130
24. The Swan of Tuonela	135
25. Pohjola's Wedding	140
26. The Golden Maid	145
27. The Younger Sister of Pohja's Maid	153
28. The Sword of the Spirit	161
29. The Boat Journey	167
30. The Playing of the Kantele	174
31. The Theft of the Sampo	182
32. Final Doubts	187
33. The Last Battle	193

IV. The Kalevala's Magic
The Occult-Historical Key

34. What is Meant Here By Magic	203
35. Then and Now: Two Human Types	210
36. Atlantean Magic in the Kalevala	217
37. At the Change of Ages	223
38. Väinämöinen and Aino	227
39. Marjatta	233
40. Marjatta's Son and Väinämöinen	239

V. Väinämöinen's Return
The National-Occult Key

41. Väinämöinen and the Nation of Finland	247
Notes	255
Bibliography	266
Additional Reading	269

Introduction

to the English Translation of
The Key to the Kalevala

inland's Heritage and National Independence. Finland, a small country so far north that it touches the Arctic Circle, preserves a fascinating ancient history and offers a unique and profound wisdom to the world. Bordered by Russia to the east, the Gulf of Finland in the south, the Gulf of Bothnia in the west, and Norway to the north, Finland is the least populated country in the Fenno-Scandia region. Up until the beginning of this century it was a little recognized Grand Duchy of czarist Russia, devoid of a national identity. However, as political events unfolded in the early 1900s, this proved to be more a matter of definition than truth. For Finns, a cohesive cultural identity was close to their hearts for thousands of years. The primary tradition that served as the glue of Finnish cultural identity was the ancient oral tradition, preserved and propagated by storytellers and shamans. They passed down starlore and wisdom-teachings in stories called runes, or runos, from the earliest times. And today, Finland is a modern nation that stands on its own, having courageously defied the Russian Revolution by declaring itself independent in 1917.

The Origins of Finnish Mythology. In the early 1800s, Finnish folklore, much of it containing ancient memories and esoteric, cosmological

knowledge, was collected into a massive epic called the Kalevala. In-
trepid folklorists working out of the universities at Turku and Helsinki,
most notably the esteemed compiler of the Kalevala, Elias Lönnrot,
struggled to record the runo stories before the oral tradition succumbed
to the pressures of modernization. These passionate folklorists, known as
rune collectors, travelled the outbacks of Finland, on foot and on snow
skis, talking with the peasants, encouraging them to speak the ancient
stories. And what a wealth of wisdom was stored in their heads! One
man, Arhippa Perttunen of Latvajärvi, could recite over four thousand
lines of poetry. These stories migrated from village to village with pack
peddlers and merchants, and thus variant versions of even the best
known myths could be found. The great challenge for Lönnrot (a
physician by profession) was to compile and cross-compare his comprehensive data bank of Finnish poetry, and, with accuracy and insight,
weave it together into a unified whole. By 1849, fifty runos consisting of
almost 23,000 lines of poetry were published. This collected work, the
Kalevala, based very closely on the original poems collected in the field,
is the Finn's national treasure, their national epic that enshrines for them
the greatness of their people's past. The Kalevala contains the songs and
stories of the ancient Finnish people, and has been translated in its
entirety into over thirty languages.

But where did these stories come from? More to the point, who are
the Finns, and where did they come from? In answering this, we can get
a sense for the unique contribution of the Kalevala, elucidating an
important mystical dimension of the human spirit. Significantly, Pekka
Ervast's insightful interpretation of the Kalevala almost single-handedly
reveals to us long lost artifacts of wisdom from our collective past.

According to one theory based upon archaeological and linguistic
studies, Finnish people migrated to Finland in the remote past from
northern Central Asia, originating from beyond the Ural Mountains,
perhaps even as far east as China and Tibet (Lehtinen 1986). According
to a different theory, one supported by German scholars, before the
Germanic tribes swept into Europe, people of the Finnish family originally inhabited large areas, from central Europe eastward to the Ural
Mountains. Afterward, parts of the Finnish group moved northward
where they remain today. In any case, the Finns speak a Finno-Ugric
language unrelated to the Indo-European language that is shared only by
Estonians and scattered remnants of shamanistic societies in northwest-

ern Russia and Siberia. The beliefs and traditions brought to Finland by the early Finns are comparable to the traditions of Asian shamanism today. The Bear Ceremony, for example, is described in the Kalevala (Runo 46) and its rituals are quite similar to the Bear Cult of the Ainu people, who live in the islands north of Japan. Although the distance between Finland and Japan is great, the indigenous circumpolar cultures, including those in Alaska and Canada, share many basic beliefs and myths. The Finns, the Ainu, the Ostyaks, the Votyaks, the Tlingit, and others—these are the people of the midnight sun, so close to the North Pole that in summer the day never ends and in winter the darkness is deep and long.

Finland has a long standing reputation as a bizarre, even dangerous backland filled with rune singers, wizards, and peasant shamans. Sailors in the late Middle Ages used to fear the incantations of the Finn, for he was reputed to be capable of invoking storms to sink the ships of enemies. Other legends attribute clairvoyance and conjuring skills to the Finnish magician.

Finnish mythology is rooted in shamanism. Seers and shamans undertook visionary journeys and they used the reindeer as their animal spirit companion. The Pole Star was for them a high god, and the nearby Big Dipper was the Great Bear, Otava, a god and animal spirit that was greatly revered. The ancient Finns were animists. They worshipped nature and believed that everything had an inner spirit, that everything, even stones and trees, contained consciousness. They also worshipped the deceased, and shamans often visited graves to communicate with departed spirits.

When the rune singers chanted the ancient wisdom, they could facilitate healings. For example, as evidenced in Runo 9, blood flow from a wound could be staunched by reciting the Origin of Iron rune, to invoke magical power over the blood. It was believed that by recalling a thing's origin, you could invoke power over it. Since the source of blood clotting is hemoglobin, and clotting depends upon iron in the blood, a quite profound knowledge of the body is hidden in this rune. Apparently, these ancient shamans utilized healing modalities that we are just beginning to understand.

Chanting was a shamanistic technique to tune the mind into distant times and places. When shaman-singers chanted the Origin of the World rune, they believed they could actually travel in spirit, in mind, back to the birth of the world. Chanting, as for Hindu and Buddhist mystics, was a way to alter the mind, and in so doing they could summon the invisible powers that create and sustain the world. After all, the words "invocation" and "vocalize" both refer to voice and language. The ancient singers mastered a complex mystical art that survives today only in remote places like Tuva in Central Asia. In Finland, this sacred vocation was fairly common up until the end of the nineteenth century.

As a result of their intimacy with the darkness, living as they do so close to the North Pole, the Finns accumulated a rich treasure trove of starlore, and some of their ancient cosmo-conceptions are preserved in the Kalevala. For example, the Sampo is a central object of mystery in the Kalevala, and it was envisioned as a spinning mill. On one level, it is a magic mill capable of grinding out food, money, or whatever you wish. But on an astronomical level, it is a cosmological image of the spinning World Axis centered upon the Pole Star which, in the Far North, is almost straight overhead. Furthermore, the Sampo's "many ciphered cover" is a metaphor for the bright, twinkling stars of the night sky. Beyond these cosmological associations, however, Pekka Ervast finds a deeper, esoteric meaning for the Sampo, one involving humanity's spiritual growth to wholeness.

The Sampo, as the World Axis, is very similar to the World Tree found in Asian mythologies. This parallel is well-known and recognized in the academic literature, suggesting trade links between Finland and Central Asia in ancient times, or perhaps a common homeland. Studies have compared Finnish and Vedic mythology, although, unfortunately, many of them are available only in Finnish. In *The Key to the Kalevala*, Ervast notes the major parallels between Finnish and Vedic thought, and the reader can consult the Additional Reading section for other sources. The major conception shared between Finnish and Vedic-Hindu cosmology is the idea that the world was born from an egg. In Chapters 7 and 8, Ervast explores this event as it appears in the Kalevala. The Viking or Eddic mythology also espouses this doctrine, and makes us wonder about possible connections between the Finns and the Germanic groups that arrived in Norway, Sweden, and Denmark beginning around A.D. 500.

There are some similarities between Viking lore and Finnish myth and culture. Significantly, some of the Kalevala stories seem to be fragmented historical accounts of invading Vikings arriving in the Finnish fringelands, bringing with them warrior gods to oust the matrifocal, shamanistic ideologies of the early Finns. In general, however, as described above, the Finns are more closely related to Central Asia than to the Germanic groups to the west, and a tenacious hold on their true identities is testified to by the preservation of their non-Germanic language up to this day. In its beauty and vision, the rich and large corpus of Finnish poetry, taken as a whole, challenges the best in oral traditions around the world, suggesting the Finn's had access to a wellspring of wisdom deeper and more wide-reaching than what may have been handed to them from the Vikings.

The Finnish people were probably in Finland since 500 B.C., though there may have been successive waves of migrations from the east. The Lappish people to the north of Finland, according to archaeological accounts, may be descended from the same people who lived in the region over 7,000 years ago. Despite the threat posed by modernization, Finland preserved its shamanistic outlook longer than, for example, Denmark, Sweden, or Norway, because of its remoteness. Christianization, and the eradication of indigenous beliefs, came late to Finland. In fact, one might say that it never completely happened, as even today there are shamans in northern Finland and Lapland.

For most of this century, European countries have had little interest in Finland's contribution to human knowledge, and less so in America. In fact, despite a growing fascination among English speakers with Celtic mythology, ancient civilizations, mystical teachings, and shamanism, Finnish mythology has remained largely unexplored. And yet it provides a window into all of these topics. Now it is time that the insights into human spiritual unfolding that are encoded into Finnish mythology are shared with the English-speaking West. The work of Pekka Ervast is the perfect place to begin, and we feel that *The Key to the Kalevala* is destined to be considered a classic.

Pekka Ervast: Finnish Mystic, Spiritualist, and Teacher. Pekka Ervast was a writer, occultist, and Christian mystic, born December 26, 1875, in Finland. Since early childhood, Ervast searched honestly for truth, but was often beset by the conflicts between idealism and reality that are so common in all walks of life. His passion was to find the real purpose of our existence and how we should live honestly, but he did not find any answers within the religious standards of his day. Finland was largely Christian in the late 1800s, but Ervast was not satisfied with Christian doctrines as they were being taught in church or even in theological seminaries.

During his early years at the University of Helsinki, Ervast became acquainted with Theosophy. At this time, the works of Theosophist Madame H. P. Blavatsky were becoming known, and eventually Ervast himself became one of two translators of Blavatsky's classic Theosophical work, *The Secret Doctrine*, into Finnish. Theosophy is a system of philosophical thought based upon spiritual insights into the esoteric, occult history of the human race and its developmental laws. The principles of Theosophy opened up the avenue of inquiry that Ervast had been seeking. Furthermore, through reading the work of the great Russian writer Leo Tolstoy, Ervast discovered esoteric Christianity. The path of the Sermon on the Mount became his path, and its cosmic law became his law.

Ervast has testified that when he began to follow the esoteric teachings of Jesus, he entered an occult path wherein totally new worlds opened up for him. He became a spiritualist who travelled to realms of knowledge where he could understand the meaning of life and could see human beings not just as living single lives, but as reincarnating spiritual beings, journeying through the school of this world in order to learn and evolve spiritually.

Ervast's insights into the fundamental laws of life transcended his interest in esoteric Christianity. Being an avid student of world mythology and religion, and having great respect for his own culture's myths and legends, he specialized in interpreting his National Epic according to Theosophical principles. As a result, in *The Key to the Kalevala*, Ervast offers a most comprehensive and inspired mystical reading of the deeply profound esoteric knowledge sequestered within the Kalevala. He saw the Kalevala as a Holy Book, a sacred text that could be unlocked with the key of Theosophy.

The literary works of Pekka Ervast consist of over a hundred volumes, many of them full-length books. Very few of Ervast's works, however, are available in English. Fortunately, Ervast was fluent in several languages, including English, and he translated at least two of his books into English: *H.P.B.: Four Episodes from the Life of the Sphinx of the*

XIXth Century (1933) and *The Sermon on the Mount* (1983), both published by the London Theosophical Publishing House. A collection of Ervast's lectures from 1929 called *Astral Schools* was translated and published by the Rosicrucian Literary Society of Finland in 1979. His book *The Esoteric School of Jesus* recently has been translated and is to be published by Blue Dolphin Publishers. Ervast's contribution to revealing the esoteric contents of the Kalevala was discussed by Finnish scholar Juha Pentikäinen in his book *Kalevala Mythology*. Pentikäinen discusses *The Key to the Kalevala* and emphasizes Ervast's unique interpretation of the Kalevala as a Holy Book.

Ervast was an avid reader and studied the writings of the best minds of his day, including Rudolf Steiner and H. P. Blavatsky. In Helsinki in 1912, Rudolf Steiner, the founder of the Anthroposophy movement, gave a talk on national epics with special focus on the Kalevala, an event Ervast mentions in his Foreword to *The Key to the Kalevala*. In 1920 Ervast founded the Rosicrucian organization in Finland, the Ruusu-Risti, which still exists today and is engaged in publishing, teaching, and translating projects. Ervast labored to bring opportunities for spiritual learning and growth to his people, and the seeds he planted continue to bear fruit.

Ervast's life was not long—he died at age 58—but his collected writings, lectures, and books are all the more valuable for this reason. During the course of his Theosophical and Rosicrucian activities between 1895 and 1934, he gave over thirteen hundred public lectures, most of them without written notes. His skills and presence as a speaker verged on the mystical, and it was often noted that he seemed to answer questions from his audience before they had been asked. He could speak clearly and intelligibly to the most profound questions of philosophy, religion, and Theosophy. His message reached truth seekers in all sectors of society, and his books can be found in tens of thousands of Finnish homes. Through his life's work in service to the truth, he remains a most important spiritual teacher to his nation. Moreover, Ervast's diverse and profound teachings as a "seer from the North" are timeless and universal, intended for all of humanity.

The 50 Runos of the Kalevala. In reading *The Key to the Kalevala*, the reader will become intimate with three important characters from the Kalevala.

These are the primary Kalevala-heroes, and we will see all of their faults, mistakes, and triumphs exposed. Väinämöinen is the ancient sage, the primal First Shaman, master word-weaver, musician, incantation slinger, and wise psychopomp to the rest of our heroes. Lemminkäinen is a young, wayward romantic. As the Arctic Don Juan, he always gets into new adventures, being led around by his impetuous nature. Finally, there is Ilmarinen, the primeval smithy. Diligent and industrious, Ilmarinen is the master architecton of the stellar dome, for he is the one who forged the magic Sampo. These are the three main characters of the Kalevala, and the principles they represent will be deciphered by Ervast, but there are several other players who we must also get acquainted with.

Louhi, the "sparse-toothed dame of Northland," is the enemy of the Kalevala-heroes and she rules the benighted land of the Far North called Pohjola. A central episode in the Kalevala, Runo 42, tells of her hoarding the Sampo, and the quest of the three heroes to retrieve it. The beautiful maiden of Pohjola, daughter of Louhi, is the young woman who the heroes set out, one by one, to win the hand of. Joukahainen is an upstart youth who challenges Väinämöinen to a singing contest, and suffers the consequences of his foolhardiness. Aino is the girl promised to Väinä-möinen, but she rebuffs him and accidentally drowns. Marjatta, thought to be a late addition to Finnish poetry and a reflection of the Virgin Mary, is the mother of the newborn boy who is destined to take Väinämöinen's place as spiritual ruler. Her child represents the arrival of Christianity in Finland, and her story is told in the last runo of the Kalevala, Runo 50.

There are others, and their roles will become clear as we summarize the fifty runos below. Though Ervast's interpretation does not draw from all of the runos, the following summary is intended to give the reader a sense of the entire scope of the Kalevala epic. Before we begin, a pronunciation guide to commonly used Finnish words and names is provided below. The most common names are given phonetically as well as according to the guidelines in Webster's Encyclopedic Unabridged Dictionary of the English Language. Less common Finnish words are simply given phonetically.

Väinämöinen. Væinæmainen. Phonetic: Vi-nuh-moy-nen.
Väi- (rhymes with *why*), nä- (rhymes with *luh*),
möi- (rhymes with *boy*), nen (rhymes with *pen*). No accent.
He is also sometimes called Väino.

Lemminkäinen. Lemminkæinen. Lemmin-ki-nen.
Lemmin- (sounds like the fruit *lemon*), käi- (rhymes with *why*),
nen (rhymes with *pen*). No accent.

Ilmarinen. Ilmurinen. Il-mah-*ree*-nen. Il- (sounds like *ill*),
ma- (sounds like *muh*), ri- (rhymes with *see*), nen (rhymes with *pen*).
The italics indicate the accent is on the third syllable.

Kalevala. Kulevulu. *Kah*-leh-vah-luh. Soft accent on first syllable.

Kaleva. Kulevu. Kah-leh-vah.

Louhi. *Low*-hee.

Aino. Uino. *I*-no.

Marjatta. Muryuttu. Mar-*yah*-tah.

Tapio. Tupio. Tah-pee-oh

Tuoni. T*wah*-nee

Tuonela. T*wah*-neh-lah

Manala. Munulu. *Mah*-nah-lah

Joukahainen. Yo-kuh-hi-nen

Pohjola. Poh-yo-*lah*. Also called Pohja.

Sampo. *Sahm*-poh. (Sahm rhymes with bomb; poh rhymes with go.)

Ilmatar. *Il*-mah-tar

Kyllikki. *Kyoo*-luh-kee

Ahti. *Ah*-tee

Kaukomieli. Kow-kuh-mee-lee

Untamo. *Oon*-tah-mo

Kalervo. Kah-*lair*-vo

Hiisi. *Hee*-see

Kullervo. Koo-*lair*-vo

Ukko. *Oo*-ko

Patoinen Poika. Pah-*toy*-nen *Poy*-kah

Sampsa Pellervoinen. *Sahmp*-sah Peller-*voy*-nen

Jumala. Yoo-mah-lah

Suomi. Swoh-mee.

Otava. Oh-tah-vah.

Runo 1. Prelude. Lönnrot, after the style of the rune singers, tells of his
yearning to sing the poems of his people. The intimate relationship
between poetry and nature is portrayed with images of nature singing; for
example, the frost sings verses and the raindrops recite poems. *Creation
and the Birth of Väinämöinen.* Ilmatar, the virgin of the air, leaves the

loneliness of the sky and moves down to the sea, where the wind impregnates her. She drifts upon the waters for ages, pregnant but unable to give birth. A magical bird flies by and lays several eggs on Ilmatar's upraised knee. As the bird sits brooding in the nest, the heat makes Ilmatar jerk her knee, and the eggs begin to change. One breaks open and the lower half becomes the earth, the upper part becomes the sky, the yolk becomes the sun, and the white becomes the moon. During her thirty-year pregnancy with Väinämöinen, Ilmatar sculpts the cliffs, coves, beaches, meadows, forests, and other features of the earth and sea. Finally, Väinämöinen forces his way out of his mother and floats on the sea for another eight years before he reaches land.

Runo 2. *The Sowing.* After many years on the barren land, Väinämöinen asks Sampsa Pellervoinen to plant trees. They all thrive, except for the oak tree. So they find another oak acorn-seed and, for fertilizer, Tursas the sea gnome burns some hay that was gathered by five water nymphs. The acorn is planted and the oak that grows from it is so huge that it blocks out the sun. No one is able to chop it down. Finally, a tiny man emerges from the sea, who suddenly grows into a giant. He confidently fells the tree with three blows of his axe. The sun shines again. Now there are trees, grass, and berries, but as yet no barley. A little titmouse tells Väinämöinen that no barley will grow until he cuts down the trees. Väinämöinen does this, leaving only one birch tree standing. An eagle flies by and is so pleased that Väinämöinen left a tree to perch on that he strikes fire to burn the fallen trees. Väinämöinen plants seeds in the fresh mulch that results and barley begins to grow. This runo ends with the happy springtime song of the cuckoo.

Runo 3. *The Singing Contest.* Joukahainen, a young man from Lapland, hears of Väinämöinen's growing fame and challenges him to a singing duel. Väinämöinen easily outdoes him, and, angry at being bested, Joukahainen threatens Väinämöinen. However, Väinämöinen sings him, that is, magically enchants him, deep into a paralyzing swamp. Väinämöinen releases him when he promises him his sister Aino as a bride. Later, Aino is upset when she learns of this, but her mother is pleased at the prospect of Väinämöinen entering the family.

Runo 4. *Aino*. Väinämöinen happens upon Aino gathering sauna switches and tells her to adorn herself only for him. Aino, upset, tears off her adornments and races home, weeping. Her mother attempts to console her, but Aino is distraught at the idea of becoming an old man's bride. She goes to the sea to bathe, and is drawn into the water where she drowns.

Runo 5. *Aino Lost Again*. Grieving for Aino, Väinämöinen asks Untamo, the spirit of sleep, to tell him where the sea maidens live. He sets out to fish for them and catches a steelhead. However, it slips back into the water and transforms into Aino, who taunts Väinämöinen for having lost her a second time. He goes home heavy-hearted, where his mother Ilmatar advises him to travel to the north and court one of the daughters of Pohjola.

Runo 6. *Joukahainen's Revenge*. Crossing a river while journeying to Pohjola, Väinämöinen is ambushed and shot with an arrow by Jouka-hainen. His horse dead, Väinämöinen falls into the water and is swept out to sea, drifting at the mercy of the waves. Joukahainen goes home, exultant.

Runo 7. *Väinämöinen's Rescue and Promise*. After drifting for several days, Väinämöinen is rescued by an eagle, the same eagle who was thankful for the tree Väinämöinen had left for birds to perch on. The eagle leaves him in Pohjola, where a maid finds him weeping on the shore. Louhi, the mistress of Pohjola, takes him in and entertains him well, but Väinä-möinen is anxious to return home. She gives him a horse to ride home on, and promises her daughter in marriage to the man who can forge the Sampo for her. Väinämöinen rides away, thinking he will get Ilmarinen to forge the Sampo, because he could not do it himself. As he departs, Louhi warns him not to look up on his way home.

Runo 8. *Väinämöinen's Wound*. However, riding home through the meadows, he does look up and sees the lovely maid of Pohjola, sitting on the rainbow, weaving. He tries to persuade her to come down and ride with him, but she refuses. They debate the merits of the single life versus the married life, and finally she makes him do a number of absurd tasks—tying an egg into a knot, splitting a horse hair with a dull knife, peeling birch bark from a stone, and so on. He does all of these, but the last task is to build a boat from the splinters of her spindle. While working three days on the boat, during a moment of inattention Väinämöinen gashes his knee with his axe. He tries to staunch the blood flow by singing magic verses, but he forgets the Origin of Iron blood-stopping rune. In pain, he sleighs off to find someone who knows it. Finally, he finds an old man who claims to have stopped worse bleeding.

Runo 9. *The Healing of Väinämöinen.* The old man also has forgotten some parts of the magical incantation, but Väinämöinen reminds him and he completes the healing spell. The flow of blood from Väinämöinen's knee stops, and the old man's son goes into the woods to gather ointments and salves to heal the wound. Väinämöinen recovers, and warns listeners not to take up impossible tasks on a dare, and acquiesce to the will of Jumala.

Runo 10. *The Forging of the Sampo.* Väinämöinen returns home and urges Ilmarinen to journey to Pohjola and forge the Sampo. Ilmarinen suspiciously hesitates and then refuses, but Väinämöinen tricks him by singing into existence an enchanting fir tree with the Great Bear (the Big Dipper) on its branches and the moon on its crown. Climbing up the tree, Ilmarinen is caught up in a whirlwind and is magically delivered to distant Pohjola. There, he is well received, and sets to work forging the Sampo. When it is done, the mistress of Pohjola locks it up in Pohjola's Stone Mountain. Ilmarinen then asks for the beautiful daughter's hand to wed, but is rebuffed. Dejected, he goes home and tells Väinämöinen that the Sampo has been built and is busy grinding things for Pohjola.

Runo 11. *The Exploits of Lemminkäinen.* Lemminkäinen is very handsome, but is also a rascal filled with wanderlust. He hears of Kyllikki, a beautiful island maiden much sought after, but disdainful of all her suitors. Lemminkäinen goes to the island to woo her, but she refuses him too, so he carries her away by force. Resisting at first, she finally gives in to his love when he promises to never go off to war. Likewise, she promises to never go to parties without him or gossip around the village. Lemminkäinen's mother is delighted with her new daughter-in-law.

Runo 12. *The Broken Promise.* While Lemminkäinen is away gathering fish, Kyllikki goes to a dance with her girlfriends in the village. Lemminkäinen finds out, and, his trust shattered, he angrily prepares to go off to war. His mother begs him not to go, protesting that he shall surely be killed. He leaves his hairbrush, saying that if he dies it will bleed. Arriving in Pohjola some time later, he defeats and scatters all the Pohjola wizards in a singing contest with them. He ignores only Wet-Hat, an ugly cow herder, believing him to be beneath contempt. Angered, Wet-Hat runs to the river where he lies in wait to get his revenge on Lemminkäinen.

Runo 13. *The Elk Chase.* Lemminkäinen asks Louhi for one of her daughters. She refuses, saying he must first catch the Elk of Hiisi (the Devil) in a ski chase. He goes to a ski maker but is secretly given skis made of bad wood. After an exciting chase through the snow filled forests, Lemminkäinen does momentarily catch the elk, but it bolts and he breaks his skis trying to catch it.

Runo 14. *The Death of Lemminkäinen.* With the help of hunters' charms and forest spirits, Lemminkäinen finally catches the elk. The mistress then demands other deeds of him, including shooting the swan in the river of Tuonela (the river of death). On his way along the river, Wet-Hat, lying in wait, shoots Lemminkäinen with a poison arrow. Forgetting the charm to cure the poison, Lemminkäinen staggers, dying, and is thrown into the river after being chopped to pieces by the son of Tuoni.

Runo 15. *Lemminkäinen's Resurrection.* Back at home, Lemminkäinen's mother and Kyllikki frightfully watch the brush begin to bleed. Rushing off to Pohjola to find her son, Lemminkäinen's mother is led astray by Louhi, but the sun tells her what happened. She asks Ilmarinen to make a rake for her, retrieves all of Lemminkäinen's body parts by raking through the river, and fits him together with the help of special charms. To restore him to life, she sends a bee to get an ointment from the

Creator's storehouse. Lemminkäinen revives and they return home together.

Runo 16. *Väinämöinen's Journey to Tuonela*. Väinämöinen sends Sampsa Pellervoinen, the little man, to fetch wood for a boat he is building. Using a solid oak log that Sampsa found for him, he begins singing the boat into shape, but forgets one of the magic verses. He decides to journey to Tuonela, the land of the dead, to find it. Arriving at the bank of death's river, Väinämöinen pretends to have died in order to get in, but Tuoni's clever daughter will not ferry him across until he tells her the truth. He eventually tells her why he came and she boats him across. On the other side, the old man of Tuonela tries to trap Väinämöinen, but he narrowly escapes back to the land of the living and warns everyone never to attempt to go to Tuonela.

Runo 17. *In the Belly of Vipunen*. Väinämöinen decides to seek his missing magic verse from Antero Vipunen, a famous giant shaman who has been asleep for ages. Surviving dangerous trials along the way, Väinämöinen finds him and, prying open the giant's mouth, Väinämöinen falls in. Once in Vipunen's belly, Väinämöinen torments the giant shaman so much that he sings out all his magical charms for Väinämöinen to hear. Väinämöinen escapes with the verse he was looking for, returns home, and completes his boat.

Runo 18. *The Rival Suitors*. Väinämöinen sets sail for Pohjola to court the daughter of Northland. However, Ilmarinen finds out and knows she was promised to him, so he also sets out. Seeing them both arriving, Louhi, the mistress of Pohjola, advises her daughter to choose Väinämöinen. But she wants the forger of the Sampo, and tells Väinämöinen as much.

Runo 19. *Ilmarinen's Labors and Betrothal*. Ilmarinen arrives at the house of Pohjola and is given a number of tasks to perform in order to win Pohjola's beautiful daughter. With the help of the maiden, he is able to accomplish all of the tasks. He claims his bride and is told to protect her. Väinämöinen leaves, disheartened, and advises older men to never compete with a younger man for a beautiful maiden.

Runos 20-25. These six runos tell of the wedding preparations, the wedding feast, instructions for the bride and groom, and the wedding party's homecoming.

Runos 26-30. These five runos tell of Lemminkäinen's various adventures in Pohjola, his singing competition with a sorcerer, his escapes from danger, a visit to the island of women, and his arduous journey across the frozen tundra.

Runos 31-36. These six runos tell of the misfit boy, Kullervo, and his struggle to find his real family. Kullervo is believed to be an orphan, the sole survivor of a clan who were completely slaughtered. As he grows up he cannot find his place in life and experiences one misfortune after another. His life seems hexed. In anger he kills Ilmarinen's bride and flees. In his fugitive wanderings he finds his true family who had, in fact, escaped being killed, but then he unknowingly sleeps with his sister. Discovering this and becoming miserable to the core and completely hopeless, he finally commits suicide by falling on his own sword.

Runo 37. *Ilmarinen's Gold and Silver Bride.* Grieving for his wife, Ilmarinen forges for himself a gold and silver woman. But he cannot bring her to life, and, distraught, tries to pawn her off on Väinämöinen. But Väinämöinen tells him to melt her down to make useful tools, and the rune ends with Väinämöinen urging people not to worship images, nor seek happiness in gold and silver.

Runo 38. *Ilmarinen's Second Courtship.* Ilmarinen returns to Pohjola to court another Northland maiden, but Louhi expresses regret at having given him her first daughter. She reprimands him and vows to not repeat her mistake. Ilmarinen asks the girl to come with him, and when she refuses, he carries her off by force. Sleighing southward through the woods, she treats him to a tongue-lashing for being so foolish, and spends the night at an Inn laughing with another man while Ilmarinen sleeps. The next morning, disgusted with such behavior, Ilmarinen changes her into a seagull and continues on his way home. He meets Väinämöinen and tells him what he did to the girl, and that the people of Pohjola are prospering with the Sampo in their possession.

Runo 39. *The Voyage to Pohjola*. Väinämöinen urges Ilmarinen to come with him to Pohjola to retrieve the Sampo. They start out by land, but find a boat and take to the river. Väinämöinen calls into existence men and women to help them row, but they are incapable of helping until Ilmarinen himself begins to row. On the way along the shore they come upon Lemminkäinen, who jumps in with gusto, happy to be along for the adventure.

Runo 40. *In the Rapids*. The Kalevala-heroes come to a rapids and get stuck on the back of a huge pike. Lemminkäinen and Ilmarinen fail to get them free, and finally Väinämöinen kills the pike and they make their way to an island. They cook the pike and eat it, leaving only a pile of bones. With them, Väinämöinen makes a kantele, a five-stringed harp. All of the others try to play it, but none can.

Runo 41. *Väinämöinen's Playing*. As Väinämöinen plays his new musical instrument, all of nature flocks to listen and rejoices. The animals, the birds, the fish, even the nature spirits weep for joy. Väinämöinen, overcome with emotion, cries, and his tears roll into the sea. A duck goes to fetch them and finds they have turned into pearls.

Runo 42. *The Theft of the Sampo*. The Kalevala-heroes arrive in Pohjola. Väinämöinen first asks Louhi if she will share the Sampo, but she refuses. He then says they will have to take it by force. Louhi, angered at such a threat, calls her warriors to attack the interlopers. However, Väinämöinen acts quickly, plays his kantele and enchants all of Pohjola into a sleep-trance. Going to the copper mountain where the Sampo is kept, the three heroes work to free the Sampo. Väinämöinen opens the doors with a chant, Ilmarinen butters the hinges to keep them from squeaking, and Lemminkäinen is chosen to heave the Sampo up. But its roots go down to a depth of nine fathoms, and Lemminkäinen fails to lift the Sampo out by himself. He enlists the aid of Pohjola's strong ox, and plows the roots up. Heaving the Sampo free, they carry it to their boat and depart. The third day on the water, Lemminkäinen decides they need some cheer and, against Väinämöinen's wishes, begins to sing. His bellowing startles a crane who flies off, squawking, to awaken Louhi from her trance back in Pohjola. Realizing that the Sons of Kaleva have taken the Sampo, she conjures up a storm, some fog, and

calls upon a sea monster to kill the men of Kalevala. Though the
Kalevala-heroes overcome these obstacles, the kantele is blown overboard and lost.

Runo 43. *The Battle For the Sampo.* Louhi gathers an army and sails in
pursuit of the Sampo. Väinämöinen, seeing they cannot outrun her,
conjures up a reef that wrecks Louhi's ship. Louhi transforms herself into
a huge bird, takes her warriors onto her wings and tail, and alights on the
mast of the heroes' ship. Väinämöinen smashes her claws with the
rudder, and her warriors fall into the sea. Louhi is able to claw at the
Sampo and it falls overboard, shattering into pieces. Väinämöinen sees a
good omen in the pieces of the Sampo spreading over the ocean, some of
them reaching land. As Louhi departs she threatens to lock up the sun
and moon and send diseases to Kalevala. Väinämöinen goes ashore,
gathers and sows the pieces of the Sampo, and prays to Jumala to protect
the people of Kaleva.

Runo 44. *The New Kantele.* Feeling that it is time to make music again,
Väinämöinen asks Ilmarinen to forge a rake to search for the pike-bone
harp. Unable to find it, Väinämöinen makes a new kantele from
birchwood, with tuning pegs of oak and strings made from the hair of a
beautiful forest maiden. Again, all of nature responds to his playing with
joy.

Runo 45. *The Plague.* Hearing the rejoicing, Louhi bitterly determines to
send a plague to the people of Kaleva. The origins of illness are invoked
and cast over the land. In response, Väinämöinen warms up the healing
sauna and with powerful incantations he sends the aches and pains away
to Pain Mountain, thus curing his people.

Runo 46. *The Bear Ceremony.* Hearing that Kaleva's people have escaped
her plague, Louhi sends a bear to wreak havoc on their cattle. Väinämöinen kills the bear and they hold the customary ceremony and feast.
The bear is treated with respect, as a welcome guest, and the feast is in his
honor. Väinämöinen sings of the birth of the bear, friend and brother to
man, born not on earth but upon the shoulders of Otava, the Big Dipper.
Väinämöinen plays and sings, delighting the gathering, and concludes
with an eloquent prayer for the welfare of the land of Kaleva.

Runo 47. *Louhi Steals the Sun and Moon.* The sun and moon come and sit in the limbs of a tree to listen to Väinämöinen's enchanting music. Louhi quickly steals them, hiding the sun in a steel mountain and the moon in a rock cave. Next, she steals fire from the people of Kaleva. Ukko, the highest god, wonders why it is dark, and strikes up a new spark of fire from which he plans to make a new sun and moon. But the maid who was appointed to nurse the spark drops it, and it falls to earth. Väinämöinen and Ilmarinen set out to find it. Ilmatar, Väinämöinen's mother, tells them that the fire, after causing great damage, fell into Lake Alue, causing the lake to boil over its banks. The firespark is swallowed by a whitefish, which agonizes until it is swallowed by a sea trout, which in turn is swallowed by a pike. Väinämöinen and Ilmarinen weave a fiber net to catch the pike, but are unsuccessful.

Runo 48. *The Capture of Fire.* Väinämöinen has a huge net woven of fine linen, with which they succeed in catching the pike. As the Son of Day cleans the fish, the precious firespark pops out, badly singes Väinä-möinen's beard, scorches Ilmarinen's face and hands, and burns down half the forests in the country. Väinämöinen finally captures the fire and returns it to its proper place in the hearths of Kalevala. Ilmarinen heals his hands with the help of a frost charm.

Runo 49. *The Release of the Sun and Moon.* Ilmarinen forges a new sun and moon, but they give no light. Väinämöinen casts lots (a divination technique), and learns where the sun and moon are hidden. He goes to Pohjola, defeats the guards, but cannot open the locks and bars which imprison the sun and moon. He returns home and has Ilmarinen forge special tools to open the locks. While Ilmarinen is working at his forge, Louhi visits in the shape of a hawk and asks what he is making. He replies that he is forging an iron collar to chain up the mistress of Pohjola. Feeling she is doomed, Louhi releases the sun and moon. Changing herself into a dove, she flies back to Ilmarinen and tells him that the sun and moon are once again in the sky, where they belong.

Runo 50. *Marjatta and Farewell to Väinämöinen.* Marjatta the virgin lived a chaste and pure youth in the house of her father. One day while herding sheep she swallows a lingonberry and magically becomes pregnant.

When the time comes to give birth, she is shunned by her family and goes off to a stable where she gives birth to a son. She keeps him away from other people, but must bring him to the old man Virokannas so that he can be christened. Väinämöinen is called upon to question her, determine who the father is, and decide whether the boy should live or die. Väinämöinen decides that since he was conceived from a berry of the earth, he should be planted in the earth, that is, left to die in the forest. But then the one-month-old boy begins to speak, and accuses Väinämöinen of false judgment. Angry and ashamed, but recognizing that his successor has come, Väinämöinen sings himself a boat and sails away. As he departs, he says that a time will come when his people will need him again, and he leaves behind his kantele and his songs for his people.

And so ends the epic. A close study of the Kalevala and its internal structure reveals that Elias Lönnrot very carefully ordered the poems such that themes appear in pairs and triplets. There are, of course, the three primary Kalevala-heroes who represent a trinity of forces. A dyadic relationship between Pohjola and the land of Kalevala occurs throughout the epic, which Ervast recognizes as the battle between the forces of darkness and light. Drawing upon this dynamic polarity, the Kalevala epic moves through three major phases. Runos 1-19 describe cosmogenesis and provide an introduction to how reciprocal relations between Pohjola and Kalevala, including the practice of exogamy, were established. Runos 20-36 go into detail regarding the courtship and marriage rituals intended to define and maintain those relations. Runos 37-50 describe the resolution of the forces of Pohjola and Kalevala, and the dawn of a new world order.

With its cohesive storyline, weaving together characters and events into a related whole, the Kalevala is a masterpiece of suspense, drama, and poetic beauty. It contains information about mundane Finnish traditions, such as the wedding ceremony, but is also filled with incantations, magic, and ancient spells. In fact, the word "rune," though now commonly used as the word for a Celtic divination glyph, is really an old Gothic word meaning spell or incantation. This is why the Kalevala chapters are called runes, or runos.

The runos of the Kalevala are like treasure chests filled with gems that operate on many levels of meaning simultaneously. As Ervast shows, a seemingly natural event, such as Ilmarinen's betrothal, echoes with deep, spiritual implications. In reading the Kalevala out loud, one can get a sense of being a rune singer, and, like the rune singers of old, one may even slip into a trance every now and then, tuning into the deep, mystical wellspring from which Finnish myth originates. The original meter of the Kalevala (the trochaic tetrameter) is identical to the one used by Longfellow in his epic poem *Hiawatha*. In fact, it has been shown that Longfellow based his famous poem—the meter as well as much of its content—on the Kalevala (Moyne 1963). The Kalevala meter is pleasing to hear, and the rune singers sang at public meetings and festivals for hours and hours until all the beer was drunk and their runo stores were emptied.

Pekka Ervast was something of a runo wizard, and was certainly Finland's greatest and most insightful Kalevala commentator. He unlocked the stores of the Kalevala's inner knowledge, and the key he used was, as he says, Theosophy, but his own ability to tune into the secret content of the Kalevala elevates his interpretations above all others.

Pekka Ervast's Key to the Kalevala. Before delving into the outline of Ervast's *Key*, I would like to say a few things about this translation and the organization of the notes and comments.

The translation of this book was an international labor of love. Fine-tuning the translation began in 1995 and continued for over a year. Everyone involved in this project was committed to seeing it manifest, convinced that its time had come. With care and attention we worked to produce a translation that was accurate to Ervast's intended meaning. For Kalevala passages, we had the great good fortune of being granted permission by Eino Friberg to use his 1988 English translation of the Kalevala. Although other complete English translations of the Finnish National Epic have appeared, in 1888 (Crawford), 1907 (Kirby), 1963 (Magoun), and 1989 (Bosley), Friberg's translation is unparalleled for its poetic beauty and its accurate preservation of the original meter of ancient Finnish poetry. The Kalevala can truly be a pleasure to read, and we feel that Friberg's generous contribution to this project adds a great deal to its aesthetic appeal.

Sources and Kalevala citations are collected as end notes, which are numbered according to the five parts. Other notes fall into three categories: comments by Ervast, comments by the translator, and comments by the editor. Most of these are also collected with the end notes. However, comments immediately pertinent to the text appear as footnotes at the bottom of the page.

The Key to the Kalevala is divided into five parts with a total of forty-one chapters. The first part offers a general introduction to the Kalevala and the then-current (circa 1916) academic understanding of it. Ervast, as an independent thinker and spiritualist, emphasizes that his approach is completely different than the academic approach. He sees the Kalevala as a Holy Book, a repository of ancient knowledge and a guidebook for those on the spiritual path. He ends the first part by revealing the "key" to understanding the Kalevala from this esoteric viewpoint: Theosophy. In Chapter 3, Ervast himself summarizes how Theosophy will be used to interpret the Kalevala, writing that "we will shed some of the light provided by the Theosophical 'wisdom of the ages' onto certain rune stories to show that the Kalevala's intellectual and spiritual background is comparable to that found in other Holy Books; we will examine the Kalevala's theology, the story of creation, its understanding of life and death and so forth."

In Part II (Chapters 4-17), we learn that the three primary characters—Väinämöinen, Ilmarinen, and Lemminkäinen—represent divine evolutionary forces. They correspond to will, intellect, and emotion. Their various adventures in the Kalevala illustrate the unique accomplishments and pitfalls that these aspects of humanness encounter while they grow and unfold within the individual and within humanity as a whole. Ervast insightfully draws from specific episodes in the Kalevala to illustrate his interpretations.

In Part III (Chapters 18-33), Ervast explains the Kalevala's inner teaching concerning human development, advising us to seek truth through initiation. The ancient mystic sages of Finland and Asia are called upon as prototypes for this goal. Ervast goes into greater detail in this section regarding the three forces of spiritual evolution within the human psyche. Ervast sees a "way of knowledge" in the Kalevala, exemplified by the ancient seers and sages of Finnish culture.

Concepts such as "works for wages" are introduced. This concept, as an example, involves three trials that are set for the truth-seekers Ilmarinen and Lemminkäinen to accomplish. Here, again, with great insight, Ervast draws from specific episodes in the Kalevala. These "works" or trials symbolize the psychological and spiritual lessons that Ilmarinen, as the representative of intellectual development, must "accomplish" before getting his "wages." His wages are none other than an initiation with his higher self, symbolized by the maiden of Pohjola. In other words, Ilmarinen—the intellect—must work hard to achieve a certain level of preparedness before he can receive an initiation into higher teachings. Ilmarinen's journey of spiritual development is found step by step throughout the epic Kalevala poem.

Likewise, Lemminkäinen must overcome obstacles unique to his growth as symbol of the emotional force within humanity. But he fails in his vain efforts, is murdered, and is ultimately resurrected through the love of his mother. His emotional lesson is one of total selflessness, self-surrender and, ultimately, redemption and rebirth. Ervast is quick to point out the similarity of this episode with Christ's resurrection and, more significantly, with the Egyptian legend of the resurrection of Osiris. While many of these processes are known and understood in Theosophical thought, the way that the Kalevala illustrates specific lessons and pitfalls is fascinating, and Ervast has a sharp eye for the Kalevala's esoteric content.

The final discussion in Part III involves the Sampo, which symbolizes the completed spiritual body. The journey undertaken by the three heroes to Pohjola, where the Sampo is kept hidden away, represents the final step in their growth to wholeness. Thus, the three evolutionary forces within humanity work together harmoniously to accomplish the final goal, that of retrieving the magical Sampo that had been appropriated by the forces of darkness led by Louhi. In so doing, the completely unified spiritual body—the light body—can fully manifest. Ultimately, a plot twist that occurs during the final sea fight for the Sampo reveals a deeper spiritual meaning that Ervast does not avoid explaining.

Having revealed the deepest esoteric meaning of the final battle over the Sampo, in Part IV (Chapters 34-40) Ervast switches gears to explore the esoteric background of Finnish magic. Finnish culture is rooted in shamanism. This section contains material from K. S. Lencqvist's classic dissertation on Finnish and Lappish magic, never before available in English. After quoting from and summarizing Lencqvist's work, Ervast explains the role of the three Kalevala-heroes as Atlantean teachers, devoted to passing wisdom to the new human type at the "change of ages." Here Ervast explains the Theosophical doctrine of seven root races of humanity and compares the inner nature of the Atlantean human with the modern (Aryan) human. Moreover, he describes the different methods that were/are used to teach these two different root races. Chapters 37-40 very engagingly describe the intimate relationship between Väinämöinen (the ancient sage), the little maiden Aino (who represents the dawning of the Aryan root race), Marjatta, and Marjatta's son, who is Väinämöinen's successor as World Age ruler.

Finally, in Part V (Chapter 41) Väinämöinen is identified as Finland's national *genii*, or tutelary deity. Ervast discusses the role of the Finnish people in bringing about global evolution, and the obligation of each nation to manifest its own special contribution. Here we sense some amount of nationalistic pride that was prevalent when Ervast was writing, which is a strong characteristic of the Finnish people. This section also contains some strikingly prophetic remarks about what was likely to happen in Europe in the coming years. Given that Ervast's book was originally published in Finland in 1916, on the eve of Finland's graduation to statehood, we might suspect that it therefore embodies something of the spirit of progressive, forward-moving thought that accompanied that era of cultural transformation.

In summary, Ervast masterfully interprets the deeper meaning hidden within the Finnish Kalevala according to Theosophical principles. Some passages are quite complex and challenging, for Ervast did not shy away from formalizing his insights into a point by point system. Many other explanations are very straightforward and accessible, for Ervast was first a speaker and teacher. One even finds the occasional humorous aside. For example, one passage relates the proverb which advises the truth-seeker not to awaken sleeping bears. Ervast adds, "especially with a stick."

As Ervast was foremost a speaker and teacher, *The Key to the Kalevala* should be read with this in mind. The personal characterization in his writing, often posing rhetorical questions or illustrating a point with hypothetical examples, should give the reader a sense of Ervast's unique voice and speaking style. One can thus be present to Ervast's spirit and his fervent desire to convey the secret teachings of his precious Kalevala to the world. Ervast was blessed with the gifts to accomplish this goal, and continuing interest in Ervast's works, now reaching to the Americas, testifies to his authority and valuable insights.

It is unfortunate for all of humankind that Ervast lived and worked in such a restricted linguistic area and within such a small, isolated country, for he was well versed in all great religions and in the mythologies of many cultures. In our thoughts he should be recognized as a universal humanist living in truth and love, a messenger of light and a bearer of blessings.

Talked with Pekka

Now this editing is finished
I am tired, my duty ended
Learned the magic of old Finland
Heard the chanting, talked with Pekka
Though the sentences all were backwards
Flipped around and somewhat awkward
I worked together with the doctor
To unkink them, lead them straightways
So that singers in our times
Magic makers in my land
Might grow wiser having listened
To the runo wizards' wisdom
Theosophical expressions
Insights of the Far North's teacher

John Major Jenkins
Lafayette, Colorado
December 26, 1997

Foreword

THIS BOOK VALUES AND DEFENDS everything in the Kalevala that the great majority of modern civilization thinks is nonsense: its fairy tales, miracles, exaggerations and irregularities. The reader will quickly discover that I find a deeper meaning in all of these things.

I am of little standing in comparison to the scholars who have already studied and interpreted the Kalevala. I would not have dared to engage in this work unless I was convinced that, ultimately, the real meaning of the Kalevala has escaped detection in scholarly circles.

I do not wish to claim that my own understanding of the deeper meaning of the Kalevala is thorough and unerring. My comprehension is undoubtedly both imperfect and subject to correction, but when properly understood my interpretations open up new directions for further investigation. In consideration of other works along these lines, such as H. P. Blavatsky's references in *The Secret Doctrine*, a journal article called "Kalevala, the National Epic of the Finns" (Lucifer, Vol. III, 1888), M. Ramstedt's (a.k.a. Martti Humu's) booklet *Kalevalan sisäinen perintö* (*The Inner Testament of the Kalevala*)—which is an instructive overview— Herman Hellner's *Kalevala ett teosofisk diktvärk* (*Kalevala, A Theosophical Epic*, Teosofisk Tidskrift, 1904) and Rudolf Steiner's Helsinki lecture of April 9th, 1912, called "Das Wesen nationaler Epen mit speziellem Hinweis auf Kalevala" ("The Nature of National Epics With Special Emphasis on the Kalevala"), printed in manuscript the same year, I take the liberty to hope that my present study will to some extent be accepted with the forgiving goodwill generally given to first attempts. If fate allows, in the future I hope to explore more deeply these interesting aspects of Finnish occultism. In the present work, only a preliminary outline of this subject can be offered.

As the Kalevala says:

Ei sanat salahan joua,	Knowledge cannot stay concealed,
Eikä luottehet lovehen,	Hidden in some secret burrow;
Mahti ei joua maan rakohon,	Words of wisdom never vanish,
Vaikka mahtajat menevät.	Though the wise men pass away.[1]

Sammatti, Finland
August 1916
Pekka Ervast

PART I

The Kalevala
as a Holy Book

*"Without the help of symbology
(with its seven departments, of which the moderns know nothing)
no ancient Scripture can ever be correctly understood.
Symbology must be studied from every one of its aspects,
for each nation had its own particular methods of expression."*
—H. P. Blavatsky[1]

What Is the Kalevala?

I N THIS BOOK, we will answer the question "what is the Kalevala" in a way that is probably strange and new for most readers. Shortly, we will introduce ideas about the origin and intrinsic value of the Kalevala that will surprise both scholars and laymen. Thereafter, as the book proceeds we will consistently explain and defend our views, and deliver them for judgment to the kind reader. We may succeed in convincing the reader of the veracity of these ideas, or he may continue to wonder and even disapprove of our extremely curious perspective.

Before we give our own answer to the question of what the Kalevala is, we want to briefly summarize for the reader what the conventional views of the Kalevala are in our land as well as the attitude of scholars who have approached its study.

The great Elias Lönnrot, who "dreamed the Kalevala out," believed that our ancestors, the ancient Permians, left their mark in the Kalevala. From the rune stories of the Kalevala arose a lively picture of the Finnish people's past, their religion, traditions, struggles, ideals and heroes. Lönnrot's vision strongly influenced other scholars and, both in Finland and abroad, they began to see the Kalevala as a valid source for investigating the history of Finnish culture. The Kalevala soon spread the fame of Finnish people around the civilized world so that everyone could see that there, in the Far North, a small nation exists in the backwoods that has an epic history unlike any other. "What an epic people," they whispered in foreign lands, "what an amazing history! A people of sages and heroes!"

This enormous enthusiasm awoke Finland from a dream that had lasted centuries. Finns now felt unified because they had a great common past and a substantial record of it. It was natural that this religious and poetic awakening was followed by another wake up call, involving the movement towards nationalization and the language program of Snellman. The Finnish people thus learned about themselves and established their place in the modern world. The prophetic words of czar Alexander the First had come true: the Finnish nation had risen as a nation among nations.

And now we live in another time. Enthusiasm has weakened. The Kalevala is no more what it was. It is certainly still considered a national epic and it is read in schools, but in scholarly circles it has lost its value as a source of historical data. The old Permian civilization is no longer found in the Kalevala. To scholars, the hope of Lönnrot was just a dream of Finland's great Elias. The Kalevala thus does not speak of any real Golden Age; the Kalevala is just an epic. It tells of the lucky dreams our people once had, and about a summerland that lived in our ancestors' imaginations. It only suggests, perhaps, how a powerful, immortal spirit of muse has always been natural for Finns.

Our scientific investigators base their modern opinions on the fact that the Kalevala is just a collection of stories, not a continuous epic preserved in the collective memory. The ancient singers celebrated the heroic deeds of Väinämöinen, Ilmarinen and Lemminkäinen in numerous variations in different regions. In one era a singer reports one version and elsewhere you hear a slightly different version. With tireless enthusiasm Elias Lönnrot travelled around the song-fields of Karelia and collected the rune-songs, gathering verses from here and there. He was the first who assembled the runes into a complete whole. What scholars before him—Porthan, Lencqvist, Ganander, Becker, Topelius the Elder and others—had accomplished, was basically just preliminary work. After Lönnrot, new field-collections were undertaken and his manuscripts and notes were carefully analyzed. Consequently, we now have a clear and comprehensive understanding of Lönnrot's Kalevala. Lönnrot himself was the last of the great rune-singers. He was so thoroughly immersed in the Kalevala's spirit that he accomplished what none other had yet been able to: he created a continuous epic narrative from scattered pieces of poetry. He embodied the Finnish spirit to the extent that he—in Eino Leino's words—was "the spirit of Finland that emerged into national consciousness during that time."[2] This is why the Kalevala was his work although he was not the author of the runes.

A detailed investigation also reveals that the different runes of the Kalevala are not all of the same age. Some are pagan, while others are from the period of Christianization; for example, the last poem—the 50th—is certainly Christian. For this reason it is impossible to fully regard the Kalevala as a historical record of the remote past. Of course we do see aspects of early Finnish life, especially elements from these peoples' religious or "superstitious-poetic" beliefs, but these do not reflect an undiluted pagan age; rather, they belong to the transitional period between paganism and Christianity. In this way, what we admire in the Kalevala is considered by academia to be, as professor Kaarle Krohn says, "poetically veiled Christianity."[3]

An argument recently put forth claims that the Kalevala is not really uniquely Finnish, and that its contents were borrowed from Germanic traditions. From the west, heroes and kings came to Finland, so the argument goes, bringing with them songs about their past, and then composed more runes about themselves. It is thus erroneously thought that Finnish myth is of foreign origin, that the Kalevala-heroes were Vikings and did not spring from the heart of our people.

These are some of the ideas presently in vogue in academic circles. If they are really true, then Lönnrot's vision was, in a sense, mistaken. His work would then simply be a beautiful composition and the national significance of the Kalevala would be a kind of sentimental anachronism. It played its role in awakening us in the last century and now it can be shelved with other ancient texts.

What would the real students of the Kalevala and friends of Finland say to this? What would happen to their glorious visions of the ancient Finnish culture, and their hopes for Finland's future? Their collective heart would lament: "Who now will heal our wounds? Is there anyone who will create the new faith?"

And now comes our turn to have our say. Now, we who see deeper meaning in the Kalevala, we who hear what it has to say about Väinämöinen, can speak loudly and proclaim, if only to soothe our own heart: "Be at peace! Nothing has been lost because nothing has yet been found. Not even scholars have finished their search. There are discoveries to come which will refute today's conclusions. But what of them! The real worth of the Kalevala lies elsewhere. Its real importance is found in its own secret content."

When we now move to present our curious new ideas about the Kalevala, and in consideration of the wounds inflicted on the national heart by misguided investigation, we can rightfully ask: Is *a man* needed to heal them? Cannot the Kalevala itself serve as doctor? Is it not possible to find a cure for the disease from the place where the disease itself was discovered? If the Kalevala, when scientifically analyzed, denies us our national dreams, perhaps when analyzed by other methods the Kalevala reveals a truth beyond those dreams! Perhaps the Kalevala is a completely different kind of book than scientists have allowed. Perhaps it is in the same category of books in world literature that are considered to be holy. Let's think about this a little. If the Kalevala, as we know it today, existed in the pagan age, what value would the Finnish people have given it? Wouldn't the people have seen, as reflected in a mirror, themselves—their best tendencies and most eternal selves? Would they not have sought in the Kalevala consolation and advice, rejoicing for the heart, and peace for the conscience? Undoubtedly. For the ancient Finnish people, the Kalevala would have been a most valuable treasure, the holy inheritance of the ancestors. The Kalevala would have been like a Bible, a Holy Book.

And if it was like that then, why can't we have the same viewpoint today? Why can't we approach the Kalevala as a Holy Book? Why shouldn't we study it knowing it is not an ordinary book?

To compare, the historical veracity of the New Testament is claimed by many to be quite vague. Some have even questioned the very existence of Jesus. But has this diminished the New Testament's spiritual power? Has it thrown all Christendom into desperate confusion? Not at all. Christian Faith is not shaken by this. Faith upholds Jesus because the New Testament witnesses his deeds. And how does the New Testament witness to and defend his life? Because it is a living book. The best cure for confusion is to read the New Testament. When one reads it—not as an impertinent critic who seeks historical flaws, but as a human being who honestly seeks truth—then the New Testament itself speaks for its own. Then the Christian professes with an exuberant and rejoicing heart:

"The Testament is holy because it opens my mental sight; Jesus is living because he awakens life in me."

What if the Kalevala's nature was like this? What if it had this same power even only for the one who, in the right spirit, could read it?

Okay—so this is how we would like to propose that these possibilities should be explored a little. We should endeavor to find out exactly in what sense the Kalevala might be a "Holy Book."

2

The Kalevala
As a Holy Book

FIRST OF ALL, what is a Holy Book? Is there, so to say, a *technical* definition of a Holy Book, one not ambiguous but precise and exact? In fact, there is. But a materialist or one with biased beliefs will not understand it. Only a free-minded person can understand the real meaning of the technical definition of a Holy Book.

In what way can the religious believer and the materialist take each other's hand? Perhaps in the sense that both of them admit boundaries for human knowledge. Both sides know that human knowledge extends far and wide in the visible, material world; we have seen the microcosmic and macrocosmic realms with the instruments of science. There is limitless potential for knowing about the visible life on earth, and likewise they do not believe a great deal is kept hidden from the intellect in the world of the soul. But both camps agree that human knowledge does have its limits. The thinking goes that a human being cannot solve the enigma of death, cannot explore unseen worlds, nor can one speak directly with the creator and giver of life. The only difference is that a religious believer says: "God denies us access to certain things, certain things are unknowable," while the materialist cuts the Gordian Knot with one stab and cries "there was no knot to begin with!" In other words, the materialist concludes there is nothing to explore beyond death nor in the unseen world because the unseen world does not exist and beyond death grins emptiness.

The arrogant materialist does not notice that he prematurely claims to possess a monopoly on secret knowledge when he denies life from death. Likewise, one with blind faith doesn't recognize that he goes through life with eyes closed, even though the possibility of realizing this exists.

As human beings we must be very open-minded and admit that human knowledge may be much more vast than what we agree on in every day life. Only a free-thinker can entertain the idea that knowledge may extend into areas that are considered supernatural. One apostle tells us that the human spirit can explore everything, even the depths of God.

If we are to understand what a Holy Book is, we must acknowledge that human beings are capable of obtaining supernatural knowledge.

On what basis does this conviction rest? It is based upon clear historical foundations. All known cultures have had intellectual giants, mysterious people who claimed to know more than ordinary mortals. These were the world's great philosophers and thinkers, great poets and prophets, saviors and great sons of God. If people turned Jesus into a god, the fault was not his; he called himself a Son of Man. If one might be suspicious of the historical existence of Jesus, Buddha's life has been historically proven. Buddha and India's wise men taught, as did Jesus: Follow me because I know the truth.

When the lives of these great seers are before us, we are not justified in criticizing, saying "what do they know?" As free thinkers we can certainly ask, "perhaps they knew something, but how can we know what they knew? Have they left behind any evidence of their knowledge?"

This line of questioning thus brings us to the Holy Books. The Holy Books contain testimonial evidence of the existence of seers. In what way? The wisdom of seers is hidden within the Holy Books. But how do we know that? We understand this when the seers' wisdom awakens in ourselves.

When the knowledge awakens in ourselves—this is really a courageous statement. Can a modern person obtain supernatural knowledge? Certainly. In what way? How can he obtain this knowledge? By going the way advised in the Holy Books.

This argument of ours clearly appears to be circular. However, we will see that it nevertheless makes a lot of sense. If one seeks the truth in the teachings of a Holy Book, the truth comes. When truth and knowledge have thus dawned, one confirms that a Holy Book certainly is holy, because the wisdom of life and death was found, hidden within. Because there is hidden wisdom in a Holy Book, those who lodged it there must have been wise seers. Thus, there must have been wise seers living in the remote past.

So, how would we now define a Holy Book? A Holy Book is a book in which are hidden the divine mysteries of life and death, a book that can guide a seeker to supernatural knowledge.

In what way can we then understand the Kalevala as a Holy Book? We certainly should not assume that every sentence and word in the Kalevala contains hidden wisdom. We should abandon orthodox theories which call for a literal, formulaic reading of holy texts. This just doesn't work for the Kalevala. A letter is not holy and form is not everlasting. So goes the saying: "A letter deadens but the spirit inspires." In the Kalevala, some compelling allegorical symbols—archetypes—can be considered holy.[4] The form in which they appear is often unambiguous, but is occasionally obscured with complex additional themes. The archetypes in the Kalevala originate from mysteries and reveal the same eternal mysteries as the images in other Holy Books.

At this point, let us accept that this is the sense of the Kalevala as a Holy Book.* As such, what kind of evidence does the Kalevala contain?

The Kalevala suggests that great seers lived in the Finnish past. It contains evidence that the ancient culture of Finland produced mentally sophisticated thinkers. Finnish culture has a history. The possibility that the Kalevala-heroes were foreign to Finnish culture vanishes to insignificance. The poetic form of the Kalevala is truly Finnish. Why would Finnish poets give form to foreign concepts, and why make an effort to remember alien stories? The flower of culture unfolds within the collective heart of a people; Finland's tongue itself tells of the ancient glory. The Kalevala sings:

Vaka vanha Väinämöinen	Old reliable Väinämöinen
Elelevi aikojansa	Lived his days in lyric leisure
Noilla Väinölän ahoilla,	In the glades of Väinölä,
Kalevalan kankahilla,	On the heaths of Kalevala,

---

*The Finnish word "runo" is equivalent to the Swedish "runa," which is an old Gothic word originally meaning "secret, secret knowledge" and "incantation," although it later pertained to runic alphabets.

Laulelevi virsiänsä,	Singing songs and learning wisdom,
Laulelevi, taitelevi.	
Lauloi päivät pääksytysten,	Always singing, night or day,
Yhytysten yöt saneli	There recalling and rehearsing
Muinaisia muisteloita,	Memories of bygone ages,
Noita syntyjä syviä,	The oldest lore of origins,
	When and how all things began—
Joit' ei laula kaikki lapset	Songs that children cannot copy
Ymmärrä yhet urohot	Nor even wise men understand
Tällä inhalla iällä,	In these dreadful days of evil,
Katovalla kannikalla	In this last and fleeting age.[5]

3

The Key to The Kalevala

I F WE NOW ACCEPT that the Kalevala is a Holy Book, that it contains secret knowledge about life and death and advises us how to obtain this knowledge, how then can the ordinary, uninitiated reader, notice the supernatural knowledge within? From this perspective, does such a person have any use at all for the Kalevala?

One must confess that the uninitiated reader does encounter difficulty at this point. They cannot as yet perceive the Kalevala's hidden wisdom. One is attracted to the Kalevala's formal beauty, its poetic spirit and its artistic sense. The Kalevala's ideas about human beings and nature challenge the best in world literature. Its genuinely human touch raises it higher than, for example, many books in the Old Testament. But how can we get a grip on the Kalevala's secret content? On what basis should we conclude that its legendary tales—such as those of the Sampo and its theft—are not merely superstitious imaginings? The Kalevala is really like a locked book, and some kind of key is needed to understand it. The seer may have this key, but the ordinary reader lacks it. Where can it be found?

There are Holy Books which are comparatively easy to read; the New Testament, for example. By this we don't mean that anyone could pick up and immediately understand the New Testament as a Holy Book. However, we are sadly afraid that many, many readers have never even considered in what way their beloved Testament is holy. We suspect that if a truth-seeker is attentive enough, he will (comparatively easily, and by his own means) discover how one needs to read the New Testament to reveal its miraculous secrets.*

This is easy because the New Testament is primarily a guide which advises how a human being should strive for the knowledge of truth. The New Testament was written for people living in an era during which the way-to-knowledge—with its risks and difficulties—was allowed to become more commonly known, because educational standards were rising. In older cultures, on the other hand, the existence of truth-knowledge was widely known, but the methods and the details of its nature were kept hidden, protected by teachers and seers. The ancient books are thus veiled in great secrecy yet encode eternal truths.

The Kalevala, although recently compiled, belongs by way of its content to the older mystery guides. Its most important aspect is, of course, its presentation of the way-to-knowledge, and the manner in which it guides the seeker to truth. Besides this, it contains (to a much greater degree than the Gospels) information about the spiritual realms experienced by the truth-seeker during initiatory visions; e.g., impressions of the conditions and beings in the unseen world and of the metaphysical philosophy of life adopted by seers. In order for the reader to understand the mystical content of the Kalevala, he would thus need to begin with a sense of the worldview held by sages, mystical poets and visionaries. Then he would have a key with which to unlock the Kalevala and other Holy Books. And once the Kalevala's mystical foundations were exposed, perhaps then it would not be so difficult to discern the Kalevala's message regarding the way-to-knowledge.[6]

Is it possible to find such a key? In our own time it is not impossible because there is a philosophy of life, which anyone can learn about, claiming to reflect the knowledge of the ancient sages. Although we should regard it as nothing more than a systematic framework of ideas, it clearly helps us in our Kalevala studies. Very quickly we notice that all wise men and seers, as far as we know, taught the same philosophy of life, which can be found in all religions as a secret wisdom—an esoteric dimension of religion. This is the so-called Theosophical philosophy

---

*We have already pursued this direction in the book *Jeesuksen salakoulu* (*The Esoteric School of Jesus*), Helsinki, 1915. English translation in manuscript, 1995.

(Theosophy), in our time elucidated by H. P. Blavatsky. Madame Blavatsky's book *The Secret Doctrine*, her other works, and a rich literature from many different languages, explain Theosophy. This modern Theosophy is not a complete doctrinal system. It only presents certain aspects of the philosophy of seers and wise men, "fragmentary features," as H. P. Blavatsky used to say. But those features are so essential that they form an intact outlook of life.

As we will later describe this Mystery of the Ages in detail, we will simply outline here what *The Secret Doctrine* speaks about: 1) The Absolute Divinity, which is the unmanifest ground and foundation of all manifest existence—the peace toward which all good and evil ultimately settle as to the depths of the sea; 2) The Manifest God or the so-called Triune Logos which generates all spirit and matter, all opposites, all disharmonies of good and evil and which is, as experiential/existential reality, the common consciousness of the world's innumerable beings, gods and deities; 3) The Law of Periodicity, which determines how creation and destruction, life and death, and day and night unceasingly follow each other so that even human experience is an ever-repeating alternation from life to death and to life again (Reincarnation). After the human soul has achieved divine knowledge and wisdom it will transcend—or be saved from—the cycle of births; 4) The everlasting Law of Balance and Causality (Karma), according to which even the most minute discharge of power in the universe does not vanish but determines consequences in the same way that it was derived from previous action; 5) The existence of wise men and teachers, the so-called Secret Brotherhood which supervises the fate and progress of humanity and, when needed, even intervenes to help it—sometimes through a messenger.

If the reader is unacquainted with Theosophy, these concepts will become clearer when we examine the Kalevala runes. For now, suffice it to say that Theosophical philosophy is the key which unlocks the symbolic meaning within the Kalevala.

Our study is naturally divided into three parts. In the first we will shed some of the light provided by the Theosophical "wisdom of the ages" onto certain rune stories to show that the Kalevala's intellectual and spiritual background is comparable to that found in other Holy Books; we will examine the Kalevala's theology, the story of creation, its understanding of life and death and so forth. In the second part we will first explain the Kalevala's psychology of human development, examine how the Kalevala advises us to seek truth through initiation, and then we will briefly assess the higher levels of human development—the secret way of holy knowledge—as given in the Kalevala. Finally, in the third part we will address the nature of the Kalevala's magical or "supernatural" abilities conferred by following this way-to-knowledge.

The reader, of course, may be surprised at these words. Does the Kalevala really contain such deep and profound spiritual things? Yes, it does, and it contains things more peculiar than even the rune singers themselves may have suspected! At any rate, it seems even Lönnrot had no presentiments of this. Well, probably not. But we now live in a new age. The culmination of materialism has already passed. We are rising again to high spirituality. Spirituality is sneaking into people's souls. The new age salutes the great value of the ancient Holy Books, and reveals to us their hidden riches. The Kalevala is received with joy by its sister traditions.

Madame Blavatsky did not act thoughtlessly when she selected verses from the Indian Rig Veda and excerpts from Kalevala Runo 1 to adorn the chapter headings in her great book *The Secret Doctrine*.[7] She did not err when she wrote: "The deeper meaning of the Kalevala is the battle between light and darkness, good and evil. Kaleva's people then represent light and goodness while the people of the North represent evil forces. We can compare this to the battle between Ormuz and Ahriman, the Aryans and the Rakshas, or the Pandus and the Kurus."[8]

PART II

The Mysterious Knowledge of the Kalevala

The Theological, Anthropological, and Soteriological Key

Was the Ancient Finnish Religion Animistic?

W HEN THE UNASSUMING READER has recovered from the surprise induced by our presentation, there may arise a suspicion. He may shake his head and cry out: "Why, it is foolish to speak about the Kalevala as a Holy Book! After all, the old Finns were animists and manists, that is, worshippers of nature and the deceased— and their seers were magicians and medicine men. It wasn't until Christianity came that our nation was saved from such pagan superstition!" Indeed. The latest academic literature re-interpreting the world-view of the ancient Finns clearly concurs with this opinion. To take a recent example, Kaarle Krohn writes in the foreword to *The Religion of the Finnish Family*: "Comparative studies have concluded that a common aspect of religion for all Finno-Ugric peoples is their worship of deceased ancestors."[1]

Kaarle Krohn's interesting study called *The Religion of Finnish Runes* (which forms the first part of the above mentioned book) clearly explicates our ancestors' religious ideas. He describes the conjuring tricks of a Finnish seer, the realm of the dead and its inhabitants, nature with its gnomes, and the far-reaching influence of Christian doctrine on old Pagan religion and beliefs. The spiritual life of the ancient Finns thus receives its scientific identifiers. It is animistic because the ancient Finns animated nature with living spirits (anima); it is manist because they

19

worshipped the spirits of the deceased (manes); and it is shamanistic because they believed that certain chosen medicine men (shaman) worked with supernatural forces. Under these circumstances, how could the Kalevala be a Holy Book comparable to the Bible? The Kalevala naturally reflects the animistic and shamanistic beliefs of our ancestors; the Kalevala is full of spells, incantations, and emotional worship of nature!

Does this distinction refute our initial claim for the Kalevala? To the materialist or the Christian, perhaps it does, but for us there is no conflict here.

I am not a scholar of the Kalevala in the academic sense. While I dare to continue presenting my ideas, even though I am well aware that scholardom will certainly remain in the opposite camp, my convictions are not rooted in any exhaustive course of study I have pursued. I have had neither opportunity nor talent to this end. My courageous attitude results from studies of a different nature, and this should become clearer as the book progresses. I only wish to emphasize the fact that I am quite convinced of the veracity of my perspective, and wonder if all those learned scholars are equally sure of their own conclusions. For example, professor Kaarle Krohn believes that the Kalevala was born in Finland between 700 A.D. and 1100 A.D. This may be true for the structural form that the Kalevala takes, but the structural format of the runes is not the same as their psychological and symbolic content. The structure certainly changed with the times, and this can be charted. But the living spirit of the runes is forever, immemorial, ancient, unchanging—it has moved secretly through various format changes. In fact, I suspect overconfidence even with Krohn's timeframe for the Kalevala's structural origin. At any rate, I believe there are pieces of the Kalevala that are thousands of years old. Let it therefore remain the task of continuing scientific investigation to further clarify the structural birth of the runes.

Although we endeavor to keep up-to-date with new academic perspectives in Kalevala studies, apparent conflicts don't upset our convictions. The foundation of our confidence results from the distinction that we explore the Kalevala's spiritual or esoteric content, whereas scientists are limited by their focus on formal, exoteric content. As we have already said, only an open-minded person will *a priori* grasp our point of view. In comparative studies of religious life and religious beliefs, one finds a familiar law of evolution, progression and regression,[2] and on the basis of this, scholars have classified religious life into categories in which a development from lower to higher forms is perceived.

Thus, Christianity fits into this hierarchical schema along with other religions. Researcher Allan Menzies writes: "We are not allowed to divide religions by setting aside Christianity as the only correct religion. No religion, in our opinion, is a mere superstition; neither do we deny the guiding role of Deity in any religion... In light of this idea of development, we can find something good even in the lowest form of religion, and we find that good and right rather than evil and wrong is the final goal of even the most insignificant religious system."[3]

In this hierarchical classification of religious forms, the worship of nature is the lowest and represents the original religion of primitive savages everywhere. A later development emerges in the National Religions of, for example, the Judaic Yahweh cult, and the highest expression is found in world-wide religion, of which there are really two: Buddhism and Christianity.

Our viewpoint doesn't conflict with this developmental theory. We readily admit that a kind of evolution has taken place and that the ancient Finns, according to current classification, were nature-worshippers—animists. But our argument highlights another consideration. The development of religion is an outer expression of a social phenomenon; it is exoteric. Side by side with the exoteric development of religion has always gone the esoteric or inner religious striving, which is an individualistic phenomenon.

This requires explanation.

Scholars of religious studies do indeed constantly use words like God, Tuonela (Underworld, Hades), spiritual world, genius,* and so on, but for many these are merely dead ideas; they don't believe that they have any correspondence in reality. The unseen spiritual world is for them forever an unsolvable thing.

It is different for spiritualists. For us, the existence of the unseen world with all its forces and beings is, in a word, axiomatic. In the visible world there exist divisions and laws and boundaries, and therefore we assume that, likewise, the invisible realm is not a chaos but an organized

---

*Editor's note. Or *genii*, a tutelary deity.

cosmos. The laws of nature apply to both. By way of the body's physical constitution, human beings are citizens of the visible world, and through our souls and spiritual natures we are also citizens of the spiritual world. The only difference is that our relationship to the physical world is external or objective while our relationship to the spiritual world is revealed through subjective, internal experience. When we accept that the unseen world is a law-bound cosmos and human beings are related to it via their essential natures, it follows that exploration of the unseen world is not impossible. We feel this to be true, but what evidence is there? What do we really know about the possibilities of the human spirit? After all, how many of those who claim we can't explore the unseen realm have seriously tried to themselves? If we can see this, can't we also see that the human spiritual monad has always been capable of exploring the inner dimensions? Religious life is entirely based on the yearning and longing to enter into right relationship with the unseen forces of life (gods or God). This spiritual yearning appears as the thirst for truth and knowledge. Nothing else is so needed as the religious yearning which awakens within. Awakening spirit to self-consciousness, the seeker yearns for truth, knowledge of life and death, and knowledge of the beings and conditions of the unseen spiritual world. It is not a long step from desire to action, from longing for the truth to seeking the truth, and "seek and ye shall find."

And now we can ask: What impelled primitive, uncivilized humans to aquire a thirst for truth? Very few are seized by it even today! We aren't suggesting that everyone seized by a deep spiritual yearning would even understand what was happening to them, as it was as rare then as it is today. But the reason why some people could ultimately realize their quest is two-fold. First, human nature has long remained unchanged and the inner world itself has remained constant, unaffected by exoteric religion. As such, the individual Christian is not closer to God or the spiritual realm than the ancient Finnish pagan. These religious variations are only external by nature or merely accentuate different aspects of the human soul; the faculties of intellect and emotion diversify to attain different values within the culture but the human Self remains the same. Secondly, we believe that humanity has always received help from higher beings, has been awakened, advised and taught by them. And so there has always been—in all times and places—people whose inner capacities and relationship with God grew richer than the average person. This is an individual who has, so to speak, gone esoteric, and treads the narrow path to gnostic knowing. Having abandoned the wide abyss of exoteric faith, this kind of person is a real seer, and their spiritual knowledge is of the inner soul of exoteric religion. When they express their wisdom, it takes the form of a mythology, theology or philosophy tailored to who they are speaking to and the time and place in which they live. When we say that the Kalevala reflects the wisdom of our ancestors, we mean that within its outer form—and animism it is—dwells the ancient Finnish sages' mystic knowledge of the secrets of the unseen realm. This wisdom teaching is, in fact, global and universal. But it was found by Finnish seers, is reflected in the Finnish soul, and can therefore be considered Finnish.

The Kalevala, which refers here to the wider context of Finnish mythology in general, is thus understood as a viable historical testament to our ancestors' unravelling of the everlasting mysteries of life.

5

Humans Or Gods?

CIENTISTS HAVE DEBATED whether the Kalevala-heroes are gods or humans. Published in the year 1551, the work *Psalter* by Mikael Agricola lists "The idols of people living in Häme and Karelia" and mentions Äinemöinen (Väinämöinen), Ilmarinen, the sons of Kaleva, as well as the name Ahti.*

Agricola's viewpoint prevailed until the early 1800's, and not until then was the notion seriously discussed that Ilmarinen, Väinämöinen, and other Finnish characters, may in fact have been human beings. Lönnrot and Gottlund both argued that Väinämöinen was a historical person rather than a mythical god. The publication of the Kalevala[4] separated scholars into two camps.

While Collan and Castrén, and later Donner and E. Aspelin, argued for the intrinsic deity of the Kalevala's heroes, the others (including Ahlquist) sought their historical provenience. Nowadays, most ascribe to the notion that the Kalevala's sages (Väinämöinen, Ilmarinen and Lemminkäinen) were originally real people but that, in time, legends and all kinds of mythic dramas were woven around them.

Our own perspective is not in conflict with these scientific views. We appreciate almost every discovery of science. We are convinced that the Kalevala-heroes were, in fact, historical people. We even believe that the names were *generic* or some kind of family names, like Hermes (Thoth) in

---

*Editor's note. In the Kalevala, Ahti is another name for Lemminkäinen.

Egypt or Zarathustra in Persia. In other words, there were probably different Väinämöinens and Ilmarinens living in many different eras. Despite this, we are also convinced that these names originally designated not "idols" as Agricola claims—or even divine "beings"—but divine *forces*, emerging as a hierarchy or "divine army."[5]

This kind of confusion of name and idea[6] is typical in the history of spiritual movements.

It has been established conclusively that mythological names were originally the names of historical people. For example, in the Icelandic *Eddas* the God of poetry, Brage, was also the name of a well-known Icelandic poet. On the other hand, the meaning of the Jewish name *messiah*, the Greek adjective *khristos* (anointed), and the Finnish word *vapahtaja* (savior) changed so that today when Christians speak about the Messiah, Christ or Savior, they do mean only Jesus the Nazarene.

Our theory thus proposes that the name Väinämöinen symbolizes a type of divine hierarchy while it was also the name of a historical person. Which was first is not important. It is probable that Väinämöinen, like Christ, first represented a divine force or concept and then became a name given to the person in whom the divine ideal was especially manifest. It is also possible—and let this be said as a comfort to those who think our theory is fantastic (although we think it correct)—that Väinämöinen was first a person's name and it later took on the meaning of the spiritual characteristics projected by that person.[7]

When we want to learn about the Kalevala's spiritual background, the mysterious references hidden in its runes, first we must acquaint ourselves with what the Kalevala-heroes—those proper nouns—represent. The Kalevala's cosmology is not expressed in straight philosophical postulates; it is secreted within the structure of a rune and the visual format of a figurative language. Thus, our attention cannot be limited to minute details, but must take a wider view and embrace the whole picture. We must trace the Golden Thread woven through numerous runes. Naturally the questions arise: Does the Kalevala speak to us about God, and what does it tell us about God? The Christian reader may hurry to respond that the Kalevala certainly has nothing to say about God because the old pagan Finns knew nothing of the one and only God of monotheism. Superficially, this seems reasonable. The Kalevala does not speak about God in the Christian sense. But does it follow then that the Kalevala knows nothing of God?

Let us dwell on this for a while. Let us refrain from boasting with that overused word "faith" while we try to answer these questions: What do we know about God? What do we know about the origin of life and existence? What do we know about the Father and Creator who cares for the world like a mother gently embracing a baby in her lap? The faithful may whisper "He is love" but in our thoughts we must confess that we know nothing more of Him than He has revealed of Himself. We see Him in His works. In all of Siberia there once prevailed the understanding that it was not possible to approach the highest god through prayer.[8]

No philosopher has been able to satisfactorily describe Him because He is beyond all images. The ancient Vedantists of India who epitomize the best in philosophical thought said that it is not possible to define the absolute Parabrahman. The only thing that can be said is *neeti, neeti,* "neither this nor that." A human being can only strive to understand, describe and worship the Manifest Creator—Brahma.

One wonders if the Kalevala contains the same attitude, even if its wisdom manifests only via its silence on the matter. The Kalevala does not describe God because our intellect can say nothing about God; the living God can only be learned about by living life. The Kalevala is limited, as it should be, to reflecting upon God's worldly projections, including those in the unseen world—such as those encountered by spiritualists. The Kalevala thus does not presume to speak about God directly with words because the Kalevala is a reflection of divine mysteries.

What does the word Kalevala mean?

It clearly means "home of Kaleva" but if, as later investigators would have it, "-la" is a modifier as in juma vs. jumala (god), it could also mean "Kaleva-like" or "one with the quality of Kaleva."* And what of this Kaleva? Lönnrot originally presumed Kaleva to mean "something horrifying; killing; being derived from the same stem as the words *kalpa, kalma, kallo, kalu (-ensis), kuolen.*"[9]

Later he thought it derived from the Russian word *golovaa,* "a head." Castrén, on the other hand, compared it to the Turkish word *aalep,* "a hero." Nowadays linguists follow Ahlquist in deriving it from the Lithuanian word *kálvis,* which means "a metal-worker, a smith." The

---

*Translator's note. In English compare water vs. watery.

Estonian word *kalev* means "a gentleman's garment." According to these recent derivations, the word *kaleva* relates to "a smith" and "a gentleman" or "a lord." Keeping with this train of thought we must then ask: the smith of what? The lord of what? And without doubt we can answer to both: the world. The lord and the creator (i.e., the smith) of the world was called Kaleva.*

There is a phrase "the fire of Kaleva" (lightning), meaning something equivalent to "the fire of the Lord," and with this we may even understand Lönnrot's explanation involving horrors. Moving on, the "tree of Kaleva" was a holy tree. Niittyvilla (Eriophorum) was "the hair of the son of Kaleva" and this is thought to be a memory from the times when those of free birth had the right to grow their hair long. And doesn't it also remind us of how the ancient prophets and initiates such as the Jewish Nazarenes let their hair grow freely? As an adjective, Kalevala thus means "one with the quality of the Creator or the Lord (God)" or simply "divine." As a substantive noun, it means "the home of the Creator or the Lord," meaning the higher planes of life or the higher zones of the unseen world. Lönnrot, it thus appears, deeply inspired with the ancient Finnish spirit, chose for his book a name which is full of promise for those who approach it as a Holy Book. Moreover, we can here compare Lönnrot's choice to Dante Alighieri's book title *The Divine Comedy*. Both titles are revealing, to the point, and full of promise to the reader.

As we have just seen, an examination of the word Kalevala suggests that we are, in fact, dealing here with divine mysteries.

---

*Compare this with the following rune-phrase: "Eessä Isä Jumalan, Kengän kau'oilla Kalevan" (In front of the Father, God . . . Kaleva).

6

The Holy Trinity

"I believe in the Trinity: the Father, the Son and the Holy Ghost."
So says the Christian and believes that this creed is unique,
especially profound and spiritual. It may come as a big surprise when,
by way of comparative religious studies, it is revealed that the Trinity
doctrine is not uniquely Christian but is also found in several "pagan"
religions.

Within the Indian Vedic tradition you have the triune god Indra-
Varuna-Agni, in which Indra is the firmament, Varuna is water, and
Indra the fire god. Another trinity of that era was Vaaju (Air), Agni
(Fire), and Suurja (Sun). Later, when philosophical thought schematized
these ideas, the Trinity was said to be *trimurti*, or "three-faced," and the
different divine personages of the Trinity were called Brahma, Vishnu
and Shiva (Creator, Maintainer and Destroyer). In India it is said:
"Learn, oh pious one, that there is no real distinction between us; only in
outer appearance does one perceive it as such. There are three aspects
which are really one."

The well-known Egyptian trinity is Osiris-Isis-Horus, but in Old
Egypt there were other trinities. In Thebes, Amon, Mut and Khonsa were
worshipped as a trinity. The true Egyptian trinity consisted of Osiris,
Knef, and Ptah. Ptah was especially esteemed in Memphis, and there
with Nefer Tuum and Sekket formed the Holy Trinity. In Old Chaldea
you have the primary trinity of Anu, Bel and Ea, and the secondary trinity
of Samas, Sin and Ishtar (Sun, Moon and Venus). In ancient China rulers
dedicated every third year to "he who is one and yet three." A Chinese

saying goes: "Fo is a person but he has three forms." The divine tripartite deity of the Scandinavians was Odin, Freyja, and Thor or, alternatively, Odin, Freyja, and their other son Baldur. Jewish cabbalists speak of the three highest *sephiroths*: Kether (the Crown), Khokhmah (Wisdom), and Binah (Understanding). All three emerge from *En Soph* and within it are one.

These examples—and there are many more—should be sufficient to demonstrate that the concept of triune deity, the Trinity, is not of Christian origin. We could thus conclude that if pagan beliefs are heresy so is Christian doctrine. However, if there is truth in the Triune doctrine itself, if it has some real basis in the ways nature and life are organized, then it seems that paganism speaks the same wisdom as Christianity. It hardly needs to be mentioned that our own understanding inclines toward this conclusion.

The meaning of the Triune doctrine is accessible for everyone. Even uneducated people understand the trinity expressed by the words Father, Mother, and Son (as in the Egyptian meaning). When celebrating the origin of the world, the doctrine that the world is the son engendered by the Father and Mother has a satisfying ring to it. One who thinks deeper on these things needs only to understand the words "father" and "mother" to derive even more profound and complex versions of the world's birth. When "father" is thought of as "consciousness" and mother "matter," the "son" (the world) is derived from the cooperation of these two foundation principles. Consciousness is by its nature essentially boundless and eternal, while matter gives rise to the possibility of limitation. The world consists of perennially recurring form-events which are restricted manifestations of eternal and boundless life. Can a philosophy be any clearer in describing the original cause of manifest existence?

Anyhow, the Triune doctrine has another meaning, which is more precise in its occult inflection. When a piece of Divine Mind emerges (is born), it is bestowed with a comprehension of its own tripartite nature. The Trinity doctrine thus describes the unified, divine "group conscious-ness" or "being" in its three different modes of action (or "personalities" as Christian theology says).

When exploring the inner worlds, a seer inevitably meets the Being who, as Father and Creator, embraces the whole solar system. This mighty Being is not the origin and ground of all space, time and existence however, for he is the manifest god, the highest ruler of our solar system but only one of countless gods who populate space. His brothers are the highest Beings in other solar systems. Beyond him and his kinsmen is the eternal Father of all space, the secret divinity about whom, as we saw earlier, nothing can be known. The Book of John describes this very simply and beautifully; accordingly, Theosophical literature refers to the manifest sun-gods as Logoi. "In the beginning was the Logos [the Word], and the Logos was with God and the Logos was God. The Logos was in the beginning with God. All things came into being by the Logos, and apart from the Logos nothing came into being that has come into being."[10] Here God is a boundless yet hidden life-force, sequestering within Himself all possibilities of matter and consciousness. Logos is the manifest individual consciousness which, by drawing from the infinite potential hidden within God, creates the world.

The Logos—the Manifest God—is triune by nature and is, above all, a psychological fact. Wise men have always agreed that the human being is a microcosmic reflection of the whole cosmos, "created in God's image." As Saint Paul said, individuals can understand the depths of God by studying their own spirit.

Every human being lives a mental life of a triune nature. European psychology has described this by saying that human consciousness has three facets: knowledge, will, and sense. Modern psychologists have, in fact, invented more factors, and some even consider will to be non-existent. However, this doesn't eliminate the original tripartite division, because modern theories seem to be more about the names than the intrinsic structure.[11]

That the conflict is a practical fact of reality is observed in a person's difficult position when his own consciousness splits so that he doesn't know "what *he* wants." Anyway, we can imagine an ideal mental life in which knowledge or reason, emotion and will are in harmony and work together to serve the highest divine goal.

To understand the psychology of the manifest God or Logos (with our imperfect way), we must imagine the ideal of a perfectly harmonious mental life. Even God is a knowing, willing, and feeling being, but in him these essential characteristics are developed to their highest potential. God's will is like a specific, complete person, as are his intellectual and emotional aspects. We may even posit a collective consciousness in which the Logos is the collection of all divine hierarchies or the living sum of innumerable individual beings. At the same time we should remember that all beings and hierarchies are fundamentally one—a self-aware totality both sublime and majestic. The creative will aspect of Logos is called "God the Father" in Christian theology. Logos as emotion, as the loving principle, is called "the Son."[12] Logos as knowing thought-action and discriminating reason is called "the Holy Spirit."* (In Hindu cosmology, Brahma corresponds to "the Holy Spirit," Vishnu to the "Son," and Shiva to "Father." Shiva is also a destroyer because the will which creates anew must destroy the old.)

What does ancient Finnish wisdom tell us regarding this discussion? Did they have any knowledge of Logos and the Trinity? What does the Kalevala have to say about all this? The Logos Trinity manifests through its activity in the world. What, then, does the Kalevala teach about the creation of the world and its perfection or, in Christian theological terms, "God's salvation"?

---

*We have already explored these things in the booklet *Kirkonopin teosofia* (*Theosophy of Church Doctrine*), Chapter I.

7

The Virgin Birth

If we understand the divine Trinity as meaning consciousness, matter, and the world-forms engendered by these, we see that the Kalevala gives a central place to these three factors. Kalevalan cosmogenesis is the story of Väinämöinen's birth.[13] We must carefully examine this remarkable event because Väinämöinen represents the manifest life of the world.

In both the Old and New Kalevala, Väinämöinen's mother Ilmatar is mentioned. In the Old Kalevala she plays a marginal role, while in the New Kalevala her identity is described in more detail. In the Old Kalevala nothing is mentioned of Väinämöinen's father, who in the New Kalevala is the wind. Here we have the original, primary trinity of the Kalevala: Father = wind, Mother = Ilmatar, and Väinämöinen is their son. The wind (air) represents consciousness or spirit, Ilmatar ("mother of the waters") represents matter and Väinämöinen represents the world-forms. The whole scenario reminds us of Judaic cosmogony in the first Book of Moses, where we read that "the spirit of God moves over the waters." From the Kalevala:

Tuli suuri tuulen puuska,	Suddenly a storm wind blew,
Iästä vihainen ilma,	Out of the east an angry blast
Meren kuohuille kohotti,	Blew the water to a foam
Lainehille laikahutti.	Heaving up the rollers high.
Tuuli neittä tuuitteli,	By the wind the maid was rocked,
Aalto impeä ajeli	On a wave the maid was driven

Ympäri selän sinisen,	Round about the blue sea surface
Lakkipäien lainehien;	By the whirling whitecaps lifted
Tuuli tuuli kohtuiseksi,	Where her womb the wind awakened
Meri paksuksi panevi.	And the sea-foam impregnated.[14]

While enduring labor pains, Väinämöinen's mother prays to Ukko, the highest deity. This may be a hint that behind all creative forces and all conscious beings is a secret divinity, about which nothing more is mentioned in the Kalevala.

The school of thought led by professor Kaarle Krohn proposed that the creation rune which relates the birth of Väinämöinen is insignificant, drawing its concepts from poems about the origin of diseases, swing-songs and what have you.[15]

This may be formally correct—I am not in a position to refute it—but this interpretation doesn't address the spirit of the rune. That the spirit of the rune clearly expresses a great creation mystery cannot be accidental. And there is a facet of the creation story which clearly indicates that its spirit is drawn from a knowledge of the mystical worlds.

When we carefully compare the Kalevala's Trinity doctrine with other cosmogonies in which the Trinity is found, it somehow feels incomplete to conclude that "the son" symbolizes all worldly manifestation. The world just doesn't spring from one momentous union of consciousness and matter. The infinite spirit and the option of finite manifestation unites in the consciousness of the individual being who is thus a creator—Logos incarnate. The primary Trinity is thus not "consciousness, matter and *the world*," but "consciousness, matter and the *manifest creator*." Only the manifest creator can be observed at the foundation of the world.

Quite correctly then, "the son" is described as a living personality: Väinämöinen who, in his own turn, creates the world. Väinämöinen is the "great human prototype," Adam Kadmon, Makroprosoopos (the "great countenance") and humanity is created in his image. He is the Logos-weaver of the world, and the product of his meditation and song is the manifest cosmos. The New Kalevala has Väinämöinen coming out of his mother Ilmatar's womb *after* his creation of the world, but in the Old Kalevala he is born first and directly participates in the world creation. The Old Kalevala is thus closer to the great mystery as we have interpreted it. (This need not be a point of contention between the Old and New Kalevala because a variant of the Virgin of the Air's name—the "Mother of the Waters"—appears to be "Väinämöinen.")

A feature that is quite important in the creation story involves the virginity of Ilmatar and Väinämöinen's official fatherlessness. His mother is described as a living being while his father is just "the wind"— a more abstract and inconsequential parentage role.

Kalevala Runo 1 quite often reads grandly and magnificently:

Yksin meillä yöt tulevat,	Lonely come the nights upon us,
Yksin päivät valkeavat,	Lonely dawn the brightening days;
Yksin syntyi Väinämöinen...	Lonely born was Väinämöinen...[16]

Professor Krohn claims that the first two verses are of foreign origin, and that the third is a creation of Lönnrot's.[17]

So be it. Lönnrot thus behaves like an authentic rune-singer, or at least like a visionary. His inspiration (we can hardly speak of what he might have known) really struck home. For in those verses he describes the birth of "God's only son," meaning born from one origin (monogenesis). Here resounds the ancient mystery of the birth of the Logos. It takes place "by itself" in the sense that the Logos is the first and only manifestation at the dawn of time and also in the sense that it is a virgin birth (from the mother alone) by supernatural means.

Krohn's claim that the Kalevala's tale of Väinämöinen's virgin birth is derived from the Christian faith is unlikely, simply because the doctrine of virgin birth is found in many religions much older than Christianity.

Osiris in Egypt was born of a heavenly virgin named Neth. Likewise, Horus was the son of the virgin Isis. In Babylonia the sun-god Tammuz was Eridu Ea's "only son"; Ea is equivalent to Ishtar, Astarte and Mylitta. In Persia, Zoroaster was conceived by a ray of divine intelligence, and his mother was a virgin. In Mexico, Quetzalcoatl was born from the virgin Chimalm, and in the Yucatan Bacab was born from the virgin Chiribira and was worshipped as a savior. Likewise for the Aztec sun-god Huitzilopochtli. In India, Krishna's mother Deevaki was a virgin, as was Buddha's mother Maya. And of course Jesus Christ was born of the virgin Mary. These stories are certainly just legends separate from the historical characters, but when a person's name is symbolic of divine forces, then the virgin birth is an accurate poetic description of great relevance to the nature of the spiritual world. In Christian theology, the Christ is truly the Logos, the Word through which the world is created. Similarly, Krishna is regarded as an Avatar or incarnation of the second divine person Vishnu, and is called Hari—"he who removes sin." His mother Deevaki calls him with the words "You, the god of gods who is all in everything." Osiris and Horus were called "the king of kings" and "the master of masters" respectively. Osiris was also referred to as "the master of the whole country." As a historical person, Väinämöinen was born like everyone else, but Väinämöinen as God and Sun-Logos was born of Ilmatar, the beautiful Virgin of the Air.

The Act of Creation

N SCIENTIFIC QUARTERS it is generally agreed that, prior to Kant's scientific exposition on the origin of the world, cosmogenesis was a topic dealt with only through philosophical speculation. By the time Laplace in the early 1800s fully developed Kant's theories, cosmology had become a topic of scientific study by way of astronomy.

As we understand it, the Kant-Laplace theory proposes that solar systems originate from nebulae coalescing through circulation around a dense center. The sun was originally a huge gaseous sphere spinning on its axis. The surface mass split off into smaller spheres spinning in the opposite direction, and these formed into planets orbiting the sun.

This theory prevailed throughout the 19th century. Among others, H. P. Blavatsky in *The Secret Doctrine* made strong comments against this model, and in fact it is no longer scientifically adequate. Science has made several observations which disprove parts of the Kant-Laplace edifice, and has attempted to present new theories of cosmogenesis, but none have been completely accepted. When the emperor Napoleon learned of Laplace's astronomical ideas, he wonderingly asked him: "Where, then, does God live?" Laplace's boastful reply defines the theory's own futile emptiness: "We no longer have any need of God." Scientists have not been able to solve the enigma of the world's origin with materialistic philosophy. Ultimately, God *is* necessary—God is the reason of the world's becoming, the first impulse and prime mover. The ancient visionaries who populated space with gods and living beings were closer to the truth than our learned but spiritually blind priests of materialism.

We are not justified in regarding ancient religious cosmologies as naïve and superstitious. Their forms may seem unsophisticated and "unscientific," but if we can adjust our eyes to the mystic vision behind the forms, we will realize how insightful they really are and that they reveal profound cosmological ideas unapproached by science. The ancient cosmology doesn't concern itself with mechanical forces which determine the solar system's formation, but rather it focuses on the invisible template which guides the process of physical manifestation. In other words, the ancient doctrine describes cosmogenesis from a higher viewpoint—from God's viewpoint—instead of from the perspective of physical being. And who else but a seer, inspired by the holy spirit of truth, would venture to fathom the depths of God?

The birth of the world has therefore always been called "the creation of the world." Creation is an activity and requires an actor, a mover, a creator. The entire process of cosmogenesis is the act of a living creator.

The creative act does not draw from an empty reservoir; it is not intellectually inconceivable nor is it a logical contradiction. Nothing can arise from emptiness. Everything that is, has always been and will forever be. Matter, in its original state, is as eternal as spirit or consciousness, and both are unified in the unmanifest absolute divinity. Creation is the action of divine, reasoning beings to project and fulfill their inspirations and desires with the help of material elements. Creation is an artistic act. Let's look at how Finnish sages described the act of creation. Consequently, we will understand how the Creator-Logos manifests, shall we say, in triplicate. In other words, it will become clear that the creative act has three phases.

In reading the text of the New Kalevala we immediately see three creative stages: 1) conception, 2) pregnancy or gestation, and 3) the actual act of creation, or birth. Because the total creative process comes from Logos—Väinämöinen—we must remember that the other beings involved are variant names for Väinomöinen's other aspects. Instead of Ilmatar (mother of the waters) we can substitute Väinämöinen, because one etymology for the name Väinämöinen has it meaning "water mother" (veen emonen = water mother).

"Lonely born was Väinämöinen, all alone, the poet immortal." So reads the Kalevala, subtley revealing a secret cosmic knowledge. In the Old Kalevala one reads "at night was born old Väinämöinen, the next day he went to see the smithy." Thus it appears that Väinämöinen was ancient when he was born—a wise seer of secret knowledge—truly, a "poet immortal." It is succinctly related here that the Creator has lived before, maybe had grown and attained wisdom in a distant past. The Creator existed before the inactive state in which, as Ilmatar, he now dwells:

Piti viikkoista pyhyyttä	Long maintained in holiness
Iän kaiken impeyttä,	Her eternal maidenhood
Ilman pitkillä pihoilla,	In the far-horizoned heavens,
Tasaisilla tantereilla.	Level meadows of the air.[18]

After previous activity, Väinämöinen-as-Creator (Ilmatar) rested in the unmanifest realm of clear consciousness:

Ikävystyi aikojansa,	But in time she wearied of it,
Ouostui elämätänsä,	Was estranged from this odd living,
Aina yksin ollessansa,	Always being by herself,
Impenä eläessänsä,	Ever living as a virgin
Ilman pitkillä pihoilla,	In those far-horizoned heavens,
Avaroilla autioilla.	In those vast and empty spaces.[19]

Thus the will to create reawakened. It kindled in the Creator's heart an idea for a new world. The Creator-Artist conceived, and the so-called "First Logos" or Will of the World was born.

Jop' on astuiksen alemma,	So at length she then descended
Laskeusi lainehille,	To the seawaves down below,
Meren selvälle selälle,	To the open clear sea surface
Ulapalle aukealle.	Out upon the open ocean.[20]

At the moment of inspiration, as soon as the proto-image is visualized in the divine imagination, the "descent into matter" from the realm of pure consciousness begins. Logos sleeps surrounded by the absolute unmanifest chaos, which is often called a "sea" in ancient cosmogonies.* The idea kindled by the Logos within the world of consciousness condenses—or materializes—a form from the idea; conceptualization underlies and guides creation. The Logos, suffering the creative act within, now becomes dual while seeking a suitable form for his new image. From the inspired idea and the inevitable splitting off of the created from the creator, now flares love. From the will to create (Father) now comes emotion or relation (Mother), and mother begins to labor.

Vieri impi Väinämöinen	As the mother of the water [Väinämöinen] Aimlessly the virgin drifted:
Uipi iät, uipi lännet,	She swam eastward, she swam westward,
Uipi luotehet, etelät,	She swam south and northwestward,
Uipi kaikki ilman rannat,	Swimming round the whole horizon
Tuskissa tulisen synnyn,	In the anguish of her birth pangs,
Vatsan vaivoissa kovissa;	In her belly's bursting pains.
Eikä synny syntyminen,	Yet the borning was unborn,
Luovu luomaton sikiö.	Still the fetus undelivered.[21]

What a splendid psychology! The human creator (the poet, artist or inventor) also moves from initial inspiration to a state of suffering when he wants to substantially manifest his idea. So many in this state must think as Väinämöinen (i.e., Ilmatar) did:

Parempi olisis ollut	Better had it been for me
Ilman impenä eleä...	To have stayed the airy virgin...[22]

and must pray within to "loose the maiden from her misery, and the woman from her womb-ache." The suffering of creation has not yet reached the overwhelming *reason* to create, and we are thus still within

---

*In Latin, sea = *mare*, the plural form being *maria*. Mary is the name of the mother of Christ (the Logos). Mother = *mater* in Latin, and matter = *materia*. There are similarities in the form and even in the sounds of these internally related words: mater, materia, maria.

the "Second Logos"—the World Emotion which by nature is bisexual, consisting of matter and spirit.

Help is needed and help will come. Now the work begins and agony is forgotten. Väinämöinen is rolling on the waves of the mother

Tuli sotka suora lintu,	When a scaup, the honest bird,
Lenteä lekuttelevi,	Came on hovering here and there
Etsien pesän sioa,	Searching for a nesting place,
Asunmaata arvaellen,	For a spot to build her home on.[23]

And Väinämöinen (Ilmatar):

Nosti polvea merestä,	Raised her knee above the surface
Lapaluuta lainehesta	And her shoulder from the wave
Sotkalle pesän sijaksi,	As a refuge for the scaup
Asunmaaksi armahaksi.	And a welcome resting place.[24]

The scaup "spied Väinämöinen's (the water-mother's) knee" and

Siihen laativi pesänsä,	It is there she builds her nest,
Muni kultaiset munansa,	There she laid her golden eggs—
Kuusi kultaista munoa,	Six were the golden eggs she laid,
Rautamunan Seitsemännen.	But the seventh was of iron.[25]

What is this "scaup, the graceful bird" which makes the Creator forget his agony? It is the mind of thought, reason and insight or more precisely, the intellect which invents form. Every worker breathes a sigh of relief when he hits upon the solution to a troubling problem. The first glimmer of the solution comes like a bird flying in from the darkness of space.

The bird is an appropriate symbol of thought. We find it in several ancient religions. In India there is "the swan of time" and in Christian faith the Holy Spirit is represented by a dove. The scaup or the eagle symbolizes the Creator's thought that touches upon (involves) many spaces. It symbolizes Väinämöinen's active reason or the "Third Logos"—the Holy Spirit—whose task is to organize the primal chaos.

What does the eagle do? He organizes the elements into various types of atoms. He identifies seven types of fundamental atoms; six golden atoms of the invisible world and one iron atom for the physical world. (The numbers may vary from three to eight because "planes" and "worlds" can be classified in different ways.)

The scaup's seven eggs are definitely atoms; they are not the planets or the sun because these will be born next. After the eggs are laid and grow warm, Väinämöinen (Ilmatar) "jerked her knee" and "the eggs rolled into the water... and were broken into bits." The fragments became the earth, moon, sun and planets. Only love with reason can create the world. Perhaps we should say that atoms join together when the world is created instead of breaking into pieces but actually it makes no difference. The latest studies in atomic theory have led to the conclusion that atoms are perfectly organized worlds—miniature solar systems if you will—almost like Leibniz's monads. So there is not a significant difference between "big" and "small." On a greater dimensional scale the cosmos as we recognize it is just a microcosmic splinter from a cosmos of many planes. By this reasoning we can say that an atom is a broken fragment (in our world) or, conversely, that the same atom is a whole cosmos (in some other world). The profound knowledge of ancient wisdom peeks out at us from the Kalevala.

Furthermore, the Kalevala clearly describes how the process of creation continues. Väinämöinen (Ilmatar):

Alkoi luoa luomiansa,	Set to work on her creations,
Saautella saamiansa...	Hastens on her handiwork...
Kussa kättä käännähytti,	Where she gave her hand a turn
Siihen niemet siivoeli;	There she put the capes in order;
Kussa pohjasi jalalla,	Where her foot struck bottom, there
Kalahauat kaivaeli;	Grottoes for the fish were formed;
Kussa ilman kuplistihe,	Where the bubbles reached the surface
Siihen syöverit syventi. j.n.e.	There the deeps were made still deeper.[26] etc.

After this we must jump to the second rune of the Kalevala, where creation continues with the story of the Big Oak. Now we shift from the level of the solar system to the level of the earth. In the Book of Moses, a desert existed before water came to form a sea around which trees could thrive. Likewise in the Kalevala we read that the Creator (Väinämöinen) dwelt for "many years"

Saaressa sanattomassa,	On that mute and barren island,
Manteressa puuttomassa.	In that dreary treeless land.[27]

Soon thereafter comes "Pellervoinen, son of the field," who represents organic life brought from somewhere else:

Kylvi maita kyyhätteli,	Leisurely he sowed the land,
Kylvi maita, kylvi soita,	Sowed the land and sowed the swamps,
Kylvi auhtoja ahoja,	Sowed the fallow open stretches,
Panettavi paasikoita.	Even sowed the rocky barrens.[28]

The earth was green and produced many trees and all kinds of plant life, but still to grow was "God's tree." Only after it grew and was felled (by the little thumb-sized man) could true agriculture begin. As Julius Krohn rightly commented, this "God's tree" (the Big Oak) was a large cloud which hid the sun and moon from view,[29] and which only the little man (a ray of sunlight) was able to break up. Rather than indicating just one event, this story really symbolizes the earth-epoch in which atmospheric moisture was extreme and rain was a constant natural phenomenon. Only when this era of rain dispersed did the sun begin to shine, so that

Kasvoi maahan marjanvarret,	Berry bushes grew abundant,
Kukat kultaiset keolle,	Golden flowers filled the meadows
Ruohot kasvoi kaikenlaiset,	And the grasses multiplied,
Monenmuotoiset sikesi...	Every kind of herb arising...[30]

Thus the stage was set for the dawn of true agriculture. At the seashore Väinämöinen finds "six grains, seven seeds" and starts sowing. Other secret traditions tell that grains of wheat were originally brought to earth from another star.

We now return to the first rune, which we left earlier, and come to quite a strange paradox. All this time the Creator Väinämöinen has been busy working, but he has not yet been "born."

Jo oli saaret siivottuna,	Now the islands were in order
Luotu luotoset merehen,	And the small isles of the sea;
Ilman pielet pistettynä,	Pillars for the sky were planted,

Maat ja manteret sanottu,	Lands and continents created;
Kirjattu kivihin kirjat,	On the rocks the writs were written
Veetty viivat kallioihin,	And the signs drawn on the cliffs.
Viel' ei synny Väinämöinen,	Yet Väinämöinen is unborn,
Ilmau ikirunoja.	Poet eternal not emerged.[31]

While reading the Kalevala we of course are misled by the fact that in certain situations the names Väinämöinen and Ilmatar are equivalent. But when we remember that they are interchangeable, one wonders why Väinämöinen is not yet, at this time, born. In the Old Kalevala he was definitely born earlier (corroborating our discussion of the Trinity doctrine). Has the New Kalevala gone astray because Väinämöinen as the true Logos has, according to our presentation, already emerged? Not at all, because the New Kalevala refers to a strange plot twist: the "second creation." Creation has begun, the worlds have already been formed, but what is lacking? It lacks human beings, it lacks the "image of God." And we need not think that there are no living things yet; the world is truly full of life, and life can exist without the presence of human life-forms. But before the creative process drives consciousness into a life-form, Väinämöinen as the Triune Logos has not yet separated from his mother's womb. Only after human intellectual, emotional and mental life awakens will Väinämöinen be fully born.

What else is the work of creation other than the Creator's intention to reveal himself? "I want to see my own image." And one image after another is rejected: "This isn't me; that's not truly me." Only in humanity does the Creator begin to see himself. And deep within the human soul dwells the Creator's will to see himself in his completeness. Therefore a person does not find tranquility until he realizes his innermost divine longing and aspires toward perfection—a perfection he was created for. God's voice prays within the seeker:

Saata maalle matkamiestä,	Guide the traveler to the land,
Ilmoillen inehmon lasta,	Child of mankind to the open
Kuuta taivon katsomahan,	To behold the moon in heaven
Päiveä ihoamahan,	And to wonder at the daylight,
Otavaista oppimahan,	Get to know the Great Bear's grandeur
Tähtiä tähyämähän!	Or just to stare up at the stars![32]

And by his own doing, God assumes the human form:

Liikahutti linnan portin	He pushed against his prison lock
Sormella nimettömällä,	Pressing with his nameless finger,
Lukon luisen luikahutti	Slid the bony bolt aside,
Vasemmalla varpahalla,	With his left toe opened it;
Tuli kynsin kynnykseltä,	Scrabbling with his nails he came
Polvin porstuan ovelta.	Crawling through the exit door.[33]

The Creator first devises his essential triune nature. Then comes the second creation, the gift of the triune nature to humanity.

From the seer's standpoint, the whole cosmogony is the creative act of a great artisan. It is agony and it is joy, and its expression in the Kalevala is pure mastery. How tranquil the cosmology of the Kalevala appears in its simplicity. In it there are no ordinary human emotions, yet it contains greater emotions, greater strength, divine thoughts and divine will. It rises before our eyes sublime, majestic.

9

The Act of Salvation

IN THEOLOGICAL TEACHINGS, salvation is said to be that divine action which leads a humanity fallen into sin towards a reunion with God. This usually happens through the Trinity's second person, the son, who is then regarded as the savior of humanity as with Christ, Krishna (Vishnu) or Horus in Egypt. However, of course the entire divine Trinity is involved. For example, in Christianity the Holy Spirit leads the church and individuals to Christ, while God the Father loves the world so much that he let his only son die as atonement for the world's sins. If there is any doctrine which Christians cherish as theirs alone, it is this doctrine of divine salvation. They exuberantly cry out, "the pagans and other primitive people did not know anything about Jesus Christ!" And we respond: "It is true that pagans had no knowledge of the savior called Jesus Christ, but it is a different thing altogether to say they knew no savior at all." The world has been around for much longer than 6000 years. To our thinking it is "blasphemy" to say that the humanity of hundreds of thousands of years, perhaps millions of years, were wandering in darkness, going to eternal damnation, until just a few thousand years ago when God the Father glanced at the earth and decided something ought to be done about it. But let us leave well enough alone. Suffice it to say that the divine act of salvation is not a moment in history—it happens through long ages of learning and development. Spiritual darkness exists today as it did ten-thousand years ago, and light is possible today as it was a million years ago. Darkness and light go hand

45

in hand until the light triumphs within the individual. Salvation is not exoteric by nature (given from without); clearly salvation is intrinsically esoteric.

This is why we are not cautious in proclaiming that the ancient Finns and other ancient cultures were aware of and experienced what we call divine salvation. We just have to remember that religious forms change but the underlying essence doesn't. Superficially seen, pagans and natives have a different concept of spiritual life and the task of humanity than do Christians. But discerned with a spiritual eye, the inner experience of an authentic pagan seer and an initiate into Christian Mysteries is the same.

When we begin to examine the way Finnish seers understand mankind's development and salvation, we must remember that in ancient symbolic systems names and words had multiple meanings depending upon their context of use. These different meanings are not arbitrary. For example, a "red string" simply exists; variations arise from differing shades of its primary meaning, different perspectives on the thing itself rather than on totally different meanings. In ancient times, names and designations were not chosen in the manner of scientific exactness as in our day; rather, the whole language of definition was allegorical or poetic.

Earlier we explained how the name Kaleva means Logos in mystic language. Then, in the creation runes we saw how Väinämöinen adopted the role of the Logos. Finally, Ilmatar and certainly even the scaup express distinct activities of the Logos. Furthermore, in other places the Kalevala relates that Väinämöinen is "Kaleva's son." This comes as no surprise when we consider that Logos has the general meaning of "son of God." Overall, we understand that Väinämöinen is only an aspect of the consciousness of Logos, or, alternatively, of Kaleva.

It is told that Kaleva had twelve sons. If we ever discover the names of all twelve sons, we will know the ancient mystic names of the hierarchy of the divine Logos. These are also the twelve signs of the zodiac. Seven of these names also represent the seven primary angels—those nearest the throne of God—who are the astrological rulers of the seven holy planets. Three of the names symbolize the three aspects of the Logos-consciousness, which indicate its full nature. This is why the Logos Trinity is said to consist of three personalities or "masks." Three names have been preserved for us in the Kalevala—as well as a few others—but at least these three are certain. And who are they? They are none other than the Kalevala's three primary heroes: Väinämöinen, Ilmarinen and Lemminkäinen.

When we decide to become fully absorbed in the psychology of the Logos, we must examine Väinämöinen, Ilmarinen and Lemminkäinen as expressions of divine forces. These forces are revealed in humanity's spiritual and mental development as well as in each individual's inner life. Grand visions unfold in front of our discerning eye when we venture deeply into these things. We outlined earlier how the psychological Trinity of the Logos corresponds to the three divisions of the human psyche or soul. First, Logos as Father is the *power* (the Crown; Kether) which corresponds to human willing. Second, Logos as Son—the ever-attractive love-wisdom—corresponds to human feeling and emotion. Third, the Logos as Holy Spirit is the actively discerning divine genius of the Light of Truth, corresponding to human reasoning or thinking. When we now compare this system to the designations in the Kalevala, Väinämöinen clearly represents the divine will, Lemminkäinen the divine emotion, and Ilmarinen the divine intellect or reason. In support of this Trinity doctrine, we specifically read about Väinämöinen in the Old Kalevala:

Min' olin miesnä kolmantena	And I, Väinämöinen,
	was the third man
Ilman pieltä pistämässä,	Began designing the hem of the air,
Taivaan kaarta kantamassa,	Lifted up the firmament,
Taivoa tähittämässä.	And put the stars into the sky.[34]

Eventually we will also look at Lemminkäinen and Ilmarinen, and if our claims here initially seem to come out of nowhere, it will be better supported as we overview what the Kalevala tells us about all three of its heroes. For example, in the Kalevala, what motivates the three of them? What is the shared goal of their activities? In the beginning, at least, their pursuits involve winning the daughter of Pohjola (Northland).

Let us focus on this. All of the Kalevala-heroes court the daughter of Pohjola—each one of them wants her for his very own.

The reader may wonder, "what is so divine about this?" And we respond: Their divine activity is revealed in this.

Hieros Gamos, or "Sacred Marriage"—generally a term referring to the highest human love—is mystical language which contains a deep psychological truth for the seer. In the Christian faith, Paul's writings relate that Christ is a bridegroom while the individual human soul, the congregation and the Church are his bride. Even the realistic and popular poem "Love's High Song" is written in a form of deeply symbolic nomenclature. Christians should also be familiar with the intriguing line from the First Book of Moses: "The sons of God saw that the daughters of men were beautiful; and they took wives for themselves, whomever they chose" (Genesis 6:2). And who doesn't know the beautiful Greek story of Amor (Love) and Psyche (Soul)?

What divine truth do these allegorical stories contain? It is the same message as contained in the words "the divine act of salvation." These stories explain and make clear how divine consciousness loves and pursues the human soul, how it endeavors to join the human soul and thereby raise it up.

Väinämöinen, Lemminkäinen and Ilmarinen all live in Suvantola, on the heaths of Kalevala, where the weather is eternally summer. In other words, they live in the higher planes of the invisible world and from there pursue the daughter of Pohjola. And Pohjola is described as gloomy, benighted—its only charm is the daughter of Pohjola herself. What else could Pohjola be but "the valley of despair." And what else could the daughter of Pohjola represent but the spiritual seed within the collective consciousness of humanity? And from the viewpoint of the individual microcosm, Pohjola is the mortal life of the body and the lovely virgin of Pohjola is the human soul within the body.

The Kalevala-heroes which court the daughter of Pohjola represent the divine, developmental forces which educate the human soul and work to create a new, better humanity. Why should we be ashamed of the Kalevala's somewhat peculiar presentation of divine mysteries when we are not ashamed to talk about—albeit in a more philosophical language—"God's love," "Christ's love for his bride" and so on?

The great wisdom of the Kalevala is evident in the simple fact that we don't read in it of human beings yearning for God and thirsting for truth; rather, we learn of God's love and yearning for humanity. Everyone intuitively knows that human yearning is only a dim reflection of the divine yearning which higher beings feel for humanity. "And God loved the world," whispers the Christian in a holy presentiment of truth, but he is surely mistaken in supposing that God did not actively love His creation from the very beginning.

And how do the Kalevala-heroes fare in their courtings? How do the divine forces succeed in their salvation project? Väinämöinen does not win the daughter of Pohjola nor Aino, and neither does Lemminkäinen. Only Ilmarinen succeeds. This fact reflects an astute psychological insight and a deep understanding of life's developmental laws. After all, which aspect of the divine consciousness catches the human soul and draws it Godward? Is it the will? No. The human soul is too full of fantasies and desires to unhesitatingly comply with "God's will." And what of emotion? No. Pride is a great weakness of the human soul, leaving it incapable of being satisfied with "God's love." In its initial awakening, the human soul yearns for divine help, strength and guidance—a maturity abundant with abilities in which one can wholeheartedly believe. And this core ability is ratiocination, the reasoning intellect.

Ilmarinen, as the exponent of thought, intellect and genius, takes the maid of Pohjola for his one and only. What would be the fate of the human soul without the light of reason? Without the faculty of independent reasoning, there can be no choosing between "good" and "evil"; there can be no free will which makes us human. The human being would be an unconscious puppet in God's hands, alive but without merits.

The Ilmarinen-forces are therefore the first to become active in the life of humanity, and the Väinämöinen-forces are the last. Among people today, we cannot yet observe a human-divine will as a common phenomenon. Human will, as psychologists point out, is so easily dissolved in a substrate of desires and emotions. True willing is something esoteric. Today it is found only in mystics and gifted people. Väinämöinen is truly the eternal seer, the Poet Immortal who accomplishes more with his songs and his willing words than all the others. Väinämöinen is the Kalevala's preferred superman *par excellence*, and his duty in the act of salvation is to the individual rather than the collective. His effects are therefore found in the later developmental stages.

The Lemminkäinen-Forces

I N THE COURTSHIP RUNES, the Kalevala does not describe its heroes as complete beings. Although they represent (in the sense we are talking about) divine forces, we find them in the Kalevala to be very human—even, at times, weak. Väinämöinen old and steadfast, experienced wiseman, has the will and strength to master himself and nature, yet in courting the young maiden he behaves remarkably unwise and foolish. So his love for the young Aino, in its weakness and blatant senselessness, can be seen as nothing less than tragic. Lemminkäinen, the handsome Kaukomieli (the far-minded), whose total being exudes enthusiasm and confidence, poetry and love, is also a quarrelsome and quick-tempered warrior who is adventurous yet fickle in the ways of love. Ilmarinen, the eternal smith, the forger of the Sampo, is industrious, capable, ingenius and skillful but is often somewhat slow, lazy, sullen, even childishly simple-minded.

By making its superhuman heroes so human, the Kalevala endears them to us so much that we almost forget their divinity. It seems as though the Kalevala wants to accentuate something by contrasting each hero's fundamental character. "Look and see," it says, "what is best in each, what develops and grows." Stagnation rests like death in its place, but the living spirit goes forward.

This developmental principle runs like a Golden Thread through Lemminkäinen's story. Lemminkäinen, who represents the raging cauldron of emotional forces within humanity's heart, manifests through his life-path the sequential developmental stages of these emotions. This has

50

been formerly demonstrated by the fact that the Lemminkäinen runes, as professor Krohn shows,[35] consist of many stories which are apparently about different people: Ahti Saarelainen (Ahti Islander), Kaukamoinen, Pätöinen Poika (the gallant boy) and so on. But in the poetry of the people's imagination, these are merely variant names for the same being. By the names Kaukamoinen and Ahti Saarelainen, Lemminkäinen makes love to the island girls and takes Kylliki for his wife. As Lemminkäinen he proposes to the maid of Pohja, and the tale of his death originates from the rune of Pätöinen Poika. Lönnrot, in the New Kalevala, with great psychological insight lets the Kaukamoinen-Kylliki episode occur in Lemminkäinen's youth, before his adventure as rival suitor for the Pohja maid. This is because the Kylliki rune belongs to an earlier period in the developmental history of the lemminkäinen-forces within humanity.

As Ahti, Lemminkäinen "grew up in a high-born home, with his most devoted mother." He

Tuli mies mitä parahin	...became the best of men
Puhkesi punaverinen,	As he blossomed out red-blooded,
Joka päästänsä pätevi,	In all points quite capable
Kohastansa kelpoavi.	And a good man all around.[36]

And he had only one fault:

Ain oli naisissa elejä	Always playing around with women,
Yli öitä öitsilöissä,	always at the all-night parties
Noien impien iloissa,	To the pleasure of the virgins,
Kassapäien karkeloissa.	At the rompings of the braidheads.[37]

The rune almost scoffingly refers to Lemminkäinen's weakness, but with a humor characteristic of the Kalevala's treatment of its heroes' misadventures. When examining the Kalevala from its esoteric or occult viewpoint, this quality must be taken into consideration. Lemminkäinen receives praise, his suave power and skills are extolled; with his songs and incantations he entrances all. But in the rune we perceive a slight mockery. How are we to understand this?

This mocking quality reflects what we might call a critical factor within Finnish wisdom (this will become more clear in the last part of the book). Wisdom knows all the facts. It knows that emotion is—at least for the time being—the greatest force in humanity. It knows that emotion's naïve egoism and indiscretions get projected into nature as superstitions and nullifying nonsense. It knows that, stimulated by emotion, humanity performs its greatest heroic acts and miraculous deeds. Meanwhile, however, wisdom also knows that humanity has not yet mastered its lemminkäinen-forces. And we clearly see this in Lemminkäinen's arrogant and despicable attitude towards Wet-Hat, the blind cowherder. At the moment before his victory, Lemminkäinen is deceived by his own emotions and his tragic death is the result. The roots of emotion go so deep in a human being's physical make-up that for good reason one must fear them until one has thoroughly "purified the heart."

To be specific, what is the original root of the emotional lemminkäinen-forces? With certainty, it is surely human sexuality. The ability for divine love and the highest potential of human emotion are clearly related, but physical sexuality awakens emotions to life by identifying an external focus for emotion. The Kalevala is right on the mark: Emotion is a wonderful thing but its weakness is that it imbibes its power from sex.

When Lemminkäinen's fickle pleasure-loving and sexually urgent emotional behavior subsides, love can be focused for a longer time on a chosen object, and the Kylliki episode begins. However, neither in Lemminkäinen nor Kylliki have the emotional forces been purified. It requires oaths and swears oaths (11:289-314) and as a result drowns.

Only in proposing to the maiden of Pohjola does Lemminkäinen overcome all kinds of obstacles—and simple daring and violence are of no help here. His victories win him merit, and as he is gradually released from his emotional selfishness and conceit he begins to understand what love is. In this way the emotional life of humanity is gradually purified and ennobled; blustery pride grows humbler and becomes faithful devotion. In keeping with the Finnish character, even in Lemminkäinen's final words the Kalevala refrains from weepy and excessive emotion. While dying, Lemminkäinen succintly acknowledges his deep reliance on his mother's love and thus reveals his own profound and faithful affection for her:

Oi emoni kantajani,   "O my mother, you who bore me,
Vaivan nähnyt vaaliani!   Suffered, watching over me!
Tietäisitkö, tuntisitko,   If you knew, if you sensed

Miss' on poikasi poloinen,	Where your miserable son is now,
Tokipa rientäen tulisit,	You would come without delay,
Avukseni ennättäisit...	Hasten hither to his aid..."[38]

And later, after his mother has raised him from the dead, he immediately remembers his deep love and affection for the maiden of Pohjola, for whom he suffered so many trials:

Tuollapa syömmykseni,	For in truth my heart is yonder
Toulla tuntoni makaapi	And my sentiments are there
Noissa Pohjan neitosissa,	Among the little maids of Northland
Kaunoisissa kassapäissä,	With those beautiful lovely-locks.[39]

Here the plural "little maids" is just a kind of *pluralis modestiae*—a formal plural.

In exploring the details of these events very carefully, we can observe in Lemminkäinen's life three overall stages which, in turn, symbolize the three developmental periods in the history of humanity's emotional growth: 1) The immature or childish phase when emotions are fickle, careless and superficial, fluttering from one attachment to the next; 2) The youthful stage in which it desires to grab hold of life, and with oaths and promises attempts to remain faithful to ideals; 3) The stage of full maturity when it knows that nothing can be achieved without constant effort and occasional victory.

There is another stage that we have not described yet: The transition from animal to human. Certain secret traditions discuss the blind or instinctive emotional existence such as we find in the animal kingdom. Has the Kalevala overlooked this?

As far as we can tell it has not been overlooked, but is only referred to in passing. When Lemminkäinen sings everyone out of the Pohjola house (12:443-473), he leaves only one alone, "a most wicked cattle herder, that old man, the shut-eye herdsman." This "blind man of Pohjola, Wet-Hat, the cow herder" asks why he was not enchanted out of the house with the others. Lemminkäinen answers:

Siksi en sinuhun koske,	"This is why I did not charm you—
Kun olet katsoa katala,	Since you're ugly enough to look at,

Kurja koskemaisittani;	Let alone the touching of you.
Vielä miesnä nuorempana,	When you were a stripling boy
Karjan paimenna pahaisna	And a worthless cattle herder,
Turmelit emosi tuoman,	You deflowered your mother's child,
Sisaresi siuvahutit,	Raped your very own, own sister,
Kaikki herjasit hevoset,	And you harried all the horses,
Tamman varsat vaivuttelit	Then abused the mares and fillies
Suon selillä, maan navoilla,	On the swamps and in the quicksands
Ve'en liivan liikkumilla.	Where the muddy waters gather."[40]

The blind cow herder is a symbol for the age when a newly born humanity consorted with beasts, a phase H. P. Blavatsky mentions in her book *The Secret Doctrine*. The light of reason was as yet so dim within humanity that they could do little more than mimic animals and rush headlong into total emotional submission to the sexual instinct. This original Fall is found in Paradise Myths and has really provided the foundation for humanity's later suffering. The sexual instinct has always been humanity's fateful weakness, causing great distress. The same humanity that now, for the most part, plays out the roles of Ahti Saarelainen and the beautiful Kaukomieli, earlier acted instinctually like the blind cow herder and thus, in this life, reaps tragedy from the karmic consequences of its original "sin."

In Theosophical literature we read about humanity's Root Races. The first two were super-physical and not until the Third Root Race did human beings actually have physical bodies. Its homeland was a continent which sunk to the bottom of the Pacific Ocean, named Lemuria by the natural scientist P. L. Sclater. The above mentioned "fall into sin" took place with this Third Root Race. After that the race "became black for sin."

The Fourth Race was the red and yellow Atlantean race. They lived on the island called "Atlantis" which sank to the bottom of the Atlantic Ocean. Plato tells us of the last fragment of Atlantis, a small island called Poseidon. In the Kalevala, both "Ahti Saarelainen" (Ahti Islander) and Kylliki lived on "the Island," and therefore in their names as well as their psychological content they belong to the Atlantean phase of emotional development. (Ahti = Vellamo also refers to the emotional plane, the symbol for which has always been water.)

According to *The Secret Doctrine*, humanity now lives in the Fifth or Aryan Root Race. A small minority of humanity are, in their emotional lives, at the level of the true Lemminkäinen, but the greater part continues in the style of Kaukamoinen.

The yet to be born Sixth and Seventh Root Races are still purifying humanity's lemminkäinen-forces so that human beings in everyday life can comprehend and fulfill the Love of Christ.

The divine act of salvation is fulfilled in the gradual development of emotion. Its ultimate fulfillment occurs when personal emotions such as "good" and "evil" are absorbed into the great ocean of divine love. Fulfilled Lemminkäinen therefore represents the highest, most sublime expression of humanity's christ-forces.

Lemminkäinen-Christ

OR A CHRISTIAN it almost might feel like we are defaming the great saint when the old wayward adventurer, the Arctic Don Juan, is set up beside the holy pure and majestic Christ. Be that as it may, our aim is not to argue that the Kalevala describes the divine mysteries of the human soul as beautifully or as sublimely as the New Testament. The wisdom of the Kalevala comes from another age; naturally its external clothing is different. Our intention is only to emphasize that the wisdom of the Kalevala is essentially the same as, for example, the New Testament, and that it knew the same facts about the development and goal of the human soul. The Kalevala describes and evaluates the emotional life in its own way. It recognizes the functions of reason and knowledge, but in its wisdom it knows that emotion is the greatest magic force and most effective regenerator of the human soul. How moving and sublime it is when the brightness and strength of the self-denying love of Lemminkäinen's mother overcomes even death!

The discrepancy between Christ's sublime purity and Lemminkäinen's apparent normalcy is really quite easy to explain. Christ exemplifies the final goal of emotional sublimation, its highest divine expression. Lemminkäinen contains at all times all the contradictions and struggles of previous emotional levels, while never forgetting the final goal. In the Kalevala we clearly find a correspondence between Lemminkäinen and Christ.[41]

The important role of Lemminkäinen's mother in relation to his ultimate resurrection—his divine salvation—proves that Lemmin-

56

käinen is the Second Logos or Son. Väinämöinen's mother, Ilmatar, is not at all a human being—she is holy divine—and Ilmarinen's mother is only a subordinate character. But in every ancient esoteric system the mother of the savior played an important role as a living human being: Christ's mother (Mary); Buddha's mother (Maya); Krishna's mother (Deevaki) and so on. Thus, the story of Lemminkäinen and his mother is very striking.[42]

Lemminkäinen's death is the only one of the three heroes' deaths about which the Kalevala tells; besides that, his variant name in the death runes is Pätöinen Poika, which means the son of God or son of Logos. Likewise, every savior in ancient wisdom teachings is somehow killed and goes to the underworld. Julius Krohn has commented on the remarkable similarity between Lemminkäinen's story and the Scandinavian tale of Baldur, son of Odin. Baldur is the God of Light, and the evil Loki lures the blind Hoder—actually leading Hoder's hand—to stab Baldur with a mistletoe branch. He dies and journeys to the Goddess Hel in Manala and after forty days he rises again from the dead. Ultimately, however, his mother is unable to save him—in this regard Baldur's story differs from Lemminkäinen's. Kaarle Krohn discusses these similarities, but attributes them to the idea that both legends are of Christian origin. In his mind, the source of these legends is found in the story of the death of Jesus, his three-day visit to the realm of the dead (Manala) and his ultimate resurrection.[43]

In this conclusion professor Krohn is absolutely wrong. In presenting similarities between pagan ideas and the story of Christ, he shows his unprofessionalism because he uses only the Baldur tale as an example—and the Baldur tale is just one of many. Even if the Christian origin of the Baldur tale could be supported with writings from the Middle Ages—in itself not very likely—Krohn's explanation falls apart when you consider the much older resurrection myths: Greek, Egyptian, Indian and so forth.

Let us look at some examples. The ancient Hindu savior Krishna was struck and killed by a hunter's arrow as he sat engrossed in meditation under a tree. So tells the ancient Bhagavata Purana, and Hindus count 5000 years since Krishna's death. After his death, Krishna descended to Manala and was later resurrected. In Egypt, Osiris was killed by his nemesis, the evil snake Typhon. But Osiris returns through his son Horus and kills Typhon, to become "the master of life beyond the grave" and "the judge of souls." Likewise, Jesus is killed while fighting evil but in his resurrection claims victory over "the old snake." The Apocalypse relates that Jesus has "the keys of death and of Hades" (Revelation 1:18) and in Acts it is written that he "is the One who has been appointed by God as Judge of the living and the dead" (10:42). After his death, the Babylonian savior Tammuz stayed for three days in the underworld (Tuonela), after which he was resurrected. To commemorate the death and resurrection of Tammuz, a yearly festival of joy and sorrow was held in which someone like a clergyman said: "Trust in your master because his sufferings have prepared salvation for you." Another well known Babylonian legend tells that Ishtar, mother of Tammuz, descended to the underworld to retrieve the waters of life with which she could revive her dead son. The Greek myth about Bacchus (Zagreus or Dionysus) most resembles the story of Lemminkäinen because when the Titans slay Dionysus he is cut into pieces. For three days he sleeps in Hades, after which Jupiter awakens him and Pallas brings him his heart. After his resurrection he takes his place in heaven. A tale that presents Dionysus as Demeter's son relates that Demeter collects and puts together the mutilated parts of her son's body and makes him young and whole again, behaving quite like Lemminkäinen's mother.

We can add more examples from Syria, Mexico and elsewhere, but what we have presented should suffice to prove that the idea of a savior who is killed, journeys to the underworld and resurrects is extremely old and universal. The Christian variant is a copy of older "pagan" forms. It is quite unnecessary and simply mindless to argue that Lemminkäinen's rune has a Christian origin. With good reason—even better reason—it can be shown to be of Greek or Egyptian origin. Because of this, we are fully justified in regarding the story of Lemminkäinen's death, his mother's self-sacrificing love and his own resurrection, as "holy" and of deep spiritual meaning, just as is the story of the resurrection of Jesus.

Psychologically understood, Lemminkäinen's rune contains a crystal clear fact. The second person of Logos, the son of Love or, that is to say, the divine emotional force which is ultimately one and undivided, is "killed" and cut to pieces, dispensed among the individual members of humanity. There is a little piece of it within every human being.*

---

*The Egyptians expressed this by setting the name of Osiris before every grave. ("Osiris N. N.")

But what a travesty has that little piece of divine emotion become! Love has changed into self-importance, hate for others, and all sorts of distorted manifestations of selfishness and vice. Not until "the resurrection" or "a rebirth" will the divine love achieve within a person its original force, purity and unity, and be able to lead and rule souls both living and dead.

The "resurrection" is, of course, an individual phenomenon and is therefore esoteric by nature. In psychological terms, "resurrected ones" are really seers who have accomplished a long and difficult mental development. Humanity as a whole is still far from its goal and never achieves it all at once. One by one each individual gets to the end of the journey by their own efforts and aspirations. Not until all the individuals of humanity are mentally reborn can it be said that the divine savior—the Son of God who within humanity's heart has been crucified—has been resurrected and freed from voluntary distress. Until then he actually wanders in death's realm, preaching to imprisoned souls in darkness.

And he could not resurrect without his mother's help—without the aid of the great mother of nature and life! It is the school of life which educates humanity. Life is like a patient, loving mother. Where would a human soul be as a plaything of his emotions unless nature and life bound his wounds, comforted him, and instilled him with renewed spirit? When his personal emotional life is destroyed, the seed of divine love within his soul can neither help nor heal him. The mother nature then hastens to the aid of Pätöinen Poika, and only the mother's gentle and careful hand can awaken the son from death.

The Ilmarinen-Forces

OF ALL THE KALEVALA'S HEROES, Ilmarinen is the only one whose original divinity is accepted by scholars. The Votyaks today call the Christian God Inmar, which phonetically recalls Ilmari; Inmar and Ilmari were originally gods of the air. In an old sailor's chant, Ilmarinen is invoked for fair wind, and on a Lapp magician's drum we find a genii called Ilmaris sending storm and gale. When classifying the deities of the Häme people, Mikael Agricola mentions that

Ilmarinen Rauhan ia ilman tei Ilmarinen is the god of peace and air
Ia matkamiehet edheswei And helps travelers.

The Kalevala reveals that Ilmarinen "forged the sky and hammered out the firmament." In the Birth of Fire rune he is found together with Väinämöinen as the primeval lightning striker:

Iski tulta Ilmarinen, Ilmarinen struck fire,
Välähytti Väinämöinen, Väinämöinen made flame flash
Sakarilla vaskisella, with a copper spike,
Miekalla tuliterällä, with a flaming sword
Päällä kuuen kirjokannen, in the six vaults of many colors,
Päällä taivosen yheksän. in the nine heavenly spheres.[44]

Professor Kaarle Krohn believes Lemminkäinen was originally a real person, but regards the Kalevala's vividly and realistically described

60

Seppo (smith Ilmarinen) as being just a generic character from the deep furrows of the Finnish psyche. "Ilmarinen is a feature," he says, "or a poetic arche-image which every Finn knows completely, and which impresses the foreigner stronger than any other." And as if to guardedly make an allowance to the school of symbolic thought, professor Krohn simply acknowledges that Ilmarinen (understood in this way) "is historically much more real than the fame of any single smith who ever lived in Finland."[45]

It is quite correct to say that Ilmarinen best represents the Finnish character. He is sulky and tardy and without initiative. He is a bit dumb and on the surface seems cold and emotionless. But when someone or something motivates him to work, he is extremely skillful and conscientious. And when his blood is fired with purpose, he is passionately willing and dedicated. Even if it be easy to pull his leg, this can be attributed to his honesty rather than to mere stupidity. The Kalevala, however, only apparently describes the Finnish character through Ilmarinen. When the Kalevala is looked at from a local or limited perspective, Ilmarinen is naturally observed in the Finnish people. In looking at the Kalevala with our cosmic key—from the universal perspective—then Ilmarinen, in embodying something of the Finnish character, also represents a fundamental feature within the soul of all humanity. And what else could this fundamental facet be besides human reason?

The characteristics listed above undeniably apply to the Kalevala-hero who represents the principle of reason within the collective life of humanity's soul. The same ilmarinen-force which later appears as intelligence and genius, in its first stage of development addresses the states of stupidity and indolence. And that the forces of reason are independent of emotion and therefore cold, is psychologically and metaphysically as true as the fact that passions and emotions can be stimulated—almost without limit—by thought and reason.

Reason or intellect is undeniably a fundamentally human characteristic above all others. Without the Promethean light of reason the human being is nothing more than an animal.

It is reason (discerning consciousness) which raises humanity above the rest of nature; it lifts humanity to the door of deity and opens up the possibility of endless development. Ancient civilizations knew this. The Indian (Hindu) names for human being are *manu* and *manusha*, derived from the Sanskrit stem *man*, which means "to think." *Manu*—the "human type"—is thus "a thinker." From the same root comes the English word *man*, the German *mensch* and the Swedish *människa*—all meaning "a human being." Also from the same origin is the Latin *mens*, "mind," from which comes *mental*, meaning "concerning thought or intellectual processes." An interesting derivation from the root-stem *mens* is *mentiri*—"to lie"—which, of course, unthinking beings are incapable of.

There is a word that no being can use before rising to the level of humanness. This word is "I". The Finnish word *minä* (I) sounds like the Finnish word *ihminen* (a human being). Is it perhaps possible to find a connection between the Finnish word *minä* and the Indo-European stem for the word "man"? And if the stem of the word *ihminen* is *ihmis*, it has to be remembered that "s" also appears in the words *mens* and *manas* (Sanskrit: "mind", "reason"). That the first syllable of the word *ihminen* is *ih* and resembles the German word *ich* ("self" or "I")* may be regarded by scholars as mere chance. At any rate, in the Finnish words *minä* (I) and *ihminen* (human being) is reflected the ancient peaceful spirit of thoughtful and discerning action.

For those with "ears to hear" these meaningful derivations of everyday words prove that "the human being" was originally conceived as a "thinking and reasoning being." Since Ilmarinen thus represents in the mythology of the ancient Finns the forces of intellect, his name is esoterically appropriate because, in Theosophical literature and other sources, we know that the element "air" corresponds to the "thought or reasoning plane." Likewise, "water" symbolizes the emotional plane, "earth" the physical plane, and "fire" the world of higher spirit. Ilmarinen thus means "the master and sovereign of the world of discerning thought." In the Theosophical literature—as every expert knows—it has become customary to speak about the duality of the human ego, the higher and the lower mind. This division that has, by the way, slipped into our literature and everyday language, is based partly on psychological analysis and partly on a secret knowledge of the history of human development.

---

*The German word *ich* ("self" or "I") is also akin to the Greco-Roman word *ego* and Sanskrit *aham* ("I").

Goethe expresses through the mouth of Faust those winged words:

"Two souls, alas! reside within my breast,
And each withdraws from, and repels, its brother;
One with tenacious organs holds in love
And clinging lust the world in its embraces;
The other strongly sweeps, this dust above,
Into the high ancestral spaces."[46]

Every human being eventually notices how the opposites of good and evil, truth and lie, love and hate, beauty and ugliness, pure and impure, and noble and mean fight for supremacy inside the mind. And it is not enough for the opposites to feel comfortable side by side within the soul. People do not often know in their own mind what is right and what is wrong because reason can defend both. In the physical body the natural tendency to selfishness thus often claims victory through the weakness of reasoning.

Psychological handbooks speak of this conflict only in passing, mentioning the existence of a pure reason, but focus only on an analysis of mental life in itself. Everything which concerns their examination is considered to be a function of lower reason, including memory, logic and imagination. But observation and memory correspond to the visual knowledge of higher reason, logical understanding to the cosmic character of higher reason (reason = Logos), and imagination to the creative force of higher reason. The higher self easily serves the higher truth, but the lower self must learn to become disentangled from the domination of selfish emotions and passions by graduating from the school of experience. Without further ado it should be clear to every philosophically-minded person that a gradual development of the constantly moving lower self is impossible without the eternal thinker—the higher reason—in the background. The ageless wisdom has always defined and defended the rights and functions of the higher self. No religion has ever called the original purity of these rights "selfish" or "sinful." All religions and all esoteric wisdom-teachings advise the seeker to fight the selfishness of lower reason and emerge victorious. The teachings of ancient wisdom are rooted in a true understanding of the birth and development of the fully human self.[47]

And what is this strange "self" which escapes the analyzing insight of even the greatest philosophers such as Hume and Kant; where does it come from? How is it born?

Only secret wisdom-teachings provide the answer. The human self has its origin in God. There is only one consciousness in the world: the God-Self. Human self-reflective reasoning is a fragment of the whole divine self; human reason is a tiny fragment of the immense genii of the Logos. And how is the human self designed and given birth?

When after long ages of developmental work the lower elements assemble an animal resembling a human being, like a spiritual lightning-strike the light of the world (the divine reason, the self-consciousness of Logos) descends into the animal, material form, and the human self is born. From the dust of earth, a human being is formed, but God's spirit is blown in from above! The Son of Reason moves from his celestial home into the human figure. The human being is truly divided from the moment of birth: One hand holds fast to his mundane hut, while the other reaches up toward the blue sky. The human self, descended from God, was born into an animal form. (More details on these ideas can be found in H. P. Blavatsky's *The Secret Doctrine*.)

From a philosophical perspective we might conclude that the highest expression of reason is achieved when it realizes itself to be Reason, that is, born from God. This is possible only with the help of the limited individual consciousness, through the purification of the lower self. As we already noted in discussing Väinämöinen and the Creation of the World, the birth of the human self is so important to the world's development that it is called "a second creation."

In the Kalevala the task of "the second creation" is given to Ilmarinen. Ilmarinen accomplishes something the others cannot. Therefore let us now examine the activities of Ilmarinen.

13

Ilmarinen, Fire and Iron

I N THE KALEVALA'S VISIONARY LANGUAGE, if Ilmarinen represents the intellectual forces of humanity, why is he always working with fire and iron, and why does he forge the Sampo? While only mentioning that a "smith" aptly describes a hard-working inventor, and this is the intellect's fundamental character, we should emphasize that Ilmarinen represents the "light of reason" and, as we will see, the smith's work has clear occult underpinnings. By describing Ilmarinen as a "smith" bustling with fire and iron, the Kalevala clearly spells out for those who have "eyes to see" that the ancient Finnish seers understood Ilmarinen's deeper occult function as well his identification with conventional traditions and designations concerning the functions of reason.

The origin and function of rational forces within humanity are presented in the Kalevala primarily as three events in Ilmarinen's life: the Birth of Fire, the Birth of Iron, and the Forging of the Sampo.

The Birth of Fire provides an ethic for the descent of the forces of intellect, divine conscience, and wisdom into a human race wandering in darkness. In the previous chapter we quoted verses from the Old Kalevala which depict Ilmarinen striking fire. In the New Kalevala Ilmarinen's name is changed to "the man of the air," but this phrase clearly refers to him. Ilmarinen, master intellect and God of Reason, is the Prometheus who delivers holy fire to the human race.

As long as humanity faithfully cares for the heavenly fire, all is well. The soul of humanity is then like the virgin of Vesta in her obedient innocence:

Neiti pitkän pilven päällä,	On the very hem of heaven.
Impi ilman partahalla	On a cloud the virgin rocked it,
Tuota tulta tuuitteli,	Rocked the fire
Valkeaista vaapotteli	and swung the light,
Kultaisessa kätkyessä,	Swung it in a golden cradle,
Hihnoissa hopeisissa.	Swaying it on straps of silver.[48]

This is the state of paradise as described in many ancient mythologies. The holy fire of the highest self enlightens the young human race which, obeying its inner light, knows little of the external world. Young Adam lives innocently within nature as its obedient servant. But the time of happiness and blessing is all too brief in the paradise of Lemuria, for the lemminkäinen-forces of emotion and passion are stirring within humanity. Human beings are divided into two genders, Adam and Eve, and the holy fire of spirit loses its brightness. The calamity is described in the rune which tells how:

Impi tulta tuuitteli,	Thus the virgin rocked the fire,
Vaapotteli valkeaista,	Rocked the fire and swung the light,
Tulta sormilla somitti,	Nursed the fire-spark with her fingers,
Käsin vaali valkeaista.	Sheltered it between her hands;
Tuli tuhmalta putosi,	But the stupid maiden dropped it,
Valkea varattomalta,	Slipping through her careless fingers,
Kätösiltä kääntelijän,	From the hands that should have nursed it,
Sormilta somittelijan.	Fingers that were meant to save it.[49]

And the fire changed into burning lightning which rushed from sky to earth, bringing destruction, suffering and distress (47:173-312). In this way, the intellect together with emotion creates all evil and moral suffering by breaking natural law (causa efficiens). Lucifer, the light bringer, who in his original heavenly abode is the same as Christ (Logos), falls to earth and becomes the damned Satan, Christ's opponent. Pure reason defends truth and virtue, but through indulgence and lust, fallen reason gives way to selfishness and falsehood. As the Kalevala tells it, the cooperation of Väinämöinen and Ilmarinen is really needed, the divine forces of will and intellect must unite to raise humanity from its fallen state. And how profound is the work of those divinely-born brothers!

The rune containing the Birth of Fire greatly impresses our minds with the scope of this task.

But at the last moment even they need help. And help appears:

Pikku mies merestä nousi,	Then a little man arose,
Uros aalloista yleni...	Tiny dwarfman from the sea...[50]

This "little man" is Päivän Poika (the son of Day)—meaning the son of Sun or son of God—or, in other words, Christ within a human being's soul. The collective drama changes now to the individual. The little man who "rises from the sea" is Lemminkäinen who has grown into Pätöinen Poika; from the churning swells of emotion emerges Divine Love.* This newly born human being is the smallest of the small, yet his power is greater than the great. He is the son of God and his Father helps him in this way:

Vieri veitsi taivosesta,	From the sky a knife came falling,
Puukko pilvistä putosi,	From the clouds
	a sheath-knife dropping,
Pää kulta, terä hopea,	Golden-hilted, silver-bladed,
Vieri vyölle Päivän pojan.	Down upon his belt directly.[51]

With this sheath-knife sent from the sky he cleaves open the pike and frees the fire-spark which had been swallowed. Pätöinen Poika, like Christ, breaks the hold of bestiality and selfishness within humanity's heart and sets free the spark of divine intellect. However, as we mentioned earlier, this now occurs esoterically, meaning within the individual.

All ancient nations considered fire to be holy and celebrated the glory of heavenly light and fire. The Ascension Day bonfire (*helavalkea*) at Whitsuntide was lit in the spring not just to celebrate the vernal light but also for the glory of reason and wisdom, and even this Christian holiday at Whitsuntide brings this to mind. Without entering into a linguistic debate, we should ask why there is a similarity between the Finnish word "hela" and the Elm's Fire of the old Germans and, further-

---

*Translator's note. See Chapter 10 for more details on Lemminkäinen's development into Christ.

more, how both of these are related to the Grecian "Fire of Hermes." (Hermes-Mercury was the messenger of the gods and God of wisdom.)*

On the other hand, the Birth of Iron rune also illuminates the human history of the intellect-forces from, we might say, the mundane viewpoint. In first reading this incantation rune, we only see some speculation about the origin of iron; at the most, "iron" might mean physical matter in general. From the beginning verses:

Ilma on emoja ensin,	Air's the first one of the mothers,
Vesi vanhin veljeksiä,	Water, oldest of the brothers,
Rauta nuorin veljeksiä,	Iron, youngest of the brothers,
Tuli kerran keskimäinen.	Fire, the brother in the middle.[52]

If "air" represents the world of thought in general and "water" the emotional realm, then "iron" is the exponent of the physical world. But since Ilmarinen plays the main role in the birth of iron** and the key to understanding Ilmarinen has already been discussed, it is clear that iron as well as fire symbolizes some process or manifestation of intellectual powers. Let us not forget the meaning of fire discussed earlier: Fire is from heaven, fire is the pure light of reason, the divine enlightenment spoken of in the Gospel of John (1:4). Remembering this, we can understand what "iron" really is.

Iron, tells the rune, is the younger brother of fire—a close relation:

Olipa aikoa vähäinen,	After a little time had passed,
Rauta tahteli tavata	Iron yearned to meet his brother,
Vanhempata veikkoansa,	Meet his elder brother, fire,
Käyä tulta tuntemahan	And to get acquainted with him.[53]

What else could iron thus be but the younger brother of pure reason, the lower reason, logic, which is often considered steely, cold and hard as

---

*Translator's note. The Finnish word hela resembles the Greek word helios (the sun); the corresponding Finnish verb is helottaa. Related meanings include brightness, shine, and to glitter.

**The one mentioned as the giver of iron's birth—"Ukko, the highest Creator, he himself the God of Air"—can clearly also refer to Ilmarinen.

iron? Iron is really soft when compared to fire,* as is our mundane reason when compared to the heavenly, divine reason, so justifiably it is said in the Gospels: "and the light shines in the darkness, and the darkness did not comprehend it" (John 1:5). However, darkness and ignorance always desire light, just as in the Kalevala we read how iron yearns to meet fire. The old nations spoke about the inevitable dark "Iron Age"—where humanity now lives—and yearningly recalled the earlier "Golden Age" when the spiritual light of the higher self freely shone in the as yet unmanifest humanity.

In the rune of the Birth of Iron we find a remarkable feature: Iron is born through the work of Ilmarinen before Ilmarinen himself is born. We can understand this occurrence in the development of humanity through the teachings of occult wisdom. Before the ilmarinen-forces of reason and thought were fully embodied, the developing ability to think was already being formed by "natural evolution." Within the animal kingdom then extant—or, we might say, in the animal kingdom of which early humanity was then a part—the crude precursors of thought emerged. We do not suggest that an ability to think independently or to follow a train of reason was yet present, but within the animal group-consciousness we can trace the will to self-consciousness and nuances of early thought: imitating, admiring, attachment and faithfulness. These same traits are abundantly found even in the animal kingdom of today. The seed of understanding had already been planted in the depths of the human soul—iron was hidden in the swamps and cliffs, as the Kalevala says—before it was allowed to emerge for humanity to see.

Only after this event does the rune shift to tell us about the birth of Ilmarinen or the awakening of the higher forces of reason:

Syntyi seppo Ilmarinen,	Ilmarinen had been born,
Sekä syntyi, jotta kasvoi,	Born and grown to manhood too,
Se syntyi sysimäellä,	Born upon a hill of charcoal,
Kasvoi hiilikankahalla,	Grew up on a cindery heathland,
Vaskinen vasara käessä,	In one hand a copper hammer,
Pihet pikkuiset piossa.	In the other his tiny tongs.
Yöllä syntyi Ilmarinen,	In the night the smith was born,
Päivällä pajasen laati.	On the next day built his smithy.[54]

*Translator's note. Iron is soft compared to fire because it is melted by fire.

Ilmarinen did not evolve from lower states, he was not like a newborn who can do nothing. He was born the "smith eternal," already complete at birth. Having been born at night, he built his smithy the very next day. He was an old citizen from another world who took the form on earth of a recognizable figure. In the Old Kalevala, when the bird sent by Louhi asks Ilmarinen why he is so "very skillful, a forger quite capable," he responds:

Siksi olen kovin osaava,	This is why I am so skilled,
Varsin taitava takoja:	Quite the skillful smithy worker:
Kauan katsoin luojan suuhun,	Long I watched the mouth of God,
Partahan jalon jumalan,	Saw the beard of noble Ukko
Ennen taivoa takoissa,	When he previously forged the sky,
Ilman kantta kalkuttaissa.	Hammered out the firmament.[55]

This passage clearly relates an instance of the fire of heavenly reason descending from the higher spheres of spirit to take up residence within humanity. "There was the true light which, coming into the world, enlightens every man" (John 1:9).*

Comprehension began to awaken through natural evolution, but it is not until the holy ilmarinen-forces of higher reason join with this dawning comprehension that the individual human consciousness is truly born. Natural scientists usually do not want to believe in this kind of "supernatural" cooperation but one of them, Darwin's well known colleague A. R. Wallace, admits that it is impossible for him to understand the origin of the human spirit by any other means than this kind of supernatural involution.

Now in the rune of the Birth of Iron there opens a window to a historical era. There is nothing told about the happy Golden Age when the light of higher spirit was supreme and iron still "laid in the swamp." Instead, the Birth of Iron story directly embarks upon telling how after the "fall into sin" the ilmarinen-forces begin their task of bringing the iron of logical understanding into the daylight so that it can be forged. Indeed, with these events, iron becomes very afraid of fire:

---

*Translator's note. In the Finnish Bible of 1913, this passage reads: "It was the earnest light, which enlightens all humans who come into the world."

Rauta raukka säpsähtihe,	Then poor iron was affrighted,
Säpsähtihe, säikähtihe,	Was affrighted and afflicted
Kun kuuli tulen sanomat,	When he heard the fire speaking,
Tulen tuimat maininnaiset.	When he caught the fiery meaning.[56]

But Ilmarinen beautifully consoles:

Ellös olko milläskänä,	'Don't you worry about all that.
Tuli ei polta tuttuansa,	Fire won't burn an old acquaintance,
Herjaile heimoansa!	He won't injure his own tribesman.
Kun tulet tulen tuville,	When you come to the house of fire,
Valkean varustimille,	To the burning barricade,
Siellä kasvat kaunihiksi,	You will grow more beautiful
Ylenet ylen ehoksi,	In the flashing of the blades,
Miesten miekoiksi hyviksi,	Sword blades* in the hands of swordsmen,
Naisten nauhan päättimiksi.	Ornaments** on women's garments.'[57]

The mundane mind does not expand easily in the fire of the holy wisdom of higher reason—it prays to get loose from this "torment of red fire"—but Ilmarinen knows that evil will win altogether if the lower mind is allowed to follow its own call:

Jos otan sinun tulesta,	'If I take you from the fire
Ehkä kasvat kauheaksi,	You may grow to be a terror
Kovin raivoksi rupeat,	And commit all kinds of outrage,
Vielä veistät veljeäsi,	Even carve up your own brother,
Lastutat emosi lasta.	Cut to chips your mother's child.'[58]

However, at this great moment of distress, Iron, the human comprehension, promises that it has no thoughts of making evil. Ilmarinen jerks iron from the fire, sets it on the anvil and begins to form it. Now all that

---

*Sword blades here means "the sword of truth."

**Ornaments here means "the charm of intellect (*esprit*)."

remains is the final trial so that human understanding can become an excellent instrument of higher reason:

Viel' oli pikkuista vajalla,	Yet some little thing was wanting,
Rauta raukka tarpehessa:	Iron needed something more;
Eipä kiehu rauan kieli,	Tongue of iron is not boiling
Ei sukeu suu teräksen,	And the mouth of steel unborn:
Rauta ei kasva karkeaksi	Iron won't be tempered ever
Ilman veessä kastumatta.	Till it's quenched in tempering liquid.[59]

The test of emotion! Logic must be dipped in the baptismal water of emotions and lusts. And Ilmarinen understands that the baptismal water must be sweet and good (Kalevala, Runo 9:207-230). But what happens? The bee from whom he requests honey for the baptismal tempering disturbs his plan:

Lenteä hyrähtelevi,	Then he flew and buzzed about
Viskoi hiien hirmuloita,	As he hurled down Hiisi's horrors,
Kantoi käärmehen kähyjä,	Spewed the venom of the viper,
Maon mustia mujuja,	And the black blood of the adder,
Kusiaisen kutkelmoita,	Then the acid of the ant,
Sammakon salavihoja,	Hidden hatreds of the toad
Teräksen tekomujuihin,	Into the tempering quench of steel,
Rauan karkaisuvetehen.	Hardening liquid for the iron.[60]

It turns out the emotions were not all beautiful. When the lower reason goes through the swirl of bestial lusts and desires, its tenuous higher light goes out and all its power flows into these emotions. Then Ilmarinen unknowingly immerses iron in the accursed water, and

Sai siitä teräs pahaksi,	This put steel in evil mood
Rauta raivoksi rupesi,	And poor iron went quite mad;
Petti vaivainen valansa,	Broke his word, the wretched creature,
Söi kuin koira kunniansa,	Ate his honor like a dog:
Veisti raukka veljeänsä,	Cut his brother, bit his kin,
Sukuansa suin piteli,	
Veren päästi vuotamahan,	Made the blood flow everywhere,
Hurmehen hurahtamahan.	Gushing in a stream of gore.[61]

With dramatic realism, the rune about the Birth of Iron thus ends its splendid presentation of the intellectual condition of humanity, introducing problems which continue today. However, the ilmarinen-forces, in the form of culture, have had a long presence.*

---

*Theosophists and astrologers know why iron was chosen as the symbol of the lower mind, the lower reason. The incarnation of the ilmarinen-forces took place only after the earth had cooled, physical iron emerged, and the animal kingdom was fully formed. According to the astrological-occultic interpretation, this was caused by Mars. Mars is the planet of iron and also bestial aggressions, war and lusts, as everyone acquainted with the symbolism of astrology knows. Not until the earth had crystallized into a hardened physical state was it able to receive the iron effects of Mars. Likewise, Mars' strong emotional prodding could not be felt within the animal consciousness. And the Sons of Reason ("maanasaputras") could not incarnate until the intellectual foundations had awakened "from below." In astrological terms, the influence of the Sons of Reason has a Mercury-like effect (wisdom). Mars and Mercury are thus two very important planets whose connections with the earth are very mysterious. In a sense, the earth represents both Mars and Mercury—its development moves from Mars to Mercury—and within Ilmarinen, who represents the humanity of earth, is hidden the gods of both war and wisdom. However, with an inventive psychological twist, the Kalevala gives the role of Mars to Lemminkäinen, letting him be the warrior hero. This emphasizes that Ilmarinen himself is innocent, virtually incapable of evil; reason's evil and weakness result only from enslaving itself to lusts and passions. It is emotion that is the actual cause and origin (causa materialis) of selfishness, unkindness and warring despotism. In a way, this also reflects the same view of the old Chaldean-Jewish story about the fall into sin: Eve (emotion) lures Adam (thought) to eat from the tree of the knowledge of good and evil.

14

Ilmarinen and the Sampo

HE MOST REMARKABLE THING that Ilmarinen forges is the Sampo. A critical key to understanding the Kalevala is therefore a correct comprehension of the Sampo. As we now understand who Ilmarinen is and what his forge represents, it should be easy to get a general idea of the nature of the Sampo. The Sampo is something produced by the forces of intellect working intensely within humanity. What could this be? "Culture" is what instantly comes to mind. Lönnrot said long ago that "the Sampo describes all the resources of livelihood current at that time." Through cultural institutions and educational tasks, the intellect that had gone astray, thrown into the lap of base passions, was again guided in the right direction. However, the Kalevala relates that it was just this Sampo that led the way to new and bigger conflicts. When Ilmarinen forged the Sampo for the Mistress of Pohjola, she took it and locked it within Pohjola's stone fortress, a place the Kalevala heroes apparently did not like. The people of Pohjola certainly prospered greatly with the protection and benefits of the Sampo, but the Sampo was designed for a greater use. Thus, it was a disadvantage for the heroes of the Kalevala to have lost it. If the Sampo offers only culture, resources, livelihood, science and art, one might suspect that Ilmarinen could just forge another one, even a better and more magnificent Sampo. But he didn't and it is left to the Kalevala heroes to steal back the Sampo, to save it from an eternity in Pohjola's hill of stone. This scenario suggests that an even more profound and secret meaning is hidden within the Sampo.

74

The solution to the riddle of the Sampo in this deeper meaning would answer the mysteries of age-old traditions. We already discussed how the secret knowledge does not have the same viewpoint as scientific studies in regard to the birth of civilizations, religions and so on. The position of the secret wisdom is often contradictory. According to this secret tradition, all civilizations and religions have been installed from above, that is, through the influence of more advanced beings. At the dawn of time, humanity was as yet inexperienced and undeveloped, and the question arises as to where these higher beings came from. And for this question too, the secret knowledge has an answer: of course, they came from some other planet, whose beings were substantially like those of early earth, but immeasurably older and more developed. Consequently, these advanced beings served as helpers and teachers. In our time when theories are being formulated for moving organic life from one heavenly body to another, this kind of idea should not feel impossible. The väinämöinen- and ilmarinen-forces do not succeed in holding the attention of humanity. Humanity would have stayed ignorant of its divine faculties if Väinämöinen hadn't urged Ilmarinen to forge the Sampo. Only after the Sampo is made does the delightful maid of Pohjola agree to wed.

Ilmarinen thus represents all intellectual forces, and not just the intellect within individual people on earth, but also the genius and wisdom of all other advisors, teachers, saviors and legislators who have influenced us from other realms.

And now what about the Sampo?

The Sampo symbolizes the secret wisdom that the original teachers of humanity brought with them from the other place, the occult knowledge embodied by the so-called White or Secret Brotherhood—the seers and wisdom-keepers in their invisible temple that "was not built by human hands." This knowledge is even contained within the word Sampo. Castrén tells of an ancient Buddhist temple whose name in the Mongolian language is *sampo* and in the Tibetan language *sangfu*. The latter word means "a secret fountain" (of happiness).[62]

There exists another Tibetan word which in our thinking can be compared to Sampo. This is *sampun* or *zampun*, which is the Tibetan "tree of life." It has three roots. The first rises to heaven, to the top of the highest mountain, the second goes down to Manala, the underworld, and the third stays in the middle and reaches toward the east. If we may indulge in linguistic speculations, we could suggest that Sampo or Sambo is related to *samboo* or *samboodha*, which in Sanskrit means "the highest knowledge or wisdom"—and why not also point out the Latin combination of words *summum bonum*, "the highest good"? Comparetti's attempt to explain that "Sampo" was derived from the artificial Swedish word *sambo* ("a dwelling for several people" or "to live together") is linguistically unsuccessful. The explanation by Fries that "Sampo" referred to the Lappish magician's drum, we will reserve for later discussion.*

And if it be true that the explanation for legendary words must be sought in their own language, perhaps, for example, "sampo" was derived from the word *samapolku* ("the path of wisdom walked by ancient wisemen")? In fact we do not consider it impossible that the word Sampo is related to the words *sampi* (a sturgeon) and *sammas* (statue or landmark) as modern linguists believe. But the conceptual meaning of the Sampo and the connection with these words will become clear when the mystery of the Sampo is opened, in Chapter 28, with our occult-psychological key.

Now let us remember, despite all this philological speculation, our original occult reading for the word Sampo. Then we can comprehend the words of the Mistress of Pohjola when, with some suspicion and some admiration, she requires Ilmarinen to perform certain tasks:

Ohoh seppo Ilmarinen,	"Oho, you smith Ilmarinen,
Takoja iänikuinen!	You, the eternal hammerer!
Saatatko takoa sammon,	If you hammer out the Sampo
Kirjokannen kirjaella	And devise the ciphered cover,[63]
Joutsenen kynän nenästä,	Make it from the point of swan quill,
Maholehmän maitosesta,	From the milk of farrow cow,
Ohran pienestä jyvästä,	From a tiny grain of barley
Kesä-uuhen untuvasta?	And the fleece of summer ewe...[64]

---

*In Lönnrot's first book there is a point which clearly shows that the Sampo is something mysterious and heavenly, and a near relative to the ilmarinen-forces. When the Mistress of Pohjola asks Ilmarinen if he could really forge the Sampo, he answers: "I could surely forge the Sampo, make the multi-colored cover... a moment ago I forged the Sampo, made the multi-colored cover, when I forged the starry sky, hammered out the lid of heaven." See *Kalevalan esityöt* (*Preliminary Works for the Kalevala*) "I. Väinämöinen", pgs. 451-458.

Ilmarinen has been presented with a superhuman, supernatural, and, to the logical mind, impossible task. He will not be able to forge the Sampo by means of a human being's undeveloped faculties; it can only happen—even just in the sense of a work of art—with the help of the gods. Only a being in whom the higher self is consciously alive and whose knowledge is not limited by sensory information and logic is capable of creating the greatest artistic work of life; i.e., only they can sculpt the secret school of life in which all humanity can be educated.*

The forging of the Sampo is, in our thinking, not very well described in the Kalevala. The original tradition was presumably obscured although it is aesthetically impressive and psychologically correct if we assume, as Juhani Aho does, that the Sampo is a work of *human* art. The words describing the act of forging were seemingly derived from the Birth of Fire sequence and from the forging of the Golden Maid. The Runo 10 verses 281-310 and 393-422 complete the forging sequence and describe what kind of Sampo Ilmarinen forged. This suffices for us to describe the forging of the Sampo.

Siitä seppo Ilmarinen,	Thereupon smith Ilmarinen,
Takoja iänikuinen,	The eternal hammerer,
Takoa taputtelevi,	Rapped and tapped, rat-a-tat-tat,
Lyöä lynnähyttelevi,	Clinking away with a clank,
	clank, clank—
Takoi sammon taitavasti:	Deftly built the Sampo mills:
Laitahan on jauhomyllyn,	On one side a flower mill
Toisehen on suolamyllyn,	And a salt mill on the second,
Rahamyllyn kolmantehen.	On the third a money mill.
Siitä jauhoi uusi sampo,	The new Sampo then was grinding,
Kirjokansi kiikutteli,	With its ciphered cover spinning;
Jauhoi purnun puhtehessa,	Ground three binfuls every morning:

---

*In one respect, the Big Oak verses (Kalevala Runo 2) are describing something very similar to the Sampo: the original light of truth behind countless variant religions and philosophies. A multitude of different methods and teachings obscure the light of the sun and moon from the seeker's eyes, and thus one despondently asks "where is the truth?" Not until the "little man" (the same being we mentioned in the Birth of Fire discussion as the intuition of love within the human mind) emerges from the sea to cut down the Big Oak will the sun of truth be seen.

Yhen purnun syötäviä,	First a bin of things to eat,
Toisen jauhoi myötäviä,	Next a bin of things to sell,
Kolmannen kotipitoja.	Last a bin of things for home.[65]

This symbolism is not difficult to understand because the teachers and messengers of the Secret Brotherhood installed the foundations of all cultures. "Flour" is bread and provides all the material needs of a human being (especially in the agricultural lands of the northern regions). But people cannot live by bread alone; spiritual food is also needed, which "comes from the mouth of the Father" as Jesus said. The symbol of this spiritual life is "salt" and truly Jesus also said, "you are the salt of the earth." Lastly, a wealth of resources (symbolized in the verse by "money") are required to make civilization possible. Creativity could not express itself in the sciences, arts, and religions were there not a continuous supply of abundance.

Is it therefore any surprise that "the Old Dame of Pohjola delights"?

When the Sampo is enclosed within the Stone Mountain of Pohjola, hidden behind nine locks, the great war over the Sampo begins. People are divided into two camps. The people of Kaleva want the Sampo, or at least a part of it, back for themselves, while on the other hand the people of Pohjola jealously guard it for their own use.

What else could this be but a recollection by Finnish seers of the old battle between "white magic" and "black magic" on the continent of Atlantis? During the time of the Third Root Race (discussed above) the great teachers incarnated among humanity. During the Fourth Root Race the "black magic" was developed in the land of Atlantis, reaching an alarming strength. Symbolically, the Sampo had gotten into the hands of the people of Pohjola. A great knowledge and wisdom was given to humanity but they misused it, chaining it to their own selfish goals. (This will be explored more deeply in the third part of the book.) "The masters of the white race" then decided to salvage what was left so that humanity would not totally self destruct. Väinämöinen, Ilmarinen, and Lemminkäinen, as great leaders, rally the people of Kaleva to journey on a great mission of salvation to the dark realm of Pohjola. Likewise, the secret tradition of the Kalevala also tells how the elder seer Väinämöinen magically sings all Pohjola into a deep sleep. Even this little feature is enough to show that the "War over the Sampo" episode (Runo 43) refers to the great war on Atlantis, spoken of in many ancient legends.

15

Reincarnation

WHEN READING THE BEAUTIFUL KALEVALA-RUNES about the death and resurrection of Lemminkäinen (Runos 14 and 15), he who is devoted to the Theosophical view of life naturally recalls an ancient doctrine which reveals to him the enigma of life, a doctrine he might also remember when pondering the Christian resurrection. This ancient doctrine is reincarnation which, when first heard of, seems rather odd.

The reincarnation doctrine implies that this life is neither the first nor the last one—we reincarnate again and again. The soul does not come from our parents nor is it created by God at the moment of birth. The soul existed before birth. But where? It comes from the unseen spiritual world, and to there it returns after bodily death. The human soul is thus like a stranger wandering on earth. It arrives through the gate of birth and leaves through the gate of death.

But reincarnation is by no means without purpose. The entire process of soul development is its goal. Without it, there can be no spiritual development. Life as a whole would just go around in circles, never able to be elevated should the individual attainments ultimately pass away. But when there exists something—the soul—to which individual experiences are drawn, like crops to the granary, then there is the possibility of continuous development over long periods. Mere physical inheritance does not guarantee the preservation of, say, the quality of genius—creative genius is seldom shared by kin—but reincarnation allows for the movement of such traits into another life. When the human soul has developed to the point of genius, that genius is preserved and the soul can even continue growing. This is possible only because the human being is really a soul, living in the invisible world and incarnating on earth to have learning experiences and to perform certain tasks.

In the Lemminkäinen rune the Kalevala beautifully emphasizes life's triumph over death. The life-work of Lemminkäinen is tragically cut short. He perishes before his work is done. Perhaps the fault for this may be found in his own doings, but we all feel bitter and sad when a promising life ends prematurely.

Se oli loppu Lemminkäisen,	This was Lemminkäinen's end,
Kuolo ankara kosian	Death of that undaunted lover,
Tuonen mustassa joessa,	In the murk of Death's black river,
Manalan alantehessa.	In the caverns of the dead.[66]

Yes, it was the end. But life is not all that bitter and hard. The truth of reincarnation dispels the fear of death. A human being is not forever banished from this world of experiences, sufferings and tasks. His mother—nature—awakens him from death and the Kalevala devotes a long rune to this Mother Love as if to impress upon us that we should not fear death. The Kalevala thus offers the same optimism as other philosophies, and a belief in reincarnation existed in ancient India and Egypt.

For the scientifically minded, it may seem too presumptuous and hasty to conclude that the ancient Finns believed in reincarnation. In the Kalevala, it is not even clearly spelled out with so many words, and it is scientifically disagreeable to decipher words to mean something else! True enough, we will answer to this, but let us not forget that, all along, we have been excavating deeper things that cannot be seen on the surface. There is nothing unscientific in this in terms of our methods. Our interpretations, however, may be unreasonable and unscientific or they may be reasonable and based upon deeper insights. Naturally, it is our duty to do this with a critical eye.

We have our own reasons for our firm convictions that Finnish seers knew about and themselves believed in reincarnation as an unshakable law of life. As for us, we do not need any external evidence for it (the reincarnation doctrine). But we do not think it wrong to seek for traces of a belief in reincarnation among the old runes of the Kalevala. We even feel that if the collectors of these runes and incantations would have taken this possibility to heart, their harvest would have been much greater. There are people even today in Finland who know by their own experiences the truth of reincarnation.

There remains for us to see other places in the Kalevala which refer to reincarnation. Such is the whole life history of Lemminkäinen, with its different periods and variant names. We discussed this earlier (see the "Lemminkäinen-Forces" chapter) and we will only remind the reader that those developmental stages in Lemminkäinen's life marvelously portray the reincarnational stages of individual growth. Let us name this individual soul Lemminkäinen; thus, Wet-Hat the cowherder refers to an earlier stage in Lemminkäinen's soul journey, Ahti Saarelainen is typical of stages occurring a little later, with Lemminkäinen himself following close and Pätöinen Poika symbolizes the final acts. And another clear instance referring to reincarnation is Väinämöinen's promise to return:

"Annapas ajan kulua,	"Let the rope of time run out—
Päivän mennä, toisen tulla,	One day go, another come—
Taas minua tarvitahan,	And again I will be needed.
Katsotahan, kaivatahan,	They'll be waiting, yearning for me
Uuen sammon saattajaksi,	To bring back another Sampo,
Uuen soiton suoriaksi,	To invent another harp,
Uuen kuun kulettajaksi,	Set a new moon in the sky,
Uuen päivän päästäjäksi,	Free a new sun in the heavens
Kun ei kuuta, aurinkoa	When there is no moon, no sun
Eikä ilmaista iloa..."	And no gladness on the earth."[67]

As experts in ancient religions or modern Theosophy know, there is another doctrine closely related to the idea of reincarnation. This is the law of cause and effect known to the Buddhists as karma. It is karma in connection with reincarnation that determines what the nature of each individual incarnation is to be. The innate physical abilities and mental faculties of a person are the "presents" of karma, that is to say, consequences of a soul's past development and effort. The family and environment one is born into are likewise determined by karma, as are the unsuspected "blows of fate" encountered during life. When dwelling upon the law of karma, the extent to which the human soul is truly "free" becomes very clear.

Finnish people have always firmly trusted in "the Creator" or "destiny." "It is so allowed"* is often the only consolation in times of grief. And there are many Finnish proverbs that describe this "fatalism" from different viewpoints. Some of these are:

What goes around comes around.
What is left behind will be found ahead.
No word is said that is not meant for something.
Along the way one finds a big stump in a burnt-out clearing.
A rich man may become poor, a beggar may become a General.
By turns the water is rowed.
The wise man learns from the mistakes of others, the miserable man
    learns from his own.
If only I had my present mind in past time!
If I have become a slave, I once owned a slave.
You knew more when you arrived.
One gets wise by misfortune, not buttercakes.
One's own problems teach understanding about the troubles of others.

In the light of reason, a strong faith in destiny clearly requires that the law of reincarnation be understood completely. Thus it seems likely that the Finnish people were taught the doctrine of reincarnation some time in the past. They were taught, and they still remember, to trust in destiny and the Creator, although half of what they knew was forgotten later in the Christian age. Even the proverbs given above take on a greater meaning when read with reincarnation in mind. One man does not necessarily go from being a beggar to a General in the same incarnation, but in separate incarnations the roles truly complement each other like actors on a stage. How many people sigh later in life with the thought, "if only I had my present mind when I was young"—if only I had the wisdom of age and experience in my younger days, I would have known how to live better. From the standpoint of reincarnation this opportunity will indeed arise.

There are people alive who truly believe that this mundane life is just one empty valley of sorrow. They don't even have the strength to

---

*Translator's note. "Se on niin sallittu" (it is so allowed) means to rely upon Providence.

consider the thought of reincarnating here. Clearly, the mundane life does not have much to offer the person who expects constant pleasure, rejoicing, and happiness. One who expects as much begins from a false assumption, and when life does not offer pleasure without distress, rejoicing without sorrow, happiness without disappointment, it is natural that the "broken (selfish) heart" will lure reason to the abyss of pessimism. But if a person starts from the viewpoint offered by the doctrine of reincarnation, then the orientation to living totally changes, and a peace of mind comes which is hard to shake.

As you see, according to reincarnation each person is the smith of their own happiness. We experience exactly what we draw to ourselves. And we have to work for our happiness. We have to thoroughly live every joy and every pleasure. Life gifts us with life itself and the capacity to feel, enjoy, and be happy. Everything else we must work to obtain for ourselves, and even our basic faculties must be educated and developed.

If it seems that we do not accomplish what we strive for, that despite all our efforts life does not live up to our expectations, this is only an appearance. When we understand that we have been here before and will be here again, then we know the difference between what we reached for and what we have achieved. In some future incarnation we will certainly achieve what we hope for in this life. And yet we need not look so far! A human being who understands the impartiality of life's laws and their ability to respond to our requests develops in his life-experience the idea that one reaps what one sows. That which ends up half-finished and incomplete is not caused by life itself. The ideal goal of humanity has itself been stunted, the ideal accomplished is still filled with weakness and ignorance, and all visible striving depends on time and place! A mentally balanced person does not expect too much, neither from life nor from himself.

This genuine Finnish balance is informed by a faith in reincarnation. Its great moral effect is that it wholly changes our comprehension of suffering and evil.

Since we arrive here on earth to learn and life is our great teacher, suffering is not an absolute evil. Suffering is nature's answer to our errors. God does not send us just any sufferings, life does not harass us with misfortune. But when we do not understand how to use our reasoning conscience and how to listen to our heart, and instead express our bestial instincts, then we invoke all the goddesses of suffering and distress from the depths of the human soul. "What goes around comes around." We ourselves define our punishment and life guides and grows us. "Through misfortune one grows wise." Suffering is only apparent evil—it is sensual evil, not spiritual. Suffering has a cleansing effect and an uplifting movement, unless a person in great hopelessness throws himself into it and becomes trapped.

Evil is not what we suffer, it is what we do. Suffering is the atonement for evil and evil consists of selfish deeds which call suffering into the world. This is Finnish wisdom.

16

In the Cottages of Tuonela

WHAT DOES THE WISDOM of the ancient Finns have to say about death and life after death? Investigators concur that the ancient Finns were not materialists. They had ideas about the continuation of life after death but their conceptions of Tuonela are gloomy and gray. Matti Varonen writes in his dissertation: "The faith in the immortality of the human spirit and its continuation after death in a similar state as it was on earth is found to be a consistent point in pagan religions around the world. Thus arose the belief that the spirits of the deceased could appear here on earth, and ancestor reverence is a basic doctrine of pagan religion. Cultures deeply rooted in this ancient belief system are so strongly attached to it that even after the arrival of Christianity we find these dim ideas mixed into folk belief."[68]

And Kaarle Krohn writes in his book *The Religion of Finnish Runes*: "Within Finnish runes, Castrén has identified two different conceptions of the place where the deceased live. According to one the dead spend a shadow life in their graves. According to the other they gather together at a specified location underground called Tuonela or Manala. In both cases Castrén supposes them to be dependent upon a special divine being. The grave master and his legion were called *Kalma* and the masters of Tuonela and Manala went by the names *Tuoni* and *Mana*."[69]

In point of fact we need not write yet another study of the ancient Finn's faith in immortality and their ideas about the afterlife; our scientists have done this thoroughly. With good intent we can recommend to our readers the above quoted works. Our task remains to show what truth is hidden behind these ancient ideas, which to scientists are merely superstitions. Clearly, scientific researchers take an essentially negative stand on these matters. All "ghost stories" are thought to be derived from superstitious ignorance and the light of Christian civilization "drives off the spirits of the deceased"; the worshipping of the deceased results from the fact that people do not know the True God.

But we should momentarily put ourselves in the place of the ancient seers and look at death through their eyes. We can do this when we let Theosophy explain to us what the Wisdom of the Ages, collected from the supersensory experiences of innumerable explorers, has to say about life beyond the grave.[70]

This realm which a human being passes through between two incarnations is divided into three phases. First is the period of the soul's distress, in which a human being learns to see his own evil as it was expressed during life. Memories becomes vivid; he meets or believes he meets all the people he had harmed in some way and he feels their pain himself, understands and repents. He is advised, taught, and guided to the right way; this realm is called Tuonela or *Kaamalooka* ("the place of desires"). It is a purgatory that purifies, it is the astral world, and so on. In the second phase the newly departed relives everything that was beautiful, innocent, and happy; it is as though he fades away from Tuonela and is once again in the world, a world without suffering or evil. His most delightful dreams come true, whatever was imagined about being happy is now presented in lively images and feelings. All living beings whom he loves surround him with warm embrace; this realm is called Heaven or *Deevakahn* ("the land of the gods"). It is paradise, the realm of higher life, and so on. The third period is the preparation for a new mundane life. At the heights of his happiness and gratefulness a human being begins to think about a new incarnation, in which he will again have the chance to experience and learn, to obtain new virtues and faculties. Thus, he abandons himself into the heart of his own soul and the embrace is so complete that the old personality vanishes into oblivion, thoroughly being dissolved. Then, after the "descent into matter" is completed, and when the appropriate parents have been found, a new human baby is born into the physical world.

It should be noted that at the boundary between this world and Tuonela there exists an ethereal transition state through which the normal deceased person passes unconsciously, and which separates him from the physical world once he has arrived in Tuonela. But if the deceased, for one reason or another, feels attached to the mundane life, he may stay in this immaterial transition state or return there at times from Tuonela. In both cases he is then in a position to connect with the physical realm and associate with the living through hauntings or through a medium.

The Kalevala demonstrates that these things were clearly understood by ancient Finnish seers. In Runos 16 and 17 we read of Väinämöinen's journey to Tuonela and his adventure with Antero Vipunen. Like Orpheus descending to Tartarus to seek his Eurydice, Väinämöinen is not dead, but is a living seeker who journeys to Manala in search of three magic words. And although the Kalevala does not relate much about Väinämöinen's observations regarding Tuonela, it lets him speak this warning:

"Elkätte imeisen lapset	"Never, you children of mankind,
Sinä ilmoisna ikänä	Never, never, forever never,
Tehkö syytä syyttömälle,	Put the blame upon the blameless,
Vikoa viattomalle!	Never hurt the innocent!
Pahoin palkka maksetahan	Drastic is the penalty
Tuolla Tuonelan koissa:	In the house of Tuonela:
Sia on siellä syyllisillä,	There the guilty have their spaces,
Vuotehet viallisilla,	Sinners have their resting places
Alus kuumista kivistä,	On a couch of searing slabstone,
Palavoista paateroista,	On a bed of burning boulders,
Peitto kyistä, käärmehistä,	Under a cover of woven serpents,
Tuonen toukista kuotta!"	Woven from the worms of Tuoni."[71]

The underlying truth of these words is clear. They precisely describe how evil gets its payback in Manala.

When Väinämöinen does not find the magic words he was seeking in Tuonela, a herder suggests he go visit Antero Vipunen:

"Saat tuolta sata sanoa,
Tuhat virren tutkelmusta
Suusta Antero Vipusen,
Vatsasta vara-väkevän..."

"You can get a hundred spells,
A thousand strands of magic verse
From the mouth of Vipunen,
Belly of the verseful one..."[72]

The difficulties of the journey do not frighten Väinämöinen, and he finds the giant seer and awakens him from his sleep of death. The giant swallows Väinämöinen and, if Väinämöinen were an ordinary mortal, Vipunen would have done away with him as he had with the rest:

"Jo olen jotaki syönyt,
Syönyt uuhta, syönyt vuohta,
Syönyt lehmeä mahoa,
Syönyt karjua sikoa,
En ole vielä mointa syönyt,
En tämän palan makuista...
Mi sinä lienet miehiäsi,
Ja kuka urohiasi,
Jo olen syönyt sa'an urosta,
Tuhonnut tuhannen miestä,
Enpä liene mointa syönyt,
Syet suuhuni tulevat,
Kekälehet kielelleni,
Rauan kuonat kulkkuhuni."

"I have eaten many a morsel,
Eaten lamb and eaten kid,
Eaten beef
and eaten boar,
But never anything like this,
Nothing with a taste like this..."
"If a man, who are you there
And what sort of human creature?
I have eaten men by hundreds,
By the thousands swallowed them
But never anything like this:
To my mouth hot coals are rising,
Firebrands on my tongue are burning,
Cinders choking up my gullet."[73]

But Väinämöinen himself is a seer, a wise truth seeker who clearly intends to go onward fearlessly toward his goal. He does not give up until Antero Vipunen consents to share his knowledge:

Silloin virsikäs Vipunen,
Tuo vanha vara-väkevä,
Jonk' oli suussa suuri tieto,
Mahti ponnetoin povessa,
Aukaisi sanaisen arkun,
Virsilippahan levitti,
Lauloaksensa hyviä,
Parahia pannaksensa,

Then the verseful Vipunen,
Oldest sage with oldest wisdom,
In his mouth the greatest magic,
In his bosom endless power,
Opened up his ark of sayings
And revealed his store of verses
For good singing,
best of chanting

Noita syntyjä syviä,	Of the deepest origins
Ajan alkuluottehia,	From the very birth of time,
Joit' ei laula kaikki lapset,	Which not every child can copy
Ymmärrä yhet urohot	Nor even grown-ups understand
Tällä inhalla iällä	In these dreadful days of evil,
Katovalla kannikalla.[74]	In this last and fleeting age.[74]

Who is this Antero Vipunen and how is this giant of wisdom portrayed? What else but the realm where the deceased experience their heavenly state! Vipunen sleeps, and truly heaven is likened to a dreaming, peaceful rest. Vipunen eats everything, and truly the deceased lose their personal identity by the end of the heaven stage. Vipunen tries to chant away Väinämöinen, who is causing a great disturbance. Likewise, distress and evil are not allowed through to the heaven realm. But when Vipunen is finally won over, he opens to Väinämöinen the treasures of his knowledge—and this is true for the human being who can retain his consciousness amidst the swirl of the after death journey. The memory stores of nature are opened to him, and he is allowed to read "the book of life" which preserves all events since the beginning of the world. (In Theosophical literature one reads of "The Akashic Records".) Antero Vipunen holds the great, secret book of nature, and only by reading this can one become a very wise sage. Every deceased person must read it, both in Tuonela and in the heaven state, but most can see nothing but their own past doings. The happy Väinämöinen and his kind, who are not distracted by thoughts of themselves, can steadily read and absorb from nature the secret knowledge that truly belongs only to unselfish beings.

We also can see that when we read the Kalevala with understanding, it speaks clearly about the nature of life after death. In the rune about the journey to Tuonela (Runo 16), we can understand the nature of the semi-material transition state which separates Tuonela from the physical world. Specifically, when Väinämöinen asks the girl of Tuoni to bring a boat so that he can "get over the river," she refuses because Väinämöinen is not dead:

"Vene täältä tuotanehe,	"We will bring the boat from here
Kuni syy sanottanehe,	Only when you tell the reason,
Mi sinun Manalle saattoi	Why you come down here to Manala

Ilman tau'in tappamatta,	Without dying of disease,
Ottamatta oivan surman,	Neither in the course of nature
Muun surman musertamatta."	Nor by other doom deceased."[75]

At first Väinämöinen tries to hide his real reason by impressing upon the girl that death by iron, water, and fire has called him to Manala. But "the shortkin girl of Tuoni, the little miss of Manala" responds every time by chiding him:

"Jopa keksin kielastajan!	"What a tongue-beater you are!
Kump' on Tuoni tänne toisi,	If my father brought you here,
Mana mailta siirtelisi,	Mana moved you from your country,
Tuoni toisi tullessansa,	Tuoni would escort you here,
Manalainen matkassansa,	Mana keep your company,
Tuonen hattu hartioilla,	Tuoni's hat upon your shoulders,
Manan kintahat käessä...	Mana's mittens on your hands...
Kun rauta Manalle saisi,	If iron brought you down to Mana,
Teräs toisi Tuonelahan,	If steel brought you to Tuonela,
Verin vaattehet valuisi,	Then your clothing would be bloody
Helmasi herahteleisi...	And the red death streaming out...
Jos vesi Manalle saisi,	If water brought you down to Mana,
Aalto toisi Tuonelahan,	On the wave to Tuonela,
Vesin vaattehet valuisi,	Then your clothing would be dripping
Helmasi herahteleisi...	And your hems would be cascading...
Jos tuli manalle toisi,	If fire brought you down to Mana,
Valkeainen Tuonelahan,	Or if flame to Tuonela,
Oisi kutrit kärventynnä,	Sadly would your hair be singed
Partaki pahoin palanut."	And your old beard badly burned."[76]

The girl of Tuoni clearly speaks about the fact that even in the ethereal transition state the cause of death should be apparent. The deceased is enclosed in the semi-material ethereal ghost whose outer appearance still resembles the physical body. This is why, when the deceased appears at the moment of death to a distant friend or relative, he looks exactly like he did when he died: Those killed by disease are lean and pale, blood streams from the wounds of those pierced by swords, and water drips from the drowned.

Väinämöinen is the type of seer who journeys to the realm of the dead. And he is by no means the first of his kind to make the journey, as can clearly be seen in the words of the girl of Tuoni:

"...Parempi sinun olisi
Palata omille maille;
Äijä on tänne tullehia,
Ei paljo palannehia."

"...Better would it be for you
To return to your own country—
Many there are who enter here,
Few there are who e'er return."[77]

Väinämöinen belongs to the few who go to Tuoni alive and return with full consciousness of the journey. These few are of many types, from the lowest magicians and mediums to the highest seers and wisemen. Kaarle Krohn is quite correct (although he does not describe the highest type of seer) when he writes: "The belief in a magician as a medium is nothing unique to northern nations but is a general belief in all ancient religions around the world. To make a connection to the spiritual world so that in a state of emergency it would already be known what sacrifices needed to be made, was the essential task of these magicians. While the average human being sometimes in sleep or stupor seems to loosen from the limits of the bodily perceptions, the magician must artificially induce this state, to excite himself into an ecstacy so the soul can depart and move freely into association with the realm of spirits."[78]

We may wonder why the ancient seers usually describe the life beyond the grave as gloomy and meaningless. We can understand this when we remember that in ancient times the souls of the overwhelming majority of human beings performed magic in the evil sense much more than nowadays. The heavenly state changes in color, meaning, and feeling with the changing growth experiences of the collective soul of humanity; the heavens of modern civilization are therefore much more interesting than the heavens of ancient nations. For people who engaged in it, sorcery and evil gave rise to frightful spectors upon death, as does a bad conscience these days. Death is a day of reckoning. Many in the past and some even today try by different means (for example, incantation) to lengthen the semi-material state and delay the inevitable plunge into the horrors of Tuonela. The deceased of ancient nations hovered between heaven and earth in comparatively large numbers, clinging with all their effort to the semi-material state. Although the appearance of this state resembles the physical body, consisting of the most subtle form of physical matter, this body is not useful for interaction or fulfillment in any sense and so serves to imprison the soul in an existence of gray inactivity. After some time these beings were, of course, forced to desist and abandon themselves to the depths of the unconscious, where waits the frightening revenge of Tuonela, in retribution for evil done during the mundane life. It is natural that mediums and magicians of the less advanced type—the majority of seers—looked into the beyond and saw only a shadow-life in the realm of Kalma or distress in the land of Tuoni. And although the noblest of seers such as Väinämöinen knew the heavenly sphere and the greatest secrets of Antero Vipunen, it was difficult to describe these things to the common people except to say that it was happy and restful for those who had lived well. As certain proverbs say:

> A good person lives well, and it is beautiful to die with honor.
> The deceased have fallen asleep.
> The child is spared in heaven.
> Wherever one dies, in heaven the same measure is used for all.
> A human being dies as he has lived.
> The deceased has used up his turn.
> Peace for those still living, rest for those deceased.

The Playing
of Väinämöinen

ESTHETICALLY, the most beautiful, eloquent and grandiose place in the Kalevala is the description of Väinämöinen playing the kantele in Runos 41 and 44. Here we see the deep reverence of the Finnish people for nature. For them, nature is not dead or strange. Furthermore, apparently "lifeless" objects are really full of consciousness and emotion and are as close to the human heart as living beings. Human beings are truly just a link in the great chain of nature, brothers to all and equal to all beings in nature. Although in the Kalevala one consistently meets with this viewpoint of the ancient Finns—that of "nature animated and personified"—the totality of this belief is well represented in the description of Väinämöinen's playing. Väinämöinen enchants all of nature and all living beings with his playing. Even though F. A. Hästesko considers the scene to have been "created by joking and free imagination,"[79] his words also suggest the commonly held opinion that this passage contains the most sublime truth for those who read it with understanding.

In fact it opens to us a new understanding of the mental landscape in which the lively truth seeking of the Kalevala's sages can be recognized.

Through his playing we here meet the Väinämöinen who is a great and perfect seer. He can no longer be regarded as an average truth seeker, for he raises himself to dizzy heights above the rest of humanity, where nobody can even touch the strings of his kantele (Runo 40:259-332).

Julius Krohn says this about Väinämöinen's superiority: "He has abandoned his private needs of happiness; he has sacrificed his entire life, all
his thoughts and feelings, to the fatherland." Or instead of "fatherland,"
"to the common good" as Rafael Engelberg remarks.[80] He—Väinämöinen—has almost achieved human perfection; he is the first-born of
his nation and is even likened to a father in this rune:

Tehessä isän iloa,	...While the patriarch rejoiced them,
Soitellessa Väinämöisen.	Väinämöinen, with his playing.[81]

Through Väinämöinen's relationship with nature, and nature's attitude toward him while listening to his playing, we can understand in what
manner the Finnish seers comprehended the relationship between an
ideal human being and nature. We can also find in this description a
grand teaching. The mightiest possession of a superman is his nearly
unlimited dominion over nature. This was not won with violence nor by
other frightful means, but by love. With a force of beauty and truth he has
captured the heart of nature and won its sympathy. Both living and
lifeless things are charmed by him, listen to him, and are obedient to him
from sheer rejoicing. Nature, the consciousness of which was not fully
known within human consciousness, has now been transformed through
the great human being whose heart pulsates with joy and the desire to
serve. With unlimited trust and without reserve, nature now gives to the
seer all the love and enchantment which it always held within its bosom
for humanity.

Let us examine this in more detail. The rune first relates how all the
animals gather to listen to Väinämöinen's playing:

Ei ollut sitä metsässä	There was not a single creature
	Of the forest, of the woodland,
Jalan neljän juoksevata,	Not a single four-foot runner,
Koivin koikkelehtavata,	Not a single hind-leg leaper
Ku ei tullut kuulemahan,	That did not run out to listen
Iloa imehtimähän...	And to wonder at the joyance...
Mi oli ilman lintujaki,	Every creature of the air,
Kahen siiven sirkovia,	Every flier on two wings
Ne tulivat tuiskutellen,	Scurries like the driven snowflakes,
Kiiätellen kiirehtivät	Swirling, racing to arrive

Kunnioa kuulemahan,	To listen to the honored player
Iloa imehtimähän...	And to wonder at the joyance...
Ei sitä oloista ollut,	There was not a living creature,
Ei ollut ve'essäkänä,	Not one even of the water,
Evän kuuen kulkevata,	Not one single six-fin swimmer
Kalaparvea parasta,	From the finest school of fishes
Ku ei tullut kuulemahan,	That did not swim up to listen
Iloa imehtimähän.	And to marvel at the joyance.[82]

And the rune specifically mentions all kinds of wild animals: squirrels, elk, lynxes, wolves, bears, eagles, hawks, sea ducks, swans, buntings, larks, pike, salmon, whitefish, crickets, and perches. All obeyed the call of the seer, and the hearts of all jumped for joy.

Is there not contained in this a remarkable lesson for human beings? "Look," says the old Finnish wisdom, "you people have tamed some animal species and made them friends and willing servants, but the forests, air, and waters are full of living beings whom you fight or whom you compel to be your servants! How far away you are from your goal! A perfected human being, one who is a seer, does not wage war against even a single creature, for he loves all and all loves him." And indeed, it seems that another wise seer, named Paul, conveyed the same meaning when writing those well known words: "For the anxious longing of creation waits eagerly for the revealing of the sons of God. For the creation was subjected to futility, not of its own will, but because of Him who subjected it, in hope that the creation itself also will be set free from its slavery to corruption into the freedom of the glory of the children of God. For we know that the whole creation groans and suffers the pains of childbirth together until now" (Paul's letter to the Romans 8: 19-22).

And this vision of the future that both the Kalevala and the Bible present is not without foundation (also, compare this with the prophet's words in the Old Testament about the lion laying down with the lamb). And if we are allowed to trust even a little bit the legends from the Middle Ages and the stories of journeys to the eastern lands, reality has many times corroborated the information given in the Holy Books. In India it is said that when a saintly yogi sits in meditation, no animal is afraid of him. The birds of the sky freely approach him, beasts of the forest feel attracted and draw near, even tigers and snakes crawl up to his feet and bathe in the glow of the love which radiates from his being.

And why should we consider these legends to be just the products of naïve imagination? Indeed, these stories are woven around a hidden core of truth, and therefore they often contain greater truth than the so-called historical presentations. And who doesn't know the legends from the Middle Ages about St. Francis of Assisi? Let us review a couple of these stories which clearly show the charming power he had over animals. Once, when he was preaching in a field to a large crowd of people, a flock of swallows came flying by and made such noise that the words of St. Francis were lost upon his listeners. After realizing this, Francis peacefully turned to the birds and said: "My dear swallow sisters, please be quiet for the time of my speaking and explaining—you too can listen!" Instantly the flock of birds stopped and hovered silently above the crowd and not a single one of them flew away before Francis had finished preaching. The other story is about a wolf. Once, upon arriving at a distant village, Francis was told of a big frightening wolf who did terrible damage to the village, almost every night demanding to eat a sheep, hen, or some other animal. In the evening, Francis walked outside the village to wait for the wolf. When the big gray wolf came along with great hunger and crudeness, without fear the great friend of all animals approached him, spoke with him and gestured to shake hands with him. The wolf raised his paw and nodded his head in understanding when Francis gently reproached him: "Brother wolf, why have you thus chosen the living place of poor folk for your hunting grounds? And why do you harass their domestic animals? It is not right, and you are not allowed to behave like that. Now promise me that you will leave the village in peace." And the legend tells that the wolf kept his promise and the village was left alone...

But the Kalevala does not only tell about animals who are charmed by Väinämöinen's playing. The vegetable kingdom also participated in the common joy:

Petäjät piti iloa,	Tall old pine trees jubilating,
Kannot hyppi kankahilla.	Tree stumps dancing on the heaths.[83]

Furthermore, as if to show that the playing of Väinämöinen was not an isolated incident but was a characteristic feature of his life, the Kalevala tells us:

Kun hän kulki kuusikossa,	When he sauntered in the fir woods,
Vaelteli petäjikössä,	Roaming among the evergreens,
Kuusoset kumartelihe,	Spruces bowed down there before him,
Männyt mäellä kääntelihe,	Pine trees turned upon the hill;
Käpöset keolle vieri,	Cones were rolling on the ground,
Havut juurelle hajosi.	And the needles showering down.
Kun hän liikahti lehdossa,	When he roamed the leafy groves
Tahi astahti aholla,	Or he walked the open clearing,
Lehot leikkiä pitivät,	All the leafy groves were merry
Ahot ainoista iloa,	And the clearings always joyous,
Kukat kulkivat kutuhun,	While the flowers waked to frolic
Vesat nuoret notkahteli.	And the seedlings set to dancing.[84]

Even the vegetable kingdom is said to be a living, conscious world, which can feel love, rejoice and grieve. And though we humans know a little bit about the soul life of the vegetable world, many of us are ready to laugh at the mere suggestion that flowers and trees—by their own nature—are mental beings. But let us ask the opinion of those who spend much of their time with plants: gardeners, flower breeders, caretakers of house plants, and so on. Surely we will hear how different trees and different flowers each have their own unique natures, that plants can be in good or bad humor, that they know clearly enough if they are being loved or not. And why are people fond of their place of birth? Why is there always a longing to return? Especially within the Finnish character there lives a deep, gnawing feeling of home-sickness. When a Finn is abroad, his mind is haunted by his homeland, its spruces and birches, its knolls and hills, its lakes and rivers. "Strawberries in ones own land, blackberries from a strange land." Or, as it is said in the Kalevala (Runo 7:285-288):

Parempi omalla maalla	Water's better drunk at home,
Vetonenkin virsun alta,	Even from a birchbark shoe
Kuin on maalla vierahalla	Than honey mead from golden bowls
Kultamaljasta metonen.	At a stranger's sumptuous table.[85]

On what does this feeling depend? Does it mean that the impressions of childhood are the strongest? Yes, but that is not all. The impressions of childhood are strong because the young heart is pure and sensitive to its surroundings, but love comes not only from other human beings: all of nature loves the child. Our attachment to our birth place depends as much upon the love inherent in that place as upon our love towards it. The feelings come from both sides and we Finns have an inborn inclination to understand our nature. In our own love-nature, there is something mute, unexplainable with words, which corresponds to the soundless feelings of trees and plants.

The Wisdom of the Ages preserves the viewpoint that the vegetable kingdom does not really consist of unconscious organisms but instead represents an educational classroom in the developmental system of consciousness. Upwards from the mineral kingdom, the realms of nature take huge steps along which living consciousness slowly ascends to the level of human consciousness. Not until consciousness reaches the level of the human form does it individualize. Before this it expresses itself as a species or group-consciousness aspiring to the personal individuality of the highest animals. From the standpoint of the secret science it is thus undeniable that nature is full of soul and emotion. When a thoughtless boy with stick in hand whips up the grass and flowers, trampling under foot whatever happens to be in front of him, nature suffers a mute pain. But when, in the autumn, the reaper mows the ripened corn, the fields rejoice. Truly, humanity has been invited to participate in the great educational work of nature. But we fulfill our duty poorly when we treat nature cruelly, coldly, or without concern. Let every Finn learn from the Kalevala the kind of lovely relationship a good and gentle person can have with our loving but mute nature.

And the Kalevala does not limit its deep knowledge of nature to the so-called organic or living nature. Even lifeless nature has within it consciousness and feeling; even it rejoices with the playing of Väinämöinen, the human seer who played so greatly that the

Vuoret loukkui, paaet paukkui,	Mountains echoed, boulders crackled,
Kaikki kalliot tärähti,	All the crags and cliffs were quaking;
Kivet laikkui lainehilla,	In the waves the rocks were splashing,
Somerot vesillä souti.	Gravel swirling on the waters;[86]

And

Kun hän soitteli kotona,	When he played in his own cabin,
Huonehessa honkaisessa,	In his simple home of pine logs,
Niin katot kajahelivat,	Rafters rattled, floorboards bounded,
Permannot pemahtelivat,	
Laet lauloi, ukset ulvoi,	Ceilings singing, doors hallooing,
Kaikki ikkunat iloitsi,	With the windows wide rejoicing,
Kiukoa kivinen liikkui,	Even all the hearthstones stirring
Patsas patvinen pajahti.	And the birchen uprights whooping.[87]

This imagery is so aesthetically natural that it seems to portray the rune singer's intention to show us how lifeless things, in their own way, respond to the soundwaves emanating from his playing. But when one knows the ideal circle of the Kalevala, one knows well enough that the rune really means that the cliffs and stones, ceilings and floors, windows and doors, fully participate in the collective rejoicing. When understood in its esoteric meaning, this viewpoint is not a great leap out of reality. What was said above about the vegetable kingdom holds true, with slight changes, even in the inorganic or lifeless world. Even the mineral kingdom feels, though in a slower and weaker way. Also, lifeless things can rejoice and love although they—and with a greater measure than living nature—can only reflect the sympathy and tenderness that we have directed at them. Look at how we become subtley attracted to and attached to our tools and furniture, our books, our pieces of art, and to our entire lifeless houses! When we take gentle care of them, attend to and talk to them, treat them like our children or our friends, they are also in a good and grateful humor, look happy and cheerful, serve us willingly, console us when we are in low spirits, and advise us when we are uncertain. What a social world can human beings create from the "lifeless things of the home!" Poets are able to do this and common people, in their ignorance, tend to pity and smile condescendingly on the dreamers.

Even scientists have finally observed that metals can become tired and everyone knows this by their own experience. After long use, nobody's razor is ever as good even though it is regularly sharpened—it has its own sense of humor! Barbers are said to have an adage: "This razor is now tired. Let it rest for awhile, so it will again work excellently." We call it weariness—but who knows what the razor itself calls it when making its own psychological studies? The fact is only that metals are sometimes lively and sometimes tired.

And what about the machines?! Let us ask the machinist if his machines are a lifeless species, so we can get to the truth of this. "Dead? Indeed! They are certainly living, living and quite capricious beings. If a stranger touches my machine, it instantly takes ill and gets out of gears." Railway engines, for example, are only in union with their own drivers and do not stand a chance with someone else. They also must rest from time to time, otherwise they will perform badly and will not have the strength to haul...

The Kalevala has gotten surprisingly deep in its look at the soul life of nature. This is clear also from the fact that the ancient Finnish seers have not merely looked at the soul of visible nature, but have witnessed in the invisible mental world the subtle expressions of life and beings which have no physical counterpart. A materialist considers these impressions to be the product of mere imagination, but the seeker of truth knows; there are people living today for whom the inhabitants of the unseen realm are as real and true as those in the visible world.

The Kalevala's rune of Väinämöinen's playing enumerates these beings and they all gather around Väinämöinen to listen to his playing:

Tapiolan tarkka ukko,	Then the watchful Tapio,
Itse Metsolan isäntä,	He, the master of the woodland
Ja kaikki Tapion kansa,	And of all the woodland people,
Sekä piiat jotta pojat	With his sons and with his daughters
Kulki vuoren kukkulalle	Traveled to the mountain peak
Soittoa tajuamahan;	To enjoy the music fully.
Itseki metsän emäntä,	Even Tapiola's mistress,
Tapiolan tarkka vaimo	Watchful matron of the woodland,
Sinisukkahan siroikse,	In blue stockings
Punapaulahan paneikse,	and red laces
Loihe koivun konkelolle,	Halted on a birch-knee, moving
Lepän lengolle levahti	To the elbow of an alder,
Kanteloista kuulemahan,	There to harken to the harp,
Soittoa tajuamahan...	To absorb the joyous music...
Itse ilman Luonnottaret,	Even nature's airy daughters,
Ilman impyet ihanat	Beautiful virgins of the sky,
Iloa imehtelivät,	Listened to the thrilling music,

Kanteloista kuuntelivat	Rejoicing with the gladness of it;
Mikä ilman vempelellä,	Some upon the rainbow's rim,
Taivon kaarella kajotti,	Shimmering on the shaft of heaven,
Mikä pienen pilven päällä,	Some upon a little cloudlet,
Rusoreunalla rehotti...	Resplendent on the roseate border...
Tuo Kuutar korea impi,	Then the Moonmaid, dainty virgin,
Neiti päivätär pätevä	And the Sunmaid, skillful damsel,
Pitelivät pirtojansa,	Busily plied their weaver's reeds,
Niisiänsä nostelivat,	Nimbly lifting up their heddles;
Kultakangasta kutoivat,	Both were weaving cloth of gold,
Hope'ista helskyttivät	Interlacing threads of silver,
Äärellä punaisen pilven,	Seated on a red cloud border
Pitkän kaaren kannikalla.	By the overarching rainbow.
Kunpa saivat kuullaksensa	When they heard the charming music
Tuon sorean soiton äänen,	Of that graceful instrument,
Jo pääsi piosta pirta,	From their hands the shuttles slipped
Suistui sukkula käestä,	And the battens of their fingers,
Katkesihe kultarihmat,	Breaking off the threads of gold
Helkähti hopeaniiet...	As the silver heddles echoed...
Ahto aaltojen kuningas,	Ahto, king of wave and water,
Ve'en ukko ruohoparta	Sedgy-bearded patriarch,
Ve'en kalvolle veäikse,	Heaves himself up to the surface,
Luikahaiksi lumpehelle,	Rests upon a water lily
Siinä kuunteli iloa...	Where he listens to the joyance...
Itseki ve'en emäntä,	Even the mistress of the water,
Ve'en eukko ruokorinta	She, the sedgy-breasted matron,
Jopa nousevi merestä,	Rises from the deep-sea bottom
Ja lapaikse lainehista...	And emerges from the wave...
Tuota ääntä kuulemahan,	There to harken to the gladness
Soitantoa Väinämöisen...	Of old Väinämöinen's playing...
Se siihen sikein nukkui,	There she fell into deep slumber,
Vaipui maata vatsallehen	Lying prone upon her stomach
Kirjavan kiven selälle,	On a many-colored writrock,
Paaen paksun pallealle.	Prone upon a solid slabstone.[88]

These are the guardians of earth, air, water, and fire whose existence is a mere fairy tale in the eyes of a blind civilization. But the ancient Finnish wisdom knew just as much as the original composers of the tales of alchemists and occult scientists from the Middle Ages, who also mention and classify the elementals of nature. Paracelsus is the father of modern medicine, and truly he was a quite modern observer in many respects. Yet he believed in the existence of nature spirits and, as in the Kalevala, lists four types: gnomes or Tapio's people who live on the ground, sylphs or the Air Virgins of Luonnotar, undines or Ahtis and Sotkotars who live in the water, and salamanders or Kuutars and Päivätärs who live in fire.

In ancient times people lived in a closer relationship with these unseen beings than we do nowadays. Because these elemental fairies have more immediate power over nature and the forces of nature than us humans, it is natural that people in past times prayed for their help, sought their favor, made unions of friendship with them and so on. All of the "fear and ignorance-based worship of nature" that our scientists propose to explain our ancestors' beautiful understanding of the elementals clouds these facts with a different meaning. If we do not see that millions and billions of beings use this miraculous planet as their home and school, if we think that this earth globe is created only for us, then we, the children of modern times, are the ignorant and superstitious ones. These beings are in a different category of nature, and have nothing directly to do with the kingdoms of nature we already know of.

In this connection, we do not wish to speak in any more detail of the elemental fairy folk. We only want to emphasize that the Kalevala's brotherly, democratic, and lofty spirit is clear to us because it always presents the beings of the secret and invisible realm as spirit familiars, equal to human beings, all of us like brothers and sisters in God's great Creation.

PART III

The Kalevala's Inner Ethic

Occult-Psychological or Practical-Soteriological Key

18

The Way of Knowledge

THE ESOTERIC ETHIC of mystery wisdom that seers of all times have been instructed in is not the same as yesterday's outdated exoteric ethics. Everyday Christian morality defines how a human being is to live and think (or trust) so that in this life one might succeed, live long, and beyond the grave achieve eternal blessedness. It makes a thoroughly bourgeois and selfish impression. Its only goal is a heavenly blessedness and since this is limited to a rather abstract rejoicing around God's throne, it remains a palpable ideal only for the ethical elitists of society. This general opinion encourages common people to be law abiding, live blamelessly and pursue their careers. Therefore any thinking human being, any truth seeker, can experience Christian ethics in the outward life, but this leaves the deepest, most personal questions unresolved: How can I understand life? How must I live?

The position of esoteric morality is different. It begins where exotericism ends. When a truth seeker finally asks himself how he must live, the inner ethic extends a hand and only then can he comprehend the counsel of the sage's ethic. Only when a human being longs for truth with the soul's entire force can one hear the mystery-wisdom whisper: The real human virtue is mental development, venturing along the narrow way of knowledge.

The goal of this journey is the divine mystery-knowledge of life and death, nature and creation, the visible and invisible worlds, good and evil, and with truth in hand, one wanders with divine love and power. But how can this knowledge be achieved? It is not a lesson that must be committed to memory; it is not taught by others, nor is the conviction of truth deduced by logic. This knowledge is based upon experience and what we might call a truly scientific knowledge. And by what means can this kind of knowledge be acquired, a knowledge of unseen worlds and of things beyond death? Indeed, this knowledge is based upon observation. We all make observations through our senses, and we proceed to construct from these observations ideas, conceptions and imaginings through various psychological processes. But what kind of observations serve as the foundation of acquiring super-sensible, supernatural and divine knowledge, and how are they gathered?

For us to understand this, we need to get free from some erroneous psychological ideas and develop for ourselves an understanding of psychology's greater depths and possibilities.

Psychology makes a distinction between sensations coming from the outside and those originating inside of us. External sensations come from stimuli in the outside world: we see, hear, smell, taste and feel the beings and states of the world around us. Inner sensations come from stimuli inside the body; for example, from chemical changes in the body. Many kinds of inner sensations work together, like feelings of hunger, exhaustion, vitality, pain and so on. According to modern psychology these many interrelated sensations constitute, so to say, our soul's experimental field. Our outer sensations carry knowledge coming from the outer world. At the same time, our inner sensations reveal our body's subjective state and influence our perception of the external world.

This is certainly in effect true, and error only derives from the fact that modern psychology believes the inner sensations are limited to subjective events; in other words, that the only observations we can make via inner sensations involve our own body. This illusion is reinforced by the fact that our scientific psychology considers our physical body to only be the residence of our personality rather than a microcosmic mystery corresponding to the macrocosm—this is what our body in reality is. The official understanding of our anatomy and physiology does not recognize the body's more delicate and ethereal features which constitute the unseen half. Furthermore, also going unacknowledged are the possibilities for development inherent in these unrecognized subtle features.

On the other hand, if we take the position of occult physiology and assume that each organ in our bodies, visible or invisible, corresponds precisely with some specific inner mechanism of the cosmos at large, then once having made this harmonic correspondence between the bodily microcosm and our surrounding macrocosm, it follows *a priori* that the former can mediate information from the latter. Thus, the possibilities for knowledge within our own soul increases unlimitedly; the experimental field is widened until it is out of sight. There would develop within our bodies a new faculty and the body itself would change from an insubordinate animal to an impartial tool for observation.

This is not a presumptuous thing to say from the standpoint of occult science. To all seers this hypothesis is an experimental fact. The morality of mystery-wisdom specifically teaches how truth seekers must cleanse themselves internally and prepare themselves so that the personality can develop into an apparatus used to achieve this knowledge. The method is based upon the psycho-physical fact that the body and soul functions are coordinated, and it utilizes the fact that the soul can affect the bodily functions. For example, if we awaken within ourselves a predetermined feeling, we can produce a predictable change in the body. The esoteric ethic is based in the knowledge that each human being has been invited to be their own master, to educate and master themself. Therefore, the first declaration of the esoteric ethic is *procul profanis*: those who do not believe in their own power must stay away.

Formally speaking, the ways leading to the ultimate goal are many, though in spirit they are all the same. In a certain sense, each human being must journey in their own way since we all have our own unique human temperment.

The ancient Finnish seers also seem to have distinguished between different temperments because in the Kalevala we see residual echoes of the initial stages in the representatives of two major types: the lemminkäinen-temper which is characteristic of an emotional person and the ilmarinen-temper which represents the active, rational character. We do not speak of a special väinämöinen-temper because in representing the will of humanity Väinämöinen is supportive of all approaches. Concerning the Logos Trinity (the väinämöinen-, ilmarinen-, and lemminkäinen-forces), we mentioned earlier that the väinämöinen-forces only present themselves later on in the development of humanity or individually in an advanced person's esoteric development. When we examine the Kalevala's developmental psychology, we must remember that while doing so we are really looking overall at the activity of the väinämöinen-forces.

Indeed, Väinämöinen appears constantly in precisely this role in the Kalevala. For example, although Ilmarinen may be on the scene as the primary actor, Väinämöinen appears as the awakener, inspirer, adviser, and in the last stages also as the primary actor.

It has become conventional to distinguish two stages on the way to knowledge. One is the way of preparation and cleansing, the other is the true way of acquiring knowledge. With the method of cleansing a person tunes his corporeal vessel to the point that it can at least begin its purpose as a true path of development while pursuing studies in the world.

The Kalevala clearly distinguishes between these two stages. The way of preparation is described in the runes about the proposal trips to Pohjola, while the true way of acquiring knowledge is found in the Sampo-cycle. With great skill, Rafael Engelberg examined the contents of the Kalevala from the aesthetic-psychological viewpoint. He observed this basic division by calling the Kalevala's first part "The Sampo is Lost to Pohjola" (Runos 1-25) and the last part "The Sampo is Won Back" (Runos 26-50).[1]

Of course his basis for making this distinction is different than ours, and he did not even suspect anything about the occult contents of the Kalevala. But since the two headings he chose quite strikingly describe the two stages of the secret way, we wanted to mention this. On the path of cleansing one can truly say that "the Sampo is lost to Pohjola." The Sampo represents occult knowledge and power. While preparing and cleansing, a human being becomes aware that secret knowledge does exist—it is like he forges the Sampo—but then he loses the Sampo and acquires in return the maiden of Pohjola. In other words, he does not achieve the secret knowledge and power but he does find his own soul. The Sampo is lost and Pohjola gets it, but the occult knowledge lives secretly within his body. It is not until this takes place that the second stage can begin. When the fight over the Sampo takes place, the Sampo is won back, and the knowledge and power hidden within the body can move into the daylight.

When we seek from the Kalevala hints about the secret ways of life, we must open the contents of the runes with a special key, the so-called occult-psychological key. We remarked earlier about the fact that we are not allowed to presume that events and characters in the Kalevala have the exact same meanings if the runes are opened with other keys. On the contrary, the meaning can change drastically and in fact there are several meanings. When we explored the Kalevala's mystery-knowledge we used other kinds of keys: cosmic and theogonic. In this we can see why separate psychological features and the "proper nouns" associated with the main characters change according to the key used. Ilmarinen and Lemminkäinen were gods in the first part, but now appear as human beings on earth and are candidates for consecration as truth seekers after the secret knowledge. And Väinämöinen, as we already mentioned, now appears on the scene as the exponent of the divine väinämöinen-forces and we can understand him to be the voice of divine spirit that speaks inside of human beings. However, especially in the first scenes, he is a human being (a seer, a master) who simply embodies the väinämöinen-forces.

19

Joukahainen

EFORE A HUMAN BEING can consciously step onto the path of purification, the soul must first be atuned to the vibration of a truth seeker. He must be prepared to offer himself up as ransom for the truth. This spiritual law of the Kalevala clarifies our understanding by dramatically and effectively describing the state of the soul. When the description is negative, the soul is closer to everyday mundane life; the scenario is more realistic and familiar and does not leave any uncertainty about what the soul's condition must be. This description is given in the Kalevala's most poetic runes, the Aino-group, in which there are two sections: the singing rivalry between Joukahainen and Väinämöinen, and Väinämöinen's proposal followed by the suicide of Aino.

Olipa nuori Joukahainen,	There indeed young Joukahainen,
Laiha poika Lappalainen,	He the lanky lad of Lapland,
Se kävi kylässä kerran,	Visiting round among his neighbors
Kuuli kummia sanoja,	Heard of wondrous charms recited,
Lauluja laeltavaksi,	And the magic songs were sung,
Parempia pantavaksi	Better runos there recited
Noilla Väinölän ahoilla,	Out on Väinölä's burned clearings,
Kalevalan kankahilla,	On the heaths of Kalevala,
Kuin mitä itseki tiesi,	Better than he knew himself,
Oli oppinut isolta.	Better than his father taught him.
Tuo tuosta kovin pahastui,	And it irked the youngster sorely
Kaiken aikansa kaehti	For he envied Väinämöinen,

Väinämöistä laulajaksi,   Jealous for him as a singer,
Paremmaksi itseänsä...   Singing better than himself...[2]

And Joukahainen made up his mind to leave home "to conquer" Väinämöinen despite the prohibitions and warnings of his parents. He harnessed his fiery gelding to a golden sleigh, got inside and carted off to the clearings of Väinölä. Meanwhile, Väinämöinen is also sleighing along and on the third day out they collide into each other, locking rails. Väinämöinen inquires as to who this might be, careering around so recklessly. And Joukahainen answers: "I am the young man Joukahainen... and from what mob are you, you miserable man?"

"Kun liet nuori Joukahainen,   "Since you are young Joukahainen,
Veäite syrjähän vähäsen,   Draw aside a little now;
Sie olet nuorempi minua!"   You are younger far than I am."

To this remark, Joukahainen answers: "Young or old, that doesn't matter,

Kumpi on tieolta parempi,   He who has the greater knowledge,
Muistannalta mahtavampi,   He who has the mightier memory,
Sep' on tiellä seisomahan,   Let him hold the road ahead,
Toinen tieltä siirtyköhön...   Let the other move aside...[3]

And he continues, "Since you must be the old Väinämöinen, let us begin a singing contest!"

Väinämöinen at first resists, saying, "Who am I to be a singer? Who am I to be an artist? All my life I've passed my days, in the solitary clearings... Listening to my cuckoo calling." But finally he consents to the singing competition and asks Joukahainen what exactly it is that he knows more than others. Joukahainen begins to rattle off all sorts of facts off the top of his head, things gathered from nature sciences and other studies, but Väinämöinen interrupts him: "Child's play, women's tattle. Say something about deep origins, things eternal!"

Now Joukahainen sings out his memory banks, pouring out more philosophical ideas, but when he dares to boast of his own great knowledge, Väinämöinen discovers he is a fraud. Then Joukahainen takes hold of his sword and invites Väinämöinen to duel, and when Väinämöinen scoffs at such an honor, he threatens to sing Väinämöinen into a pig. But now Väinämöinen becomes embarrassed and angry and begins to sing:

Ei ole laulut lasten laulut,	They are not the songs of children,
Lasten laulut, naisten naurut,	Songs of children, women's laughter,
Ne on partasuun urohon...	They're the songs of a bearded man...[4]

And this singing effects Joukahainen badly; the song of Väinämöinen sinks Joukahainen up to his neck in a swamp:

Jaksotteli jalkojansa,	When he tried to free himself
Eipä jaksa jalka nousta,	Could not even lift his feet;
Toki toistaki yritti,	Tried one foot and tried the other
Siin' oli kivinen kenkä...	But his feet were shod with stone...[5]

How lively is this description which evokes for us the human state of soul experienced by Joukahainen: "I have learned a lot from elders, I have read many books and passed examinations at universities and academies. I know the sciences and the arts and have achieved an understanding of all modern knowledge; all that education has to offer has become my second nature. If I talk straight and clear, who can be more educated and skillful than I?" This self-oriented, vain and materialistic mind may have the good fortune to hear a revealing message: "Do not believe, my friend, that your knowledge is the highest and most comprehensive! There exists another kind of knowledge, the ancient wisdom. This is the ancient mystery-knowledge against which your learning is child's play. There is mental development which confers a very different kind of understanding than your schooling could ever provide."

The joukahainen-soul does not fully accept this as truth but does acknowledge that fate has spoken. Because the joukahainen-soul is not thoroughly materialistic, it can at least laugh, but, however, it reacts suspiciously: "If this is so, I want to see for myself who is wiser than I— then I'll surely show him a thing or two." Like a caring mother, the soul within whispers to be careful, because maybe a deeper knowing does exist... but the joukahainen-soul defies its fate: "Is that so? Well, let life show me!"

And indeed, life does show him. Väinämöinen gets in the way of Joukahainen. New experiences can be humiliating for the young soul.

They throw him into a swamp of sorrow, distress and suffering. Where does a proud attitude go when the iron fist of fate steps in? The world grows gloomy and no fixed frame of reference can be found. "What is life, what does it mean to be human? Does God even exist?"

Jo nyt nuori Joukahainen	Now young Joukahainen realized
Jopa tiesi, jotta tunsi,	And the youngster understood
Tiesi tielle tullehensa,	That his journey's end had come,
Matkallen osannehensa,	That his road had taken him
Voittelohon, laulelohon	To the contest, to the singing
Kera vanhan Väinämöisen.	With the genuine Väinämöinen.[6]

And then in its distress the soul humbles itself:

Oi on viisas Väinämöinen,	"Wise Väinämöinen,
Tietäjä iänikuinen,	knower eternal,
Pyörrytä pyhät sanasi,	Now reverse your incantations
Peräytä lausehesi,	And call back your magic spells!
Päästä tästä pälkähästä,	Let me out of this tight spot,
Tästä seikasta selitä,	From this awful tangle free me!
Panenpa parahan makson,	I will pay the highest ransom,
Annan lunnahat lujimmat!	Give the tightest guarantee."[7]

Now the human being is prepared to promise something to the powers of life: "I understand now that there is a deeper knowledge, which I have not achieved, secrets which I have not fathomed, faculties of which I had no inkling. If I can only be returned to my prior happiness and balance, I will gladly relinquish my little pleasures which you, life, know I do not need." The soul is ready to give up the small enjoyments of life and address the deeper questions in a serious way.

But life doesn't really care about the soul's little indiscretions, not about its sins nor its virtues. So Väinämöinen sings Joukahainen still deeper into the swamp.

Oi on viisas Väinämöinen,	"O Väinämöinen, wisest wizard,
Tietäjä iänikuinen...	O thou knower, seer eternal...
Kun pyörrät pyhät sanasi,	If you will reverse your magic
Luovuttelet luottehesi,	And recant your incantations

Annan Aino siskoseni,	I will give my sister Aino,
Lainoan emoni lapsen	Let you have my mother's darling
Sulle...	For you...[8]

"I will give my only sister, the other side of myself; I will give you myself!" And then the spirit of truth answers: "Now you have chosen correctly, now you have made the right decision. I want you. I can permit only you to grow up and develop into my helper, to become an heir to my wisdom."

Siitä vanha Väinämöinen	Hearing this, old Väinämöinen
Ihastui iki hyväksi,	Was delighted beyond measure:
Kun sai neion Joukahaisen	Winning Joukahainen's sister
Vanha päivänsä varaksi.	For his old age—sweet provision![9]

Joukahainen has extracted himself from his dilemma. The soul has gotten free from the distressing situation and the intense väinämöinen-sound of life has dissipated. The soul has been returned to its old self, but it is not completely returned to its former condition. For it experienced and learned something and now life is waiting for the fulfillment of the promise. "I caught a glimpse of life's majesty and at the moment of my weakness I promised myself to him. Now I must change myself, work on myself . . . now I must sanctify myself in the service of truth . . . whoas me!"

And the joukahainen-soul's youth and inexperience is reflected in the fact that it

Läksi mielellä pahalla,	Guilty-minded,
Syämmellä synkeällä	Heavy-hearted,
Luoksi armahan emonsa,	Started homeward to his mother,
Tykö valtavanhempainsa...	To his well-respected parents...[10]

This drama is not just the story of one life. A human soul can stay in the state of Joukahainen for many incarnations.

Aino

AINO is the joukahaninen-soul's best and most delicate side; naïvely helpless, it is the virgin spirit hidden deeply under the surface of every human being. . . .

Now the artistically sensitive reader shakes his head: How can the Kalevala's Aino be explained symbolically—that miraculous and charming story of Aino! It is assuredly a simple adaptation from life, a poetic work of art rather than a great mythic symbol. Our most prominent poets and artists have drawn from it inspiration for their creative works. The Kalevala's story of Aino, that living proof of the Finnish nation's developed sensitivity to beauty, challenges the best in world literature.

We heartily agree with this position, because we also admire that young innocent girl whose heart had not yet awakened to love, who so valued her own poetic comprehension of nature and humanity that she preferred to completely give up this life than sell herself.

At any rate, there is something in the rune of Aino which has never satisfied us in the aesthetic sense. This feature is the appearance of Väinämöinen as a suitor. If the intent was to describe Aino and the special qualities of her character, why choose Väinämöinen as a suitor? The role is fit for anyone who displeased Aino yet pleased her mother. Why did it fall to Väinämöinen, the steadfast old wise one, the seer eternal, to deal with that impossible situation, making him look pitiful and even ridiculous? Why should it be this way? Perhaps there is a hidden message here. The joining of Aino's story with the singing contest of Joukahainen suggests that the Aino story has its own lesson. . . .

Because of these considerations, we dare to see Aino, as we already mentioned, as the side of the joukahainen-soul that is the very holiest. We do not suggest here that Aino is Joukahainen's higher self—this is more clearly represented by Väinämöinen—rather, she is the most beautiful side of Joukahainen's personality.

The joukahainen-soul has peeped behind the curtain. It has caught a glimpse of life's wisdom; in great distress it has felt its force. In defiance it approached this wisdom, overwhelmed by fear it promised itself to it, and then sullen and downcast it departed. From the joukahainen-state the soul shifts to the aino-state.

Sisar nuoren Joukahaisen	Joukahainen's sister Aino
Itse itkullen apeutui,	Now herself began to cry;
Itki päivän, itki toisen,	Wept a day, wept a second
Poikkipuolin portahalla,	Crouched across the outer stairway,
Itki suuresta surusta,	Wept for great and simple sorrow
Apeasta mielalasta.	Welling from her heart's despair.[11]

But the body (Aino's mother) is joyous. Instinctively it knows that mental development comes as a welcome relief: Every atom of ones being is purified, life becomes lighter. As the passage from the Bible mentioned above makes known, "All of creation sighs and waits for the sons of God to appear." The body, as a voice heard within, speaks to the soul: "What are you afraid of, why do you grieve? If you are forced to leave your old life, happiness can also be expected in the new."

But the aino-soul still grieves. It is terrified at the prospect of wisdom. This wisdom is for it old and joyless, strange and cold. This divine life appears to be like an empty, bottomless chasm, in which the soul would be lost. As the aino-soul looks at its own youth and elegance, the pearls of its many faculties and virtues, the adorning rings, crosses and bracelets, the gloomy voice of wisdom speaks:

Eläpä muille, neiti nuori,	Not for anyone else, young maiden,
Kun minulle, neiti nuori,	Not for anyone else but me,
Kanna kaulan helmilöitä,	Young maiden,
	wear that beaded necklace
Rinnan ristiä rakenna,	Or the crosslet on your bosom,

Pane päätä palmikolle,	Put your hair up in long braids
Sio silkillä hivusta!	Tie them round with silken ribbons.[12]

Then the soul becomes overwhelmed by such distressing words that it disregards its beauty and adornments. Everything that brought gladness before and which was admired by others, now has lost its charm. Now all its beloved pasttimes must be abandoned to prepare for an idle life within the body:

"En sinulle enkä muille	"Not for you or anyone else
Kanna rinnan ristilöitä,	Will I wear this crosslet here
Päätä silkillä sitaise,	Or tie my hair in silken ribbons.
Huoli en haahen haljakoista,	I don't care for foreign fashions
Vehnän viploista valita,	Nor for wheat bread sliver-sliced;
Asun kaioissa sovissa,	I can go in plainer clothing
Kasvan leivän kannikoissa	And can live on heels and crusts
Tykönä hyvän isoni,	With my good and kindly father
Kanssa armahan emoni."	And my mild and tender mother."
Riisti ristin rinnaltansa,	Then she tore off all her trinkets,
Sormukset on sormestansa,	Cross from breast and
	rings from fingers,
Helmet kaulasta karisti,	Beaded necklace from her throat
Punalangat päänsä päältä,	And red ribbons from her hair;
Jätti maalle maan hyviksi,	Left them on the earth for earth
	For the good of grove and woodland.
Meni itkien kotihin,	Then in tears she hurried homeward,
Kallotellen kartanolle...	Crying to her father's farmyard...[13]

We want to mention here that the aino-state of the soul is not such an unusual phenomenon. Talented and artistic human beings often experience it completely. Over many lifetimes these souls have cultivated beautiful talents that many covet, with the inner ambition being the desire to be loved and admired. As long as they have served these idols in peace and faith, their souls will be happy. But then arrives the day when truth in the guise of life's experiences, or by some other means, reveals how trivial, selfish and narrow their work has been from the spiritual viewpoint. Then they become overwhelmed by chronic exhaustion and dissatisfaction. If they continue serving themselves, enthusiasm does not suffice to complete any work. If they work harder because others flatter and inspire them, their faith in themselves disappears. Emptiness yawns around them. Why should they work at all? They do not know the truth, and the higher self is strange to them. Who and what should be served? Their souls are wandering in the conflict and distress of Aino. They disguise their unhappiness from themselves and others. Only when they are alone can the inner soul confess the truth to the body: "My soul is torn up and unhappy. I do not know what I want and don't want, or what I should want. God says: serve me! But how can I serve him? I do not know him, I do not love him. My life is dead."

A new charm is needed so that their lives do not turn out like Aino's. They are lucky if they have a relative or friend whom they can love—whom they can learn to love and serve. The way from talent to genius is long. But Aino did not have the strength to travel this path, although the voice of nature (her mother) advised her to.

"Alä itke tyttäreni,	"Do not weep, my darling daughter,
Nuorna saamani nureksi!	Begotten of my younger years!
Syö vuosi suloa voita,	For a year eat fresh sweet butter
Tulet muita vuolahampi,	To grow plumper than the others;
Toinen syö sianlihoa,	For the second year eat pork
Tulet muita sirkeämpi,	To become more desired,
Kolmas kuorekokkaroita,	And the third year
	eat sweet creamcakes
	To become the loveliest.
Tulet muita kaunihimpi;	
Astu aittahan mäelle,	Go to the storehouse on the hill,
Aukaise parahin aitta,	Open up the richest storeroom;
Siell' on arkku arkun päällä,	There are treasures crate on crate,
Lipas lippahan lomassa,	Piled up high in chest on chest.
Aukaise parahin arkku,	Open up the richest locker,
Kansi kirjo kimmahuta,	Clang the pictured cover up.
Siin' on kuusi kultavyötä,	There you'll find six golden girdles,
Seitsemän sinihamosta,	Seven blue dresses which were woven
Ne on Kuuttaren kutomat,	By the daughter of the moon,
Päivättären päättelemät."	Finished by the sun's own daughter."[14]

The mother's voice speaks to Aino as the body's instinct advises the soul: "Why are you not brave? If you now leave your old dreams, if you courageously make that first step away from your own egoism, a great future awaits. Do you think that I don't hold future treasures for you? Oh, what value have your faculties and talents gained up until now compared with those that await! In my secret caches are hidden all possibilities. As I grew and developed, before you had taken up your residence in me, the gods presented me with all their own secrets and charms. I will give them to you, all of them are for you to use, if only you begin to seek them. Wake up, get to work and be courageous."

But the aino-soul does not listen to its own instincts. It prefers to live in its dreams. It does not wish to know its own weaknesses, nor about its possibilities and strengths. It rationalizes in its own way—and the Kalevala certainly alludes to an open-mindedly tolerant and gentle message: no words of blame. Conversely, the extraordinary poetic quality and charm of the aino-state fully emerges in the Kalevala's description:

Ei tytär totellut tuota,	But the daughter did not heed her,
Ei kuullut emon sanoja,	Did not even hear the words
Meni itkien pihalle,	As in tears she rushed outdoors
Kaihoellen kartanolle,	To the farmyard wildly weeping,
Sanovi sanalla tuolla,	Moaning to herself aloud
Lausui tuolla lausehella:	In these melancholy words:
"Miten on mieli miekkoisien,	"How describe the happy mind
Autuaallisten ajatus?	And the feelings of the blessed?
Niinp' on mieli miekkoisien,	This is what their moods are like,
Autuaallisten ajatus,	The happy and the fortunate,
Kuin on vellova vetonen,	Like the bubbling up of water
Eli aalto altahassa;	Or ripples running down a trough.
Mitenpä poloisen mieli,	Why is the mournful mind compared
Kuten allien ajatus?	To the long-tailed duck, the woe-bird?
Niinpä on poloisen mieli,	As the wailing of the woe-bird
Niinpä allien ajatus,	So the grieving of the wretched,
Kuin on hanki harjan alla,	Deep as drift beneath a ridge
Vesi kaivossa syvässä...	Deep as water in a well...
Parempi minun olisi,	"It would be much better for me,

Parempi olisi ollut	Surely would have been much better,
Syntymättä, kasvamatta,	If I never had been born,
Suureksi sukeumatta,	Not grown up to be adult
Näille päiville pahoille,	In these dreadful days of evil,
Ilmoille ilottomille;	In this joyless atmosphere.
Olisin kuollut kuusiöisnä,	Had I died a six-night infant,
Kaonnut kaheksanöisnä..."	Or had perished on the eighth night..."[15]

And Aino's grand persona is exemplified by the fact that she prefers to die. . . .

Now a memory spontaneously arises about another young girl who did not resist marrying an older man: Mary, who married Joseph and delivered Jesus. But the mary-state of the human soul is truly a high and noble one. Oh, how far it is from Aino!

Nevertheless, with the foundation offered by the legend of Aino we can form for ourselves an idea of the conditional requirements of seeking for esoteric truth. One is not allowed to seek truth with the pride of Joukahainen, and neither should one approach it with the fear of Aino. One must seek the truth with a humble mind and a pure heart. One must approach it with love—with love and devotion.

Lemminkäinen

EMMINKÄINEN IS ALSO A SEEKER AFTER THE TRUTH. By nature he is an emotional and sparkling idealist. In his earliest incarnations he was a passionate lover, even a love maker. An ideal of faithful love has slowly been formed in his soul, a love that is not deceptive nor suspicious but which contains a promise that is absolutely reliable. This is an insatiable love that is tireless, and with ever-renewing freshness always charms its beloved. That kind of love cleanses and develops its participants, and helps human beings to rise up in freedom! And while sleighing along with Kyllikki under the wintry sky, Lemminkäinen imagines he has achieved the ideal of his love:

Siitä vannoivat valansa,	Then they vowed their vows together,
Laativat ikilupansa	Gave their everlasting pledges
Eessä julkisen Jumalan,	In the face of Jumala,
Alla kasvon kaikkivallan,	Under God's own countenance
Ei Ahin sotia käyä,	That Ahti would not go to war
Eikä Kyllikin kyleä.	Nor Kylli gad about the village.[16]

How bitter then is the disappointment when reality does not live up to the ideal: Lemminkäinen kept his oath, but Kyllikki broke hers. The disappointment is outwardly small, but symbolically decisive. All of Lemminkäinen's faith and trust are gone. Explanations and apologies do not help anything. Lemminkäinen's old nature rises, this time more manly and more resolutely, and he leaves for war.

121

And this war is not a typical, ordinary war. It is not motivated by a lust for material benefit:

"Jos markan soasta saanen,	"If I win a mark in battle,
Parempana tuon pitelen,	I will value it far more
Kun kaikki kotoiset kullat,	Than the golden hoard at home
Auran nostamat hopeat."	With the store of plowed-up silver."[17]

It is a battle of principle because Lemminkäinen has heard about and anticipates miracles:

"Mieleni minun tekevi,	"I am waiting,
Aivoni ajattelevi,	I am thinking,
Itse korvin kuullakseni,	I myself would like to hear it,
	Like to hear it with these ears,
Nähä näillä silmilläni,	See it with these eyes of mine:
Onko neittä Pohjolassa,	If there is a girl in Northland,
Piikoa Pimentolassa,	Virgin in that dismal Darkland
Jok' ei suostu sulhosihin,	Who will not accept a lover,
Mielly miehi'in hyvihin."	Will not take the best of men."[18]

Lemminkäinen has heard the wise men talk, and his own nature whispers within him that the yearning for love is fundamentally the search for the Self: "As long as you do not understand to seek the Self within, you will seek it in others and find disappointments along the way. Stop believing in others and start believing in your Self. When you find your Self, you will discover eternal love." This Self is the girl of Pohja who lives hidden within the body.

Eons ago the lemminkäinen-soul left its aino-state, which is so filled with timidity and doubt. Now it does not need urging or advice from its mother, the body. However, the body resists this independence and warns: "There will be many dangers during your journey and the way in which you, my son, without knowledge or skill, dare to storm Pohjola" (12:129-142). But Lemminkäinen does not hesitate for a moment. He knows that there is no peace nor happiness left in his life: He must seek the Self, now or never, and must know the truth. And so he readies himself for the journey.

Let us remember that this is not a mundane journey; it is an examination of the self to deepen the connection with ones essence. It is the search for the eternal life within. This seeker will be well-equipped. Sincere and honest with himself, clothed in the iron shirt of truth and with fire-bladed sword, he deals straight and true words. He must feel within him the advice of the ancient ones, things former seekers have taught, so that he will not fall into lies. And who else will support him in this endeavor, in times of distress, and grant him the necessary power besides God, the ancient father in heaven! At last, before starting the journey, his thoughts and prayers turn to God (12:217-296).

And thus the journey to Pohjola begins. Lemminkäinen visits two houses (12:311-368) before he arrives at his goal. In the first house he inquires if his journey is to end there. "A child on the floor, a boy from the stair" answers that there is no one around to undo his racer's shaft-bows.

What does this house represent? It is the day-consciousness of the truth seeker. "Can I understand my higher self with this everyday consciousness? Is my reasoning so advanced that it can do that?" "No, no," answers the voice of experience, "I am yet a child and my understanding is that of a child. You cannot find the truth if already you are turning to me for help."

The journey continues to the second house. Lemminkäinen calls, "Is there anyone here who can undo my racer's breastband?" And an old woman at the stove answers, "Yes, in this house there are hundreds. You will get such help that you will be home before sunset."

This second house is the imagination's sleep-consciousness. "Is it not possible for a seeker to find his higher self in dreams and revelations? One-third of life is spent in dreamland, where consciousness shifts to other surroundings, and thoughts and feelings are more effective, so why couldn't one quickly find the self by examining it there? That precious state of being would otherwise be wasted, and seers have told us how much that world can teach!" "Not yet, not yet," answers the voice of experience, "don't you see that I am an old witch? What have you really experienced in that world? Every vain and ugly thing. If in your day-consciousness you have hidden your higher self away, so in your dream-consciousness you have freely indulged in your lower self. Look at what I am, you have made me what I am. And you imagine that I could become your higher self, the lovely virgin of Pohja! You've made a big mistake.

You may get to see hundreds of delusions—here those indeed exist—but not the truth." And so the seeker correctly concludes:

"*Olisi akka ammuttava,*   "May such hook-chins all be shot
Koukkuleuka kolkattava."   With an arrow through the jaw."[19]

Not until after these obstacles are overcome is Pohjola found. Lemminkäinen must get to the Pohja hut in secrecy, so all the dog's mouths must be shut with an incantation. After coming into the yard, Lemminkäinen

Lyöpi maata ruoskallansa,   Smacked his lash against the ground,
Utu nousi ruoskan tiestä,   From it rose a mighty vapor;
Mies pieni u'un seassa;   In the mist a dwarf appeared
Sepä riisui rinnuksia,   Who undid the horse's breastband,
Sepä aisoja alenti.   Lowered the sleigh shafts
                                                       to the ground.[20]

Now Lemminkäinen secretly listens and peeps into the house of Pohjola. The house was full of rune-singers, musicians and conjurers, "howling out the hymns of Hiisi." Then Lemminkäinen magically slips into the hut through a wall. The old woman of Pohjola steps onto the floor and wonders how the stranger came in "without notice of the barkers." Lemminkäinen exclaims that even he is a singer and begins to weave chants and conjure. His song was so powerful, his incantation so grandiose that people were dispelled from the house. Only Wet-Hat the cow-herder remained because Lemminkäinen did not care to touch him at all. After this show of force the singer asks Pohja's old woman to bring her daughter to him.

Now what is this third house? It is the hidden side of consciousness, sometimes called the subconscious and sometimes called supercon- sciousness. It is the great and unexamined world of inner sensations. It is Pohjola, in which is hidden, somewhere, the delightful virgin—the seeker's higher self. The lemminkäinen-soul has suddenly and unex- pectedly found an ecstatic state of connection to this secret world. His outer senses are lethargic—the dogs do not bark—and the mist that separates these different realms of consciousness rise from the whipping lash in front of him. Although his experience is that of a small man just beginning, he knows that he has arrived at the right place, and the breastband is undone. Prior to this he had already won his mundane waking-reason. Likewise, he previously overcame his fanciful and unreliable dream-consciousness. Now available to him is a brighter reason, a sharper vision, a more clairvoyant eye. He experiences the consciousness where the higher I hides itself, although he does not meet her just yet. And he knows that hidden within this realm is much knowledge, that it has an ancient past even though it is obscured by the same sparse-toothed old woman of Pohjola who was present in the second consciousness. Created over eons of time, this human wickedness and ignorance in whose possession he has left his own body, now confronts the courageous seeker as if to ask what he was doing. And the seeker demonstrates that he is on the right track and driven by the right motives. He is not surprised or frightened. The force of his whole soul gathers itself together and his singing expresses an eternal yearning. His grandiose song pours out: "I am a human being, I am what I am! Away with all weakness, hesitation and sin!" His entire consciousness is cleansed. Hiisi's people are dispersed. All evil vanishes from his memory. As a hero he stands there, as a seer, victorious. And what does he care about Wet-Hat, that one miserable person left? What is that low vice? He cannot even remember such a thing in himself. It is contemptible, despicable. In disgust he turns away from it. And with victorious confidence he cries out in ecstacy: Now I want to see my Self!

22

Ilmarinen

LMARINEN IS ALSO A TRUTH-SEEKING SOUL although his determination to seek awakens later than Lemminkäinen's. Ilmarinen is a man of action and sound reason, a realist who is free from sensitivity and vanity. His joy has always been in his work and his noble ambition to work well. He does not possess other ideals and therefore he lacks independent initiative. He must be incited to new efforts by something outside of himself, then he is perfectly diligent and able.

Finally the day of fate dawns for him. Väinämöinen visits and tells him about the wonderful world where our immortal selves live:

"Onp' on neiti Pohjolassa,	"There's a girl at Pohjola,
Impi kylmässä kylässä,	Virgin in that chilly village,
Jok' ei suostu sulhosihin,	Who will not accept a lover,
Mielly miehi'in hyvihin,	Does not like the best of men.
Kiitti puoli Pohjan maata,	Half the Northland sings her praises,
Kun onpi kovin korea:	She's so very beautiful:
Kuuhut paistoi kulmaluilta,	From her brow
	the moonlight glimmers,
Päivä rinnoilta risoitti,	Breasts as rosy as the dawn,
Otavainen olkapäiltä,	Great Bear shining from her shoulders,
Seitsentähtinen selältä."	From her back the Seven Stars.[21]

126

And then he encourages Ilmarinen to pursue the maiden:

"Kun saatat takoa sammon,	"If you hammer out the Sampo
Kirjokannen kirjaella,	And devise its ciphered cover,
Niin saat neion palkastasi,	You may have the maid as payment,
Työstäsi tytön ihanan."	Have the lovely for your labor."[22]

Väinämöinen here refers to the forging of the Sampo and when we apply our occult-psychological key we can understand the personal meaning in this sentence. Later, we will explain in detail what the Sampo means for humanity's secret development. In this connection, the forging of the Sampo clearly means that one may now withdraw from day-consciousness and intentionally shift to the world of inner consciousness. Lemminkäinen could not do this. His consciousness was suddenly and unexpectedly enhanced to the point of ecstacy (as often happens in the initial stages). Is Ilmarinen susceptible to this? Not likely, one concludes from reading the rune. Ilmarinen knows that this is by nature a dangerous undertaking, that things could go awry if he unlocks the secret world of his consciousness. Therefore he does not want to take leave and propose to the maid of Pohja. Instead, he almost mockingly replies to Väinä-möinen:

"Ohoh vanha Väinämöinen,	"Oho, you old sly one, you!
Joko sie minut lupasit	So already you have pledged me
Pimeähän Pohjolahan	To the twilit Pohjola
Oman pääsi päästimeksi,	For the safety of your own head,
Itsesi lunastimeksi!	As a ransom for yourself?
En sinä pitkänä ikänä,	Never, for a long forever,
Kuuna kullan valkeana	While the golden moon still glimmers
Lähe Pohjolan tuville,	Will I go to Northland homesteads,
Sariolan salvoksille,	Those log cabins of dark Sedgeland,
Miesten syöjille sioille,	To those man-devouring regions,
Urosten upottajille."	To the sinkers down of men."[23]

But Väinämöinen does not give up. Ultimately, through him the fate of Ilmarinen must come. He changes the subject and awakens Ilmarinen's curiousity:

"Viel' on kumma toinen kumma	"There's a wonder on a wonder!
Onp' on kuusi kukkalatva,	On the edge of Osmo's field
Osmon pellon pientareella;	Stands a fir tree flower-crowned,
	Flower-crowned and golden-leaved.
Kuuhut latvassa kumotti,	On the crown the moon is gleaming
Oksilla otava seisoi."	With the Great Bear on its branches."[24]

When Ilmarinen does not believe this, Väinämöinen sets out to prove it and engages Ilmarinen's imagination. Once he has captured Ilmarinen's awareness, momentarily concentrating it and drawing it into his hands, it is comparatively easy for the seer to distract it "with the aid of a tornado" from the senses' surroundings and draw it into the inner world. When Ilmarinen regains consciousness, he is already in the land of Pohjola. It happened to him as with Lemminkäinen: the dogs do not bark. Louhi meets him and wonders who this is that the dogs will not bark at. Amazed and embarrassed, Ilmarinen can only answer that he has not come for the barking of dogs. When it comes out who Ilmarinen is, and Louhi treats him with respect, Ilmarinen's confidence and self-awareness returns and he exclaims that he is certainly capable of forging the Sampo. It is as if Ilmarinen thinks to himself: If the forging of the Sampo is no more difficult than this miraculous journey, I can certainly do it.

Then he got to see the girl of Pohjola.

We can observe the difference between Ilmarinen and Lemminkäinen. Lemminkäinen is a fire-soul. He seeks things out impetuously, he grabs heaven for himself with violence, he desires things but struggles against his own unreadiness. On the other hand, Ilmarinen is cold. He is less selfish, he does not claim for himself what he does not know he deserves. Fate takes care of him and makes sure that, in time, he gets what he has earned.

Ilmarinen does not even arrive in Pohjola by his own means. The fact that Ilmarinen was helped by destiny in the form of Väinämöinen shows that Ilmarinen was prepared, that his time had come. Lemminkäinen, on the other hand, robbed what was intended for Ilmarinen and therefore he could not keep it. That Ilmarinen was mentally prepared to receive the new experience can be deduced from the fact that, although the Sampo was not forged in everyday consciousness, in his ecstacy state he thought he had made it. Within the secret state of consciousness Ilmarinen knows for certain what key is needed to access the world of inner sensations, but that knowledge does not carry over to his everyday consciousness. During Ilmarinen's awakening, Väinämöinen asks him if the Sampo has been prepared. Ilmarinen answers on the grounds of his memory that he believes it has been made, but it is hidden within the body somewhere and he does not have it with him (10:495-510).

Ilmarinen does not win the maid of Pohja. On that subject he is in the same position as Lemminkäinen, though he has actually seen the maid. For many ages afterward, Ilmarinen forgets his fateful experience. Much later the yearning reawakens in him—that yearning which is not extinguished before the goal is reached and the higher Self is found—and then with his own conviction he starts out to propose to the maid of Pohja. Though he succeeds in reaching Pohjola, the delightful maid does not immediately consent to go with him. "You must first perform these works for wages so I can tell if you love me." The "works for wages" are, from the occult viewpoint, similar to the forging of the Sampo task. But they also have a broader and more versatile meaning. You see, before the higher Self consents to an eternal union with the lower self, the lower self must cleanse and prepare itself to prove that it will honor and keep the union holy. The same thing is demanded of Ilmarinen that was demanded of Lemminkäinen!

However, it should be noticed that it is Ilmarinen who successfully performs the works for wages. It might even be said that Lemminkäinen did not complete all of his works for wages. Because the rune of Lemminkäinen tells of a seeker who did not win the heavenly spouse, we must assume that Lemminkäinen, with his fiery character, immediately tries to tackle the most difficult work for wages and fails according to his karmic nature. The Kalevala does relate that Lemminkäinen finishes the first two works for wages but in so doing, it colors Lemminkäinen's behavior in such a striking way as to emphasize his hasty and defiant style (13:31-270 and 14:1-372).

On the other hand, Ilmarinen, who neither torments nor lingers, performs all the works for wages calmly and honestly and then claims his payment.

Now our task remains to study what these "works for wages" are.

23

The Works for Wages

T HERE ARE THREE WORKS FOR WAGES. Ilmarinen's tasks are to plow the field of adders, bridle Tuonela's bear, and catch Tuonela's pike from the river of Tuonela. Lemminkäinen, on the other hand, must ski down the Elk of Hiisi, bridle Hiisi's gelding, and shoot the swan of Tuonela. These works for wages have the same meaning; it is the cleansing of the lower self in "preparation for the wedding." As we said, this lower self consists of three "houses" or states of consciousness: day-consciousness, sleep-consciousness, and inner consciousness. These three must be cleansed—and that is what the works for wages are for.

The first work for wages is designed to cleanse the day-consciousness. How is this possible? This can be accomplished, answers the Kalevala, by either skiing Hiisi's Elk or plowing the field of adders. And what does this describe? We can understand this if we recall what is the most essential and most self-conscious character in our day-consciousness, our closest companion. What else could this be but our reason, our understanding, our thoughts! Indeed, our thoughts are like Hiisi's Elk, and our logical understanding is, from the higher viewpoint, certainly comparable to a field of adders.

To "ski down Hiisi's Elk" means to learn to calm ones thoughts. Hiisi's Elk is very swift-footed—and what is faster than thought? It must be skied upon, the scenery passed through is wintery—and how cold and unconcerned, how independent from the heart can thought be! This is "Hiisi's" (the Devil's) Elk because thoughts are disposed to serve selfish-

130

ness and evil. In the attack of the first enthusiasm of spirit one cannot master ones thoughts right away, and Lemminkäinen had to meet this challenge (13:31-270). Not until he bows down to pray for help from both nature and God, and sets out "to ski slowly," does he bend his thoughts and surrender to the ordered flow (14:1-270).

Ilmarinen's works for wages are defined by Pohja's old woman with these words:

"...*Kun sa kynnät kyisen pellon,*	"...When you plow the field of adders,
Käärmehisen käännättelet	Turn the turf of serpents' meadow
Ilman auran astumatta,	With no movement of the plow,
Vaarnojen värisemättä;	With no tremor of the plowshare.
Senpä Hiisi ennen kynti,	Long ago the demon plowed it,
Lempo varsinkin vakoili	And the devil furrowed it
Vaarnasilla vaskisilla,	With a plowshare made of copper,
Auralla tuliterällä,	With a plow point fiery-bladed.
Oma poikani poloinen	Even my poor boy, my son,
Heitti kesken kyntämättä."	Left it only halfway done."[25]

"The field of adders" represents logical understanding because it "has been plowed before by Hiisi." Since the beginning it has been in service to selfishness and evil and gets its power to grow from it. When Pohja's "own son"—the human being's personal "I"—tried to "plow" it, tried to develop it towards useful and good ends, the work was left half-finished because it was not possible for him to finish the task. The field must be plowed "without the touch of the plow"; understanding must be cleansed so that not even a trace of evil remains, and the force to do this must be taken from above.

Ilmarinen is not lacking for advice. He has met his higher self, and he can appeal to it as someone who trusts and knows in his spirit that he can discuss anything with his God. He immediately asks the maid of Pohja: How, at this moment, must the field of adders be plowed? We do not truly need to think that his own intuition will tell him the answer; maybe he has heard about this task from seers. Ultimately, it is clear that his awakened intuition immediately counsels him that whatever the method is, it will be effective and one must obey it. The advice given sounds like this:

"Ohoh seppo Ilmarinen,	"Oho, you blacksmith Ilmarinen,
Takoja iänikuinen!	You eternal hammerer!
Aura kultainen kuvoa,	Make yourself a plow of gold,
Hope'inen huolittele!	Artfully adorned with silver,
Sillä kynnät kyisen pellon,	With it plow the field of adders
Käärmehisen käännättelet."	Turn the turf of serpents' meadow."[26]

"Forge yourself a golden plow," that is to say, model for yourself through the discipline of thinking and meditation a clear view of life from the best knowledge and concepts you can find. With this method you will clear the thought-contents of your real I. And when you, in meditation with the golden plow of your faith, plow the field of your understanding, to your astonishment you will see how many "adders and serpents" are upturned. Be sure to dress yourself with the iron shirt of honesty and the steel belt of truth so that you do not stumble into conflict and fall astray into lies. Harness the fiery gelding of your strength and enthusiasm so that you do not tire and do not leave the meditation half-finished (19:59-74).

Being accustomed to thinking work, Ilmarinen successfully performs the difficult task. He observes that he has cleansed his mind and mastered his thoughts. And so Pohja's mistress gives him the second task:

"...Kun sa tuonet Tuonen karhun,	"...When you bring the bear of Tuoni,
Suistanet suen Manalan	Bridle up the wolf of Mana
Tuolta Tuonelan salosta,	From the wilderness of Tuoni,
Manalan majan periltä,	From behind the house of Death.
Sata on saanut suistamahan,	Hundreds have gone there to do it
Tullut ei yhtänä takaisin."	But not one of them came back."[27]

"Bridle up the big gelding, Hiisi's brown horse, Hiisi's foal, foamy muzzle, from the back of Hiisi's meadows"—this sounds like the same work for wages given to Lemminkäinen.

This work for wages involves the cleansing and mastering of the second "house," the sleep-consciousness. One wonders why it is a big fiery horse, bear, or wolf—animals who have killed so many? This is because the sleep-consciousness is the realm of imagination and emotions, the power of which is great and frightful. It contains a part of the mental life which our scientists call the subconscious, that part which a civilized human being keeps under control or hidden but which freely vents its strength while the body sleeps. From the occult point of view, the subconscious reveals a human being's moral state and, as the Kalevala says, many have stumbled against it. The passions of humanity are truly like wild beasts. A proverb says, "don't beat a bear with a twig," to which we would add: "especially when it sleeps." At any rate, the cleansing and mastering of this level of consciousness is unavoidable for those that journey on the inner way. The winning of emotions and passions is comparatively easy for one who is practiced in meditation because he has already directed and purified his imagination.

When Ilmarinen asks his maiden for advice, she answers without hesitation:

"Ohoh seppo Ilmarinen,	"Oho, you blacksmith Ilmarinen,
Takoja iänikuinen!	You eternal hammerer!
Teräksestä tehkös suitset,	Forge yourself a steely bit
Päitset rauasta rakenna	And an iron bridle also
Yhellä vesikivellä,	On a single waterstone
Kolmen kosken kuohumilla,	In the foam of triple rapids.
Niillä tuonet Tuonen karhut,	With them bring the bear of Tuoni,
Suitset suet Manalan."	Bridle up the wolf of Mana."[28]

An expert perceives the competence of this advice. A rapids is to be created in ones thoughts; that is to say, a mental image of some emotion in its full fury. On a stone in the middle of this foaming fury a bridle of steel must be made. In other words, one must learn to perceive the reasoning thought which gives rise to the imagined emotion. When this kind of steel-mittened and steely-hard thought of the truth is used to bridle imagined feelings, real feelings also spontaneously begin to be restrained. And when one directs this practice into the sleep-state with the help of a firm decision prior to sleeping, consciousness preserves its determination in the sleeping world and there learns to calm the beasts so that they do not suspect any evil. This is what is said about Ilmarinen (19:135-143).

Still remaining is the taking possession of the third house, mastering the inner consciousness. This third work for wages is described to Lemminkäinen:

"...*Kun ammut joutsenen*	"When you shoot the beautiful bird,
joesta,	
Virrasta vihannan linnun,	Shoot the swan of Tuonela
Tuonen mustasta joesta,	Swimming on the death-dark river
Pyhän virran pyörtehestä,	By the sacred river's whirlpool
Yhellä yrittämällä,	With one shot and one arrow,
Yhen nuolen nostamalta."	Taking but a single arrow."[29]

The same message is given to Ilmarinen:

"*Kun saat suuren suomuhau'in*	"When you catch the giant scale-pike,
Liikkuvan kalan lihavan	Monstrous fat and agile fish
Tuolta Tuonelan joesta,	From the river of Tuonela,
Manalan alantehesta	From the depths of Manala
Ilman nuotan nostamatta,	Without hauling up a seine,
Käsiverkon kääntämättä;	Without flipping out a handnet.
Sata on saanut pyytämähän,	Hundreds have gone fishing there
Tullut ei yhtänä takaisin."	But not one of them came back."[30]

This is the final work for wages. The one who performs it happily has, so to say, learned to forge the Sampo, and he will marry Pohja's delightful virgin.

24

The Swan of Tuonela

THE SHOOTING OF THE SWAN OF TUONELA turned out to be fatal for
Lemminkäinen. For us to understand this and to also understand why Ilmarinen succeeded in his endeavor, we must study
something about the secret consciousness of inner sensations and its
correlation to the physical body.

According to occult psychology, phenomena of the soul are divided
into three categories: 1) momentary thoughts and emotions; 2) varying
but more stable emotions, moods, sentiments, mental images, ideas and
ideals; and 3) stable and innate characteristics such as instincts, habits,
abilities, qualities and passions. This division correlates directly with the
division of the states of consciousness presented earlier such that 1)
momentary thoughts and emotions belong to the day-consciousness,
although the day-consciousness is certainly affected by deeper feelings
arising like goddesses or sea-monsters from the depths (states 2 and 3
mentioned below being expressions of the soul's life); 2) emotions,
sentiments, moods, and so on, belong to the sleep-consciousness, although certainly this state reflects thoughts and emotions aroused during
day-consciousness, and somewhat effects the habits and instincts of the
inner-consciousness; and 3) innate instincts, abilities, and so on, belong
to the inner-consciousness, which is very weakly affected by the other
states.

Besides the correlation of these states of consciousness to the human
being's (formal) I and to the physical body, there is also the following: 1)

day-consciousness is closest to the (personal) I and the strength of this I is most closely associated with the thoughts and emotions belonging to the day-consciousness; the day-consciousness is the most remote from the physical body and thus is least dependent on it; 2) the sleep-consciousness is a step further from the personal I and thus the personal I's power over it is correspondingly smaller; likewise, the sleep-consciousness is a step closer to the physical body; 3) the inner-consciousness is the most remote from the personal I and is essentially independent from it; at the same time, though its activities are hidden within the ethereal domain, the inner-consciousness is actually the closest to the body. Therefore it is nearly impossible for a human being to change his habits, characteristics, abilities and so on, because he—quite rightly—feels that he must make changes in his own physical body. And if we say that the day-consciousness is mediated by the cerebrum, the sleep-consciousness by the cerebellum, spinal cord and sympathetic nervous system, and the inner-consciousness by the body's secret force-centers, it is clear that if we want to connect our day-consciousness to our subconscious, we must, so to say, dig more deeply into our body.

Anyhow, this happens in the purification work, but not in a totally complete way. It doesn't result in a human being having free use of the super-sensuous and magic forces of the inner consciousness—far from it. These belong to the way of secret knowledge. Purification is meant to cleanse the body of dangerous habits and instincts, especially hate, lovelessness, apathy, cold-heartedness, desire for own gain and from other forms of selfishness.

This is the third work for wages in the Kalevala's runes, and it is impossible to perform without the help of the other two works for wages. We have already mentioned that practicing meditation to cleanse thoughts has lasting effects on the more permanent moods, and we can add that it also affects habits and instincts but this takes time. A positive background must be found with the third work for wages that gives the results of meditation to the day-consciousness to use.

"The Swan of Tuonela must be shot," says the Kalevala, "in Tuoni's black river, by the holy river's whirlpool." While these words may seem hasty to the reader—after all, what do our customs and habits have to do with Tuoni, with death?—these words reveal the facts of a deep occult knowledge. In the first place, our evil habits have a very close association with death because it is them that cause us to die and reincarnate. (From the standpoint of spiritual development, however, bad habits must die.) Secondly, evil habits have a quite special relationship with the river of Tuoni, which we will see shortly.

What is this "black river of Tuoni"? Like the Greek river Styx, it is both boundary and gulf between the two worlds of the living and the dead. The dead live in that unseen world which our physical, external senses cannot perceive. However, we can develop a connection through meditation and the awakening of our inner senses. As the day-consciousness mediates our connection with the surrounding physical world, so our inner consciousness mediates our connection with the ever-present unseen world. "The river of Tuoni" is simultaneously the boundary and gulf between our waking consciousness (including the sleep-consciousness) and our secret consciousness; it is "black" because it is dark or unconscious. As an example, if we in our day-consciousness suddenly rush into the inner-consciousness (as a result of either external or internal causes), it is said that we were "unconscious" and we remember nothing after awakening. Likewise, if we, while sleeping, move into the inner-consciousness, it is said that we sleep a deep, dreamless sleep. (Exceptional situations naturally include ecstacy states, prophetic visions while awake, and auguries received in dreams.) Our state of Self, of course, was not unconscious—only the journey of traversing the inner-consciousness to the waking state is usually unconscious—and this is the journey over "the black river of Tuoni."*

Our customs and habits, the weaknesses and faults of our characters, as well as our virtues and abilities, live in our inner consciousness. Because of this, they are separated from our conscious self and are as if undercover. In relation to our good characteristics, there is advantage in this, for we cannot reach them and kill them completely without further ado. Likewise, however, it is also difficult to get free from our evil habits and character traits—we cannot immediately change, improve, or kill them. We are seemingly forced to rely on methods like practicing meditation, which little by little will civilize our habits and characters.

---

*Louhi, the mistress of Pohjola, who is the master of our inner-consciousness, is therefore also Manala's master. This is also observed in this rune's variants and elsewhere; compare with J. Krohn, *Suomalaisen kirjallisuuden historia, I. Kalevala* (The History of Finnish Literature, I. Kalevala), pp. 253-4.

But the Kalevala says: The Swan of Tuonela must be shot "with one single act, taking but a single arrow." It also says that the giant pike must be caught "without hauling up a seine, without flipping out a handnet." Here the Kalevala obviously refers to the fact that the way must be discovered by which one can develop and change the habits and instincts hidden within the body's secret places and, in addition, urges us to learn how to shift consciousness to the inner world at will. The Kalevala not only refers to the fact that discovering this way is unavoidable, it expressly mentions it. It is not difficult for us to comprehend what way the Kalevala means.

You see, why did Lemminkäinen fail in his work for wages? Obviously, because he did not discovery this way. And when we think over his past experiences, we can understand the reason why he failed. Lemminkäinen is killed at the river by "Wet-Hat the cow-herder." Lemminkäinen chose not to enchant this man out of Pohjola's house when he first arrived, insulted him with his words, and from that moment on the man had vengeful thoughts toward Lemminkäinen. What fated characteristic was it that compelled Lemminkäinen to behave so? It was the pride of his own heart, his hate and contempt. How could Lemminkäinen change his character, develop and cleanse his instincts and habits so that they would be good enough for the heavenly bride, unless his heart were already thoroughly cleansed? And though he might do this, how beneficial could it be if the possibility of pride, hate, and contempt still lived within his heart?

As we pointed out earlier, Lemminkäinen's failure reveals that, in reality, he had not even performed the first two works for wages. He certainly should have known that to shoot the Swan of Tuonela somehow involved the heart, allowing the character to be recreated in the future and, moreover, to have the ability to move consciously into the inner world. He did not realize this because in his heart he did not have compassion nor exuberant love and sympathy.

Now, we can understand what the way is about. "To shoot the Swan of Tuonela" means to immerse ones consciousness into the heart and enliven the force-center hidden there, to awaken the force-channel which goes from the heart to the brain. When this is done, the human being's heart becomes new and the entire life is regenerated; he is good, he is compassionate, he is sympathetic. That would have been easy to do for the lemminkäinen-character had not his great enemy lived within his own heart. How beautifully does the Kalevala describe Lemminkäinen's fate. Encouraging all seekers—especially those with fiery souls—it impresses upon us the great truth of reincarnation. Truly, we all experience, as Lemminkäinen did, the Mother Nature which is always compassionate, always loving, and which always lets us try again. When we fall in battle, the Mother revives us and gives us a new body and a new personality. Better equipped than before, we can begin to solve the mystery of the Sphinx.[31]

In Ilmarinen's work for wages "the pike" also means the heart. Ilmarinen understands what the question is to be about and hurries to get advice from the maid of Pohja. And she helps:

Ohoh seppo Ilmarinen,	"Oho, you blacksmith Ilmarinen!
Ellös olko milläskänä!	Don't you worry about that now.
Taop' on tulinen kokko,	Go and forge a fire-swift eagle,
Vaakalintu valkeainen!	Hammer out a flaming griffin.
Sillä saanet suuren hau'in,	You can catch the big pike with it,
Liikkuvan kalan lihavan	Monstrous fat and agile fish
Tuonen mustasta joesta,	From the death-dark river of Tuoni,
Manalan alantehesta."	From the depths of Manala."[32]

Is this not like his higher self advising and comforting: "You, do not be afraid that your heart will cause you harm. You are a man of action. Simply perform more good works, and aid will come to you at the critical moment. Make works of love and mercy, be helpful to others and obliging. This is not difficult for your character."

Ilmarinen follows this advice and speeds on the wings of his good works to the gate of his own heart. His good karma (as Buddhists say) helps him through the difficulties and then disappears to heaven, to God, but Ilmarinen feels for himself that he has only succeeded in enlivening his heart, which according to his own modest critique is only worth a pike's head (19:185-318).

Ilmarinen has now performed all the works for wages, and therefore his wedding with Pohja's delightful virgin begins.

25

Pohjola's Wedding

FOR POHJA'S GRAND WEDDING and Ilmarinen's homecoming with his young mistress, the Kalevala dedicates a total of six runes (20-25). Though the mystical experience implicit here is captivating and grandiose, it is obvious that the size of this episode derives from the rune's attention to popular customs which have no direct connection with the mystical content. And so for us it seems that the only place where can be found descriptions of a mystic wedding is in the preparations for the wedding (Runo 20), especially the following verses:

Silloin Pohjolan emäntä	Said the mistress of Pohjola,
Pani kutsut kulkemahan,	Sending out her invitations,
Airuhut vaeltamahan,	Messengers to make the rounds:
Itse tuon sanoiksi virkki:	
"Ohoh piika pikkarainen,	"Little maid, most faithful servant,
Orjani alinomainen!	
Kutsu rahvasta kokohon,	Call the common folk together,
Miesten joukko juominkihin,	Crowd of menfolk to the drinking.
Kutsu kurjat, kutsu köyhät,	Call the wretched, call the poor,
Sokeatki, vaivaisetki,	Call the blind and even cripples,
Rammatki, rekirujotki,	Even sleigh-bound paralytics!
Sokeat venehin soua,	Row the blind here in the dories,
Rammat ratsahin, ajele,	Have the lame ones come on horseback
Rujot re'in remmätellös!	And the cripples in the sleighs!

Kutsu kaikki Pohjan kansa,	"Summon all the Pohjolanders,
Ja kaikki Kalevan kansa,	Summon all the Kalevalanders
Kutsu vanha Väinämöinen	And invite old Väinämöinen
Lailliseksi laulajaksi,	As official singer for us—
Elä kutsu Kaukomieltä,	But don't ask the man far-minded,
Tuota Ahti Saarelaista"!	Not that Ahti Islander!"[33]

These are remarkable verses because they call to mind Jesus' parable about the wedding of the king's son. When the wedding lacked "a qualified singer, a proper cuckoo," Pohjola's mistress sends invitations around the lands and villages; in a similar way, the king takes it badly when invited guest do not come, and orders his servant: "Go out at once into the streets and lanes of the city and bring in here the poor and crippled and blind and lame" and "Go out into the highways and along the hedges and compel *them* to come in, that my house may be filled" (Luke 14:21, 23; compare Matthew 22:9). And as the mistress of Pohjola refrains from calling Lemminkäinen to the wedding, likewise the king orders to throw out the guest who was not dressed in wedding clothes (Matthew 22:11-13). The similarities are so striking that one immediately comprehends the same mystic truth hiding behind both allegories.

At Pohjola's wedding, Ilmarinen, seeker of the truth, is married in holy union to the maid of Pohjola, his higher self. A human being's "higher self" is the I-consciousness of his divinely born self; the "lower" or "personal I" is a reflection of the higher self and resides in the brain. (Following the customary usage in the Theosophical literature, we use the words *individuality* and *personality* in a precisely defined and more limited meaning than one commonly finds in spoken or literary usage. The Theosophical usage is derived from Madame Blavatsky's remark that the Latin word persona originally meant "mask," through which an actor's sound was heard (per-sonare). The immortal I or individual who incarnates many times on earth plays many different roles, taking on different personalities, and is truly comparable to an actor.) An ordinary unregenerated human being is not aware of this inner I-consciousness; he is just a mortal personal being. On the other hand, the higher or "individual" I is immortal. Only on the way of preparation does the journeyer—or "propositional excursionist," to use the Kalevala's designation—sometimes get to feel the presence of the divine self within his soul. At that moment an effect streams from the inner consciousness to the day-consciousness. But only when the propositional excursionist succeeds in all his works for wages, as Ilmarinen did, will he be married inseparably with his inner self. This does not mean that a human being, from that time on, will completely know in every moment of day-consciousness the immortal I in all its characteristics and faculties; to the contrary, one can almost say that he does not yet know anything about his true self. However, in the marriage an unbroken bridge is built between the higher and lower, the eternal "connection with God" has been accomplished that truly makes it possible for him "to study the depths of God's spirit," to become absorbed in the secrets of the inner ocean of his own being. As we said, not until now is the way of knowledge and power open in front of him—but also opened is the way of unexpected error and grief.

Once more let us make it clear what the initiation to our higher self means on a practical level, what Ilmarinen as a seeker of the truth really attains at the wedding of Pohjola.

Before the initiation a human being easily makes the mistake of thinking that his physical body or his many feelings and thoughts comprise his true self, the "real I" about which psychology speaks. But on the way of purification he gradually learns to distinguish himself from his corporeal habits and predispositions, emotions, and thoughts. As a propositional excursionist he will learn to step outside of his real I, he will understand that the thoughts he controls and directs are not really himself, that the passions and desires, emotions and moods which can now be checked, are not really himself, and that habits and inclinations which he can change and develop, are also not himself. Thus "the formal I" develops within him from a subjective idea to a living, anticipating being who, in the initiation, receives its own inner contents.

Before initiation a human being can build for himself and believe in any kind of theory about life. Selfishness and evil may be hidden within his nature which he does not suspect at all, but which jumps out at critical moments. He can believe in the power of love, admire it, but at the same time hate can also live in his heart. How different it is for the truth seeker who has been initiated with his higher self! Now the meaning of the body's life is revealed to him. He knows that love is the only divine law of life. No evil within him can stay concealed from his eyes; it must be drawn out into the daylight and conquered. Hate has no place in his heart, which is exuberant with warmth and love towards all human beings. He has already struggled with all of this himself when he was a propositional excursionist, and he has reached a wreath of triumph in Pohjola's wedding.

Why is it that Lemminkäinen was not invited to the wedding? Why is it that at the wedding of the king's son there is a guest who is not dressed in wedding clothes? All memories of failed attempts, about castles in the air and petty theories, are wiped from the mind. But the poor and the miserable, the blind, lame and crippled, must be invited to the banquet because either no qualified singer has yet been found or the original guests do not come. All of the old and decent ideas about life, righteous ideas committed to memory, innocence and virtue—everything a human being has received through religion, civilization and science, and that one might expect to see at the wedding—are all conspicuously absent because none of them can sing life's real song. On the contrary, it is the human being's sins and weaknesses, faults and inadequacies that participate in the joy of the wedding; the heart's overflowing love and compassion dress them for awhile in wedding clothes and teach of their own lessons. In a decent human being's eyes, all of the foolish and nonsensical views of life, all of the old superstitions and ideals, should be invited to the wedding because the truth is hidden at their cores and they can at least pause to listen when old Väinämöinen—the eternal wisdom—sings the wedding song:

Siinä lauloi Väinämöinen,	There old Väinämöinen chanted,
Pitkin iltoa iloitsi,	Making merry all the evening.
Naiset kaikki naurusuulla,	Women all with laughing mouths,
Miehet mielellä hyvällä	All the men in joyful humor
Kuuntelivat, kummeksivat	Listened breathless in their wonder
Väinämöisen väännätystä,	At Väinämöinen's vast production
Kun oli kumma kuulianki,	For it was a marvel to them,
Ime ilmanki olian	Even to all airy beings.[34]

Can one even describe in words the blissful rejoicing which overwhelms a human soul when he, while joining to his higher self, feels the unlimited force and wisdom of the divine love? The voice of a human master, a seer, echoes through his being, so humble but at the same time so magically grandiose. He knowingly feels that he will someday arise to become a creator himself, and his words will honor the essence within and the beings of all realms so that everything will change for the better. How modestly but effectively is this sensation expressed in the last verses of Väinämöinen's wedding hymn:

"*Mitäpä minusta onpi*
Laulajaksi, taitajaksi,
En minä mitänä saata,
En kuhunkaan kykene;
Olisi luoja laulamassa,
Suin sulin sanelemassa,
Luoja laulun lauleleisi,
Lauleleisi, taiteleisi.
Laulaisi meret mesiksi,
Meren hiekat hernehiksi,
Meren mullat maltahiksi,
Suoloiksi meren someret,
Lehot laajat leipämaiksi,
Ahovieret vehnämaiksi,
Mäet mämmikakkaroiksi,
Kalliot kanan muniksi.
Lauleleisi, taiteleisi,
Saneleisi, saatteleisi...
Annap' ainaki Jumala,
Toisteki totinen luoja,
Näin näissä elettäväksi...
Näissä Pohjolan tuvissa...
Jotta päivin lauleltaisi,
Illoin tehtäisi iloa
l'ällä tämän isännän,
Elinajalla emännän!"

"What in fact am I at all
As a singer, as an artist!
Having in myself no power,
Not truly fit for anything?
Were the great Creator singing,
Chanting with his flowing voice,
It would be the song of songs,
Chant of chants, and art of arts.
"He would sing the seas to honey,
And the sea sands into peas;
Into malt the ooze of ocean
And its gravel into salt;
All wide woodlands into cornfields,
And the clearings into wheatfields;
All the hills to sugar cakes,
And the boulders into hen's eggs.
"He would sing with perfect art,
Sing his magic and create...
"Jumala, thou true Creator,
Grant the same some other time
So that all of us may live...
In these halls of Pohjola...
That our days be filled with singing,
And our nights with merrymaking
In the lifetime of the master,
In the lifetime of the mistress.[35]

When a truth seeker has carried through with the grand experience of Pohjola's wedding, he can no longer be suspicious about the meaning of life nor can he be without belief in his god. He now feels his own divinity and he knows that the same divinity is hidden within the soul of every human child. But afterward his reason may become covered in fog and he may forget to be united with his divine I.

26

The Golden Maid

HEN AN ASPIRING TRUTH SEEKER enters into a holy alliance with his higher I, he is said to be "a homeless wanderer" (*parivraadshaka*) in the Hindu Holy Books. This recalls the words of Jesus: "The foxes have holes, and the birds of the air have nests; but the Son of Man has nowhere to lay His head" (Matthew 8:20). In Theosophical literature this means that a human being who is initiated with his higher I is truly homeless on earth because his real home is in the heavenly state of his divine self; in his mundane life he is like an envoy who "fulfills the will of his divine Father." He neither has nor wants "a permanent home" here on earth because wherever he fulfills God's will by serving humanity, that is his home. The Hindu term and the words of Jesus given above do not complain, they express the rule.

As true as this is, we can also approach this from a different viewpoint. To our minds, the Kalevala also expresses psychological aspects of initiation. After the wedding, we read of how the young couple moves to Ilmarinen's home where the Pohjola maid will permanently live. In other words, though the union between the higher and lower self occurs in Pohjola, that is, in the inner consciousness, a real home for the higher self is made within Ilmarinen's day-consciousness. While in the day-consciousness a human being certainly must remain united with his higher I. And this is how it goes in the beginning. For awhile after the initiation one lives blessedly happy and feels protected like one has built a cozy home to live in. But then comes a catastrophe: the higher I vanishes from sight.

This will happen sometimes in the same life or more likely when the human being is born anew on earth. When the human being reincarnates, he does not retain in his day-consciousness any memory of his initiation. He just feels an unspeakable yearning and loss, deep pity towards others who are suffering and a certain feeling that he lacks something which ought to be found. The Kalevala describes this eventuality through the death of Pohjola's maid and Ilmarinen's resulting sorrow. With good reason we can say that Runo 37 begins a new page in the book of Ilmarinen's life, that now it is a question of Ilmarinen's new period of incarnation:

Se on seppo Ilmarinen	Craftsman Ilmarinen wept
Naista itki illat kaiket,	Every evening for his woman,
Yöt itki unettomana,	Weeping sleepless through the nights
Päivät einehettömänä,	And fasting through the days;
Aamut aikaisin valitti,	In the early hours complaining,
Huomeniset huokaeli,	Every morning sighing for her,
Kun oli kuollut nuori nainen,	Lamenting for his lovely lost one,
Kaunis kalmahan katettu;	For his dear one in the grave.
Eipä kääntynyt käessä	For a month he swung no hammer,
Vaskinen vasaran varsi,	Did not touch the copper handle,
Kuulunut pajasta kalke,	And the clicking forge was silent.[36]
Yhen kuuhuen kululla.	

A human being in this state is truly in a curious position. He is a different personality who remembers nothing about the old one, but in the inner consciousness of his individual I he has experienced love's great initiation and now he continually tries to participate in the day-consciousness of his new personality. This awakens an invincible yearning for divine truth, the solid trust that the truth is to be found within the human being's own self. It also awakens tireless, unrelenting work and mental exertion. Though the aspirant cannot stray far from his god's side, his own eagerness and yearning invites mistakes which will teach him through sufferings and sorrows.

We also are fully justified in asking: Does this mean that the human being has been returned to the same position of the propositional excursionist, though he previously traversed the way of cleansing? Isn't this a regressive development? Isn't this unjust? Why strive to achieve anything if the hard won fruits must vanish from ones hands? On no account do we wish to blindly defend nature. Objectively understood, a human being always loses something at death, i.e., while he is resting. Death is to an individual life what sleep is to a personality's life. For example, if an artist is preparing a great work of art, rest always breaks his concentration and he cannot immediately afterwards get back into his creativity. The more skillful he is, the quicker he returns into the rhythm of it, but in life and nature the cyclic law of periodicity prevails, and a human being cannot change it. The Kalevala clearly points out this fact. Winning Pohjola's maiden as ones own assumes that the human being has already accomplished a specific work: the forging of the mystic Sampo. This means he has succeeded—either before his true cleansing or through his works for wages—to find his inner consciousness. It means that the day-consciousness visited the invisible world, as Ilmarinen did when he went to Pohjola first through Väinämöinen and later by his own doing. In this mystical-psychological meaning, the forging of the Sampo before initiation is unavoidable.

However, when Ilmarinen again enters the scene after his happy marriage, we discover that the Sampo nevertheless remained in Pohjola! Consequently, Ilmarinen must either have forgotten how the forging was done or he reincarnated and was thus prevented from remembering.

Now, from the point of view of nature, is this unjust? Or can we understand these things from the other side? The other viewpoint also exists as a matter of fact.

Though he has already been initiated, Ilmarinen still has work ahead of him, but he is not conscious of it. He must retrieve the Sampo from Pohjola or, we could say, he must forge the Sampo again, this time in day-consciousness. This is, in other words, the widening of day-consciousness towards the inner consciousness, or making the inner consciousness more present in day-consciousness.

Now there is a possibility here of misunderstanding. During initiation we might suspect that when the inner consciousness presents itself to the day-consciousness as the higher I, it may deplete itself or completely reveal itself to the day-conscious I. We might also suspect that the inner consciousness, as "the divine" I, never changes or grows. This assumption is misleading. During initiation the inner consciousness presents only a personified part of itself to the day-consciousness because the divine self is unlimited. And far from the belief that the inner I cannot develop, it is truly the inner consciousness that reaps the fruits of all development: Because the higher I is immortal, it has unlimited possibilities to grow. The self-education of an initiate is thus not allowed to set limits on the free growth of the inner I, which happens when the day-consciousness tries to express the glimpses of the inner I experienced during initiation. Therefore it is inevitable that the higher I withdraws from the day-consciousness to a hiding place and so one is forced once again to seek it out to widen ones ideas and understanding. This is a fairly common rule because it is very difficult for the lone initiate to understand things. Only in the presence of a great and wise teacher can the development proceed quickly. As a rule, many reincarnations are passed through in these efforts, and the law of development demands that the initiate loses all knowledge of his previous initiations before reincarnating on earth—and thus the Pohjola maid dies away from Ilmarinen...

At first Ilmarinen does not even suspect that a great task awaits him, that of acquiring the Sampo. In reality, he doesn't know anything about the Sampo. He can only surrender to his sorrow and yearning, the feelings of loneliness, compassion, and sorrow for the world. But this does not last for long:

Seppo naisetta elävi,	For a time he lives on wifeless,
Puolisotta vanhenevi;	Growing old without a woman.
Itki kuuta kaksi, kolme,	After mourning two months, three months,
Niinpä kuulla neljännellä	On the fourth he went to work.
Poimi kultia mereltä,	From the sea he gathered gold,
Hope'ita lainehilta;	From the billows gathered silver
Keräsi kekosen puita,	And collected stacks of firewood,
Kolmekymmentä rekoista,	Thirty sledge loads altogether;
Puunsa poltti hiililöiksi,	Burned the firewood down to charcoal,
Hiilet ahjohon ajeli.	With the charcoal fueled his furnace.[37]

Now a will to action is awakening within Ilmarinen. And truly there are grieving people everywhere. The world is full of suffering. Maybe if he set to work and created something new he might forget his own distress. Maybe he would find peace again if he gave form to his yearning, if he created some ideal out of himself.

Otti noita kultiansa,	Then he took those golden coins
Valitsi hope'itansa	And he chose those silver pieces,
Syksyisen uuhen verran,	Just the weight of autumn ewe
Verran talvisen jäniksen,	Or the heft of winter hare.
Työnti kullat kuumentohon,	Put the silver and the gold
	Into the furnace of his smithy;
Pani orjat lietsomahan	Set the slaves to fan the fire
Palkkalaiset painamahan.	And the hirelings pumping on.
Orjat lietsoi löyhytteli,	So the slaves then worked the billows
Palkkalaiset painatteli	With the hirelings pumping on,
Kintahattomin kätösin,	With no mittens on their hands
Hatuttoman hartioisen;	And stripped naked to the waist,
Itse seppo Ilmarinen	While smith Ilmarinen himself
Ahjoa kohentelevi,	Was attending to the forging,
Pyyti kullaista kuvaista,	Trying to form a golden image,
Hope'ista morsianta.	To create a silver bride.[38]

And now the Kalavela proceeds with the strange and familiar story of the forging of the Golden Maid.

This story brings to mind, of course, the Greek tale of Pygmalion, who sculpted for himself in marble the image of a delightful woman: Galatea. Pygmalion fell in love with his Galatea but because the marble statue was cold and lifeless, he prayed to the gods to give life to his image. The gods consented, Galatea came to life, and Pygmalion was extremely happy.

It did not happen like this for Ilmarinen and his golden bride, however, and we will shortly see that the Kalevala's psychological description expresses more completely and fittingly the mystical message of the story, a meaning which the Greek tale missed.

The Golden Maid is not created in an instant. According to the New Kalevala a ewe or sheep first emerges from the forge; according to the Old Kalevala it is a sword. On the second attempt, after working laboriously a foal (N.K.) or a stallion (O.K.) appears. Not until the third attempt did the Golden Maid emerge fully formed from the forge. On the previous attempts, "the others were very delighted" but not so for Ilmarinen. Finally, on the last attempt, Ilmarinen was satisfied, and the others "were badly afraid."

This is, for our mind, a description of the activity of a creative genius in the field of the arts, sciences, philosophy, religion, politics, and so on. A human being wars against the injustices of the world or he creates, for example, a delightful work of art. He gains appreciation and honor from the world but his loving heart stays empty because the world does not understand it. Finally he believes he has discovered the means to satisfy his own heart: he must create from his own personality an image of that perfect human being which reflects the hidden ideal, a creation the whole world can love. The demand for perfection awakens in his thoughts: "I want to be a perfect, righteous personality." And he sets himself about the giant task:

Siitä seppo Ilmarinen	Then he hammered without ceasing
Takoi kullaista kuvoa,	To create the golden image,
Takoi yön levähtämättä,	Working all night without resting,
Päivän pouahuttamatta.	All the daytime without pausing;
Jalat laati neitoselle,	Legs and arms he fashioned for her—
Jalat laati, käet kuvasi:	
Eipä jalka nousekana,	But the legs, they cannot walk,
Käänny käet syleilemähän.	And the hands cannot caress him.
Takoi korvat neiollensa:	Then the ears he molded for her—
Eipä korvat kuulekana.	But the ears, they do not hear him.
Niin sovitti suun sorean,	When he made a sweet mouth for her
Suun sorean, sirkut silmät.	It could speak no welcome to him;
Saanut ei sanoa suuhun,	When he made those bright eyes for her
Eikä silmähän suloa.	They could not look sweetly at him.[39]

The fruit of his efforts does not satisfy. The bride is beautiful but she is lifeless. But soon Ilmarinen observes that while his heart stays empty his personality has changed into something so delicate and blameless that it can claim all moral virtues:

Siinä seppo Ilmarinen	On that first night, Ilmarinen
Heti yönä ensimmäisnä	Feels the cold and wants more covers,
Kyllä peitettä kysyvi,	
Vaippoja varustelevi,	So he gets himself more covers,
Kahet, kolmet karhuntaljat,	Puts on two or three more bearskins,

Viiet, kuuet villavaipat	Five or six more woolen blankets
Maata kera puolisonsa,	To warm himself beside his wife,
Tuon on kultaisen kuvansa.	By the side of that gold image.
Se oli kylki kyllä lämmin,	Now, his side against the blankets—
Ku oli vasten vaippojansa,	That was warm enough for comfort,
Ku oli nuorta neittä vasten,	But the side against the maiden,
Vasten kullaista kuvoa,	Toward his precious golden image—
Se oli kylki kylmimmässä,	That was cold and freezing
	with hoarfrost
Oli hyyksi hyytymässä,	
Meren jääksi jäätymässä,	And was freezing into sea ice,
Kiveksi kovoamassa.	Stiffening into stony hardness.[40]

Ilmarinen made a mistake, a great error. What was it? It is the mistake we mentioned earlier: he tried to create a final form and image for the living spirit of his own inner consciousness, and so he limited its infinite possibilities for growth. He fell into the sin which a commandment warns us about: Do not make graven images of Me because I am your God. All images of perfection made by human hands are limited, images of idols. Life seeks form without the interference of human beings.

Ilmarinen himself became scared: "I really have nothing to do with this blameless personality. My God, what am I to do?"

Viepi neien Väinölähän.	I will take it to Väinölä,
	Take it to old Väinämöinen
Sitten sinne tultuansa	So he took it to him there.
Sanan virkkoi, noin nimesi:	
"Oi sie vanha Väinämöinen!	"Here, old Väinämöinen," he said.
Tuossa on sinulle tyttö,	"Here's a virgin made for you,
Neiti kaunis katsannolta..."	Beautiful for you to look at..."[41]

And the wise man, whose voice is the same as Ilmarinen's innermost feeling, says:

"Oi on seppo veikkoseni!	"O you smith, my little brother!
Tunge neitosi tulehen,	Shove your girl into the fire.
Tao kaikiksi kaluiksi...	Forge it into useful tools
Ei sovi minun su'ulle,	It would not befit my kindred

Ei minullen itselleni	And it would not suit me either
Naista kullaista kosia,	To go courting after gold
Hope'ista huolitella."	Or go chasing after silver."[42]

Neither life nor the God of life has need of externally perfect personalities. Images of idols exist solely that they will be broken.

Kylmän kulta kuumottavi,	'Frozen is the gleam of gold,
Vilun huohtavi hopea.	Icy is the shine of silver.'"[43]

27

The Younger Sister of Pohja's Maid

ILMARINEN FELL INTO ANOTHER ERROR, which taught him certain things and from which he benefited. As he aspired to personal and moral perfection, and while renewing his efforts on the way of cleansing without awareness of his previous works for wages, Ilmarinen began to make remarkable observations regarding his sleep life. Now, in the same way as it happened for him as a propositional excursionist (though, of course, he did not remember it), his sleep-consciousness grew clear and his dreams became astonishingly vivid and filled with meaning. Accompanying these dreams was a feature that most surprised Ilmarinen. First, while sleeping and dreaming Ilmarinen felt himself to be very much in his daytime self; he could observe, think, control himself, perform deeds and make decisions in quite the same way as when awake. Gradually, he observed himself to have a body although it was not his physical body—he could sometimes even observe his physical body sleeping—but this new body, available for him to use, was light and so extremely delicate that it could even go through walls. This nighttime vehicle looked the same as his physical body, and wore similar clothes.

Ilmarinen did not waste much thought on these matters, as long as he had other things on his mind. From his experiences he concluded that magicians and seers, perhaps "in Lapland," probably used this delicate night-body apparatus "when falling into a trance."*

When Ilmarinen tired of aspiring to exemplary morality and observed that the results were empty, he returned to these nighttime experiences and gave them his due attention. He thought: "Because many mysterious possibilities are hidden within my soul, I want to begin to study and develop them. In that way I will find the true life and the peacefulness of God that I desire."

The Kalevala tells nothing about the interlude during which Ilmarinen makes these observations because it would have to be expressed with complete realism and the Kalevala speaks the truth in veiled allegories. One must read the Holy Books frequently so that one understands what has been omitted in the text.

The Kalevala throws itself into the middle of a new adventure and begins to reveal how Ilmarinen tries to seek the living contents of his inner consciousness through the mediation of the younger sister of his inner consciousness, that is to say, through his sleep-consciousness. In other words, Ilmarinen left for Pohjola to propose to the younger sister of Pohjola's maiden:

Tuop' on seppo Ilmarinen,	Ilmarinen, smith eternal,
Takoja iän-ikuinen	
Heitti kultaisen kuvansa,	Cast aside his golden image,
Hope'isen neitosensa;	Threw away his silver bride.
Pisti varsan valjahisin,	Then he harnessed up his colt,
Ruskean re'en etehen,	Hitched up Browny to the sleigh;
Itse istuvi rekehen,	He himself sits in the sleigh,
Kohennaikse korjahansa.	Mounts up in his basket sleigh.
Lähteäksensä lupasi	He decided to set out,
Sekä mietti mennäksensä	And as he went he contemplated
Pyytämähän Pohjolasta	Begging for another daughter,
Toista Pohjolan tytärtä.	A second wife from Pohjola.[44]

---

*Compare the word *lovi* (trance) with the names Louhi (Pohjola's mistress) and Lovitar (the suffix -tar indicates female gender).

By the conclusion of the Kalevala's 38th rune, Ilmarinen quite clearly remembers his previous union with the girl of Pohja. Louhi's first question when she sees Ilmarinen concerns the well being and circumstances of her daughter (Ilmarinen's wife). After all, she was, "Living as a daughter-in-law, in the homestead of her husband, as a woman in the home of her mother-in-law." But let us remember that the Kalevala tends to condense the experiences of many lives into a single life; thus, for Ilmarinen, the aesthetic impression of completeness requires a poetic style that is not compatible with a literal description. Consequently, we are allowed to skip the places in the rune that tell of Ilmarinen's ex-wife, to keep ourselves in the main design.

When Ilmarinen asks the mistress of Pohjola for her younger daughter, he is denied. And when he encounters the girl in a hut, a child sings from the floor:

"Neitonen, sinä sisari,	"Do not, maiden, you my sister,
Elä sulho'on ihastu,	Fall in love with such a suitor,
Elä sulhon suun pitohon,	For the sweet talk of his tongue
Eläkä jalkoihin jaloihin!	Or his noble turn of leg.
Sulholl' on suen ikenet,	By his gums he is a wolf,
Revon koukut kormanossa,	In his pockets foxy tricks;
Karhun kynnet kainalossa,	Hiding bear claws in his armpits,
Veren juojan veitsi vyöllä,	At his belt blood-drinker's knife
Jolla päätä piirtelevi,	To chop a head or slash a spine."[45]
Selkeä sirettelevi."	

And the maid answers Ilmarinen:

"En lähe minä sinulle,	"No, I will not go with you
Enkä huoli huitukoille...	Nor respect such trifling suitors...
Onpa tässä neitosessa	But in this girl there is something
Paremmankin miehen verta,	Worthy of a better husband,
Kaunihimman varren kauppa,	Match for a finer-figured man,
Korkeamman korjan täysi,	Meant to grace a finer sleigh,
Paikoille paremmillenki,	Better homesteads, higher stations
Isommille istuimille,	

Ei sepon sysi-sioille,	Than a blacksmith's charcoal sheds,
Miehen tuhmaisen tulille."	Hearthfires of a dullard husband."[46]

But Ilmarinen does not give up. And when nothing else works, he turns to violence:

Saa'utti tytön samassa,	As he snatched the girl up to him,
Käärälti käpälihinsä,	Grasped her in his mighty paws.
Läksi tuiskuna tuvasta,	Like a snowstorm rushed outdoors,
Riepsahti rekensä luoksi,	Dashing to his waiting sleigh;
Työnnälti tytön rekehen,	Tossed the girl into it quickly,
Koksahutti korjahansa,	Slung her in his basket sleigh
Läksi kohta kulkemahan,	As he sped off on his journey,
Valmistui vaeltamahan,	Ready to travel fast and far,
Käsi ohjassa orosen,	One hand on the stallion's reins,
Toinen neien nännisillä.	The other on the maiden's nipples.[47]

For Ilmarinen, no joy will ever come from this violent deed. Along the way the girl weeps and complains, scolds and curses. Ilmarinen works hard to find peaceful answers to the girl's abusive words. When they stop for the night in a village, Ilmarinen falls into a deep sleep.

Toinen naista naurattavi	While another man is laughing,
Mieheltä unekkahalta.	Laughing with the sleeper's woman.[48]

In the morning Ilmarinen wakes up and understands his own wife's unfaithfulness and, because he has not yet gotten the girl as his own, becomes angry at "that kind of bride" and sings her "into a sea mew, to scream about the barren skerries." Then he sits himself down in his sleigh and, in bad humor, travels back to his own country.

Despite all the effective realism here, this is really a striking allegorical description of Ilmarinen's psychological efforts.

While Ilmarinen journeys along the psychic way, guided by his sleep-consciousness, mysterious abilities and forces hiding within his body begin to awaken. So he devotes himself to the game, the game which wise men have long warned dear humankind about. As the child on the floor sings, Ilmarinen is still like a bear in this respect; he does not have the reason and the knowledge with which he could control those new abilities. And without wise and humane guidance, the new psychic abilities are like Pohjola's younger daughter: wicked, arbitrary, deceitful. They promise a great deal: "Our name is clairvoyance; increasing the distance of your sight, and granting power over the elements and human beings, we will take you to the gods' secret negotiations and bring you all that you desire on earth." But they take a human being to ruin unless he is their master.

Ilmarinen awakens within his physical body the clairvoyant and the clairaudient senses, which have the following quality: In front of him unfolds Tuonela and the realm of death where the deceased dwell in their longings and distresses. All of these beings now rush to his side, each asking for different kinds of help. One requests Ilmarinen's co-operation in arranging something on the earth; another desires to have sensory feelings of enjoyment again and prays on his knees for Ilmarinen to loan him his body, just for a moment; still another is awkward being in Tuonela and asks Ilmarinen to help him escape. All day long these unhappy beings gather around Ilmarinen and do not give him a moment's rest. Ilmarinen's heart is overflowing with compassion and he tries to help the poor but soon observes that this is not possible. First of all, there are too many begging for help, and secondly, his own sense of justice often conflicts with their requests. And when he does not help them, they swear at him and torment him by other means!

"Where have I come to," he cries out, "to the company of the devil! What must I do?" He realizes that the fault is truly in his own clairvoyance, and with his soul's entire force he tries to free himself from it, to conjure it away from himself, and finally succeeds.

Ilmarinen cannot master the abilities he has awakened but he is delivered from being destroyed at their hands. For what reason? By virtue of his own internal sense of truth and justice. He has this internal sense as an inborn inheritance from his initiation. Because Ilmarinen has already carried out the great mental initiation, which planted the spirit of love into his heart, he is now saved and avoids "the dangers of psychic powers." On the other hand, how different will be the results for the many

who, without benefit of the inner experience of initiation, try to awaken
the supersensual forces!*

Ilmarinen was initiated into love, and he thus cannot fall under the
power of evil. He can make mistakes and his experiences are very difficult
but at the moment of distress his intuition saves him. After his eyes have
been opened, he first thinks, "Should I kill her?" And he answers himself,
"No. No violence with the sword of truth. I will just sing her away from
my consciousness and memory" (38:262-286). He leaves the temptations
of his sleep-consciousness and returns to his old familiar day-consciousness.

On his way home he meets Väinämöinen, who asks him with subtle
mockery:

"Veli seppo Ilmarinen!	"Smith and brother Ilmarinen!
Minne heitit naisen nuoren,	Where did you leave her,
	that young woman,
Kunne kuulun morsiamen	That young sweetheart
	that we heard of,
Kun sa tyhjänä tuletki,	Since you come back all alone,
Aina naisetta ajelet?"	Riding womanless as ever?"[49]

But Ilmarinen answers that, vexed, he sang "such a woman into a sea
mew on a skerry."

And now it quite seems as if we can read between the lines a little
more. Väinämöinen, the wise seer, the master, finally approaches the

---

*In this connection we would like to repeat what J. Krohn says about the *tuno* [seer,
magician] of the Votyaks in his book *Suomen suvun pakanallinen jumanlanpalvelus* (*The
Pagan Divine Service of the Finnish Family*): "Anybody who is able to supply himself with
the required knowledge can pretend to be a *tuno*. The knowledge must be obtained from
gnomes who appear at night in the shape of an old man dressed in a long caftan. The
power of the *tuno* is not the same for all, it varies according to the power of the gnome
who served as teacher. It also depends on the pupil's own susceptibility. The best
teaching is that given by *Inmar*, the most superior god. *Inmar* appears to a magician-
candidate at night in the company of a fully taught *tuno* and guides the candidate to all
kinds of odd places, all the time playing the kantele so as to assuage his fears. Finally the
god takes him to the banks of a very wide river, over which the strings of a kantele have
been stretched. Over these strings he must jump and dance; every time he falls from
them he loses a part of his coming influence. The most powerful *tuno* will be the one who
completes this trial without staggering even once" (p. 101).

struggling soul and speaks to it, not with irony, but with compassion: "Oh, you soul, do you continue to think that you really travel alone?" Haven't you opened your eyes yet to the fact that the real Pohja girl is already your own? Don't you remember your wedding in Pohjola? Don't you know that you are already one with your higher self? Look, you have already been to Pohjola, and you have already forged the Sampo!"

And Väinämöinen asks Ilmarinen:

"Veli seppo Ilmarinen!	"Well, my brother, Ilmarinen,
Mit' olet pahoilla mielin,	What has made you look so gloomy,
Kahta kallella kypärin	With your peaked hat doubly crooked
Pohjolasta tullessasi?	Coming back from Pohjola?
Miten Pohjola elävi?"	How's the life up there
	in Northland?"[50]

The memories awaken in Ilmarinen and he answers: "Truly, everything is all right in the secret world of my inner consciousness because within it the knowledge of the truth is hidden, not in the psychic realm of the sleep-consciousness." In the Kalevala's words:

"Mi on Pohjolan eleä!	"How's the living there in Pohjola?
Siell' on Sampo jauhamassa,	There they have the Sampo grinding,
Kirjokansi kallumassa:	Many-colored cover spinning:
Päivän jauhoi syötäviä,	One day grinding things to eat,
Päivän toisen myötäviä,	On the second things to barter,
Kolmannen kotipitoja.	Third day things to keep at home.
Jotta sanon, kun sanonki,	"What I say, I say in truth
Vielä kerta kertaelen:	And repeat what I relate:
Mi on Pohjolan eleä,	How they live in Pohjola
Kun on Sampo Pohjolassa!	Since they got the Sampo there!
Siin' on kyntö, siinä kylvö,	There's the plowing and the planting,
Siinä kasvo kaikenlainen,	There are crops of every kind,
Siinäpä ikuinen onni."	There prosperity unending."[51]

"Well," remarks Väinämöinen, "now you understand, brother Ilmarinen, that the Sampo must be taken from Pohjola! You had the right intention when you began to develop your psychic abilities, but your method was wrong. The Sampo must be brought from the inner consciousness, not from the sleep-consciousness, and not with the aid of the daytime sleep-consciousness, but by the secret!"

And he invites Ilmarinen with these runo words:

"Ohoh seppo Ilmarinen,   "Oho, good smith Ilmarinen!
Lähtekäämme Pohjolahan   Let us go to Pohjola
Hyvän Sammon saa'antahan,   To get that precious Sampo there,
Kirjokannen katsantahan!"   To behold the ciphered cover."[52]

That is to say, now the inner consciousness and the secret, invisible world, must be studied. Ilmarinen has already discovered the deep law of the visible world's life, but the invisible world has passed by him unexamined. And only in this invisible world can the secret of knowledge and power be found: The Sampo.

28

The Sword of the Spirit

ILMARINEN CERTAINLY APPROVES of Väinämöinen's proposition, but also remarks about the difficulties of the voyage:

"Ei ole sampo saatavana,	"But we cannot seize the Sampo
Kirjokansi tuotavana	And behold its ciphered cover
Pimeästä Pohjolasta,	From the dark of Pohjola,
Summasta Sariolasta;	From the foggy land of sedges.
Siell' on Sampo saatettuna,	There the Sampo has been taken
Kirjokansi kannettuna	With its many-colored cover
Pohjolan kivimäkehen,	Into Pohjola's stone mountain,
Vaaran vaskisen sisähän,	Hidden in a hill of copper
Yheksän lukon taaksi;	And secured behind nine locks;
Siihen juuret juurruteltu	Rooted there nine fathoms deep,
Yheksän sylen syvähän,	
Yksi juuri maa-emähän,	One root down in mother earth,
Toinen vesiviertehesen,	Second by a water run,
Kolmas on kotimäkehen."	Third one on the homestead ground."[53]

When Väinämöinen answers, "Let us build a mighty warship, on it we will take the Sampo," we understand that Ilmarinen is willing to go but would rather travel by land: "Travel overland is safer, let the devil go to sea" (39:23-35). A little reluctantly, Väinämöinen agrees to this:

"...*Kun et mieline merisin,*
Niin on maisin matkatkamme,
Rantaisin ratustelkamme!"

"...But then, if you do not like it,
Do not wish to go to sea,
We can travel overland,
Following the shore road there."[54]

But at the same time he asks Ilmarinen to "hammer me a sword, forge a new and fiery blade." Ilmarinen immediately sets to work, and with iron, steel, gold, and silver,

Takoi miekan mieltä myöten,
Kalvan kaikkien parahan,
Jonka kullalla kuvasi,
Hopealla huolitteli.

He hammered out the blade at will,
The sword, the very best of blades,
Which he then embossed with gold
And embellished then with silver.[55]

As Väinämöinen tests the new sword, observing, he turns and asks, "Will the sword match the man, will the blade befit the bearer?" (39:93-100). And he observes that it is so:

Olipa miekka miestä myöten,
Kalpa kantajan mukahan,
Jonka kuu kärestä paistoi,
Päivä paistoi lappehesta,
Tähet västistä välötti,
Hevonen terällä hirnui,
Kasi naukui naulan päässää
Penu putkessa puhusi.

Yes, the sword will match the man,
And the blade befit the bearer.
At the point a moon was gleaming,
On the flat a sun was shining,
And the hilt with stars was studded;
On the blade a horse was neighing,
On the knob a tomcat mewing,
While a hound bayed
on the scabbard.[56]

Being satisfied,

Sylkytteli miekkoansa
Vuoren rautaisen raossa,
Itse tuon sanoiksi virkki:
"Jo minä terällä tällä
Vaikka vuoret poikki löisin,
Kalliot kaha jakaisin."

Väinämöinen swung the sword
As if to split an iron mountain,
And he said: "Now with this weapon

I could even split a mountain,
Or could crack a crag in two."[57]

And before leaving on the journey Ilmarinen puts on his "iron shirt and belts of steel" (39:115-126).

What this steel equipment is, and especially the meaning of the firebladed sword, is not difficult to understand. In his letter to the Ephesians, Paul says: "Therefore, take up the full armor of God, that you may be able to resist in the evil day, and having done everything, to stand firm... And take the helmet of salvation, and the sword of the Spirit, which is the word of God" (Ephesians 6:13, 17).

Väinämöinen's firebladed sword is the weapon of truth and solid faith; it is a clear conceptualization of the task ahead and a firm faith in it. Ilmarinen creates this vision for himself from the teachings of other initiates and here, a comment from us is required. We will be able to touch the greatest achievements of mystic psychology here and, as weak as our own abilities truly are, we hope that the reader receives from our presentation a glimpse of the Kalevala's remarkable knowledge and wisdom in these matters.

For Ilmarinen and for all human beings aspiring to the truth, the true way of knowledge begins at this moment. Now he becomes a "Sampo-excursionist" or a "Sampoan," as before Pohjola's wedding he was a "propositional excursionist." As a propositional excursionist he cleansed his personality and thus became a proper bridegroom for Pohja's maid. Mentally understood, his work was negative and passive or, shall we say, "female" in quality. To contrast this, now as the Sampoan excursionist he has before him a wholly "male" (active and positive) goal in life. We have already seen how in the initial preparations—in the "forging of the Golden Maid" and in the "proposal to the younger girl of Pohja"— energetic activity was required although this was to some extent essentially a cleansing.

What then is the essential task of the truth-seeking human being? As we have already mentioned, the task is to create an immortal apparatus out of his own perishable human body, to be filled and used by knowledge and power, into which the consciousness of Logos or God can descend when the salvation of humanity demands it. An initiate, you see, does not work for personal benefit, to attain something for himself. His motivation is his deep and invincible love for truth, for God, for humanity, and driven by this love he may initially, like Ilmarinen, stray, until it becomes clear what truly needs to be done. When he sets out to create from himself an immortal apparatus, his goal is for the consciousness of Logos or the Holy Wisdom of the universe to freely use him—if not immediately in the beginning, then when the time comes—for the purposes of a divine goal.

He could not have undertaken this great work prior to his initiation. Before initiation, he does not have the self-conscious I which is independent from the physical body. In other words, his personal I is as mortal as the body. Consequently, how can the immortal be derived from the mortal? The initiation personalizes his immortal I and thus his true I-consciousness rises above the physical body and becomes independent from it. Although after reincarnating he is not aware of his inner achievement while in his day-consciousness, this ignorance lasts only as long as it is useful for him to learn from errors; when the necessary learning has taken place an inner certainty and harmony returns. And then the work of building can begin. From within and from above he must fashion from his body a magic apparatus which death does not touch.

What is the nature of this work? Is it the transmutation of the perishable and mortal body—by some kind of magic—into something imperishable? No, but it is the creating of something imperishable through the aid of the body. Like the Kalevala says, it is accomplished by retrieving the Sampo from its hiding place within the body. Here we finally meet the occult-psychological meaning of the word Sampo: Sampo is the new, immortal, magic body that an initiate creates for himself through the mediation of the physical body. In this connection we will recall the following words of Paul, lest the reader think we speak without foundation: "For this perishable must put on the imperishable, and this mortal must put on immortality. But when this perishable will have put on the imperishable, and this mortal will have put on immortality, then will come about the saying that is written, 'Death is swallowed up in victory. O Death, where is your victory? O Death, where is your sting?'"[58] Paul calls the sampo-body the "heavenly" and "spiritual" body as we read in the following extract from the same epistle: "There are also heavenly bodies and earthly bodies, but the glory of the heavenly is one, and the glory of the earthly is another. There is one glory of the sun, and another glory of the moon, and another glory of the stars; for star differs from star in glory. So also is the resurrection of the dead. It is sown a perishable body, it is raised an imperishable body; it is sown in dishonor, it is raised in glory; it is sown in weakness, it is raised in power; it is sown a natural body, it is raised a spiritual body. If there is a natural body, there is also a spiritual body."[59] And also: "However, the spiritual is not the first, but the natural; then the spiritual. The first man is from the earth, earthy; the second man is from heaven. As is the earthy, so also are those who are earthy; and as is the heavenly, so also are those who are heavenly. And just as we have borne the image of the earthy, we shall also bear the image of the heavenly."[60] And to emphasize that he is not speaking here about physical resurrection (reincarnation), but about mental rebirth, Paul adds, whispering: "Behold, I tell you a mystery; we shall not all sleep, but we shall all be changed."[61]

The heavenly magic body, the Sampo, is also said to be "the sun-body" or the "multi-colored cover" because it gleams like the sun when completely formed and is seen in the sage's eye as a very shiny light-wheel (aura). In the middle of this can be dimly seen the delightful features of the completed human being, "the Master in heaven," or augoides, as the Greek philosophers who were initiated into the mysteries would say. (Likewise, Ilmarinen's mental image gleams like the firebladed sword, the golden sword, and so on.)

The building of the spiritual body is divided into different periods, each with corresponding achievements, which in modern Theosophical literature (following the old Greek habit) are called "initiations"; one learns of the first level of initiation, the second, and so on, and the abilities and knowledge attained in each is explained. The terms and divisions vary according to the system used but, essentially, the goal and the way is the same.

The ancient Finnish system mentions two main places on the pilgrimage. One is the wedding at Pohjola, which completes the long journey of the propositional excursionist. The second involves obtaining the Sampo, which ends the troubled journey of the Sampoan. However, as the propositional excursionist had several works for wages to fulfill, so also the Sampo-excursionist has several tasks to complete before managing to achieve the Sampo for himself, and the Kalevala presents these in comparable detail.

There are, as we mentioned, different periods in the creating of the heavenly body, different points during the long journey to Pohjola, and the Kalevala identifies four divisions, naming them as follows: 1) the rowing of the boat; 2) the playing of the kantele; 3) the taking of the

Sampo; and 4) the final battle, in which the Sampo is shattered. In the rowing of the boat the sun-body is shaped to the point of becoming a "water-body." In the playing of the kantele it becomes thinner, is made into an "air-body." And in the taking of the Sampo it is formed into a "fire-body" which, in the final battle, sends its force outward, like the sun, into the world.*

At each stage the Kalevala expresses the evil corresponding to each achievement of good: The rowing of the boat ultimately teaches Ilmarinen the lesson of psychicality and mediumship; he began to learn this when he left to propose to the younger daughter of Pohjola. The playing of the kantele, on the other hand, clarifies the distinction between right and wrong influence. The taking of the Sampo makes known the distinction between good and evil sorcery, and the final battle identifies the difference between human self-righteousness and divine sacrifice.

Perhaps these things which are very difficult to understand will become clearer if we explain them one by one. There is something we must keep in mind. Though the Kalevala's primary heroes—Väinä-möinen, Ilmarinen, and Lemminkäinen—participate in the Sampo ex-pedition, they do not represent separate people in the psychological sense. One of them, Ilmarinen, is the initiated truth-seeker. Väinä-möinen and Lemminkäinen represent different sides of Ilmarinen. Väinämöinen is certainly a master seer but he is also Ilmarinen's will and the innermost divine sound or conscience through which he speaks as a master. On the other hand, Lemminkäinen is Ilmarinen's internal senti-ment of love and blessedness, which he attained by himself and so is, in a way, Pohja's virgin in a new form.

---

*In this connection we see why the word Sampo can be compared to the Finnish words *sammas* and *sampi*. Sammas is understood as a boundary stone or boundary pillar which separates the different periods or bodies in the building of the Sampo; it corresponds on a practical level to an initiation. Sampi, on the other hand, has the meaning of "fish" and recalls the Christ symbol of the fish (*ikhthys* or, as they say, *Iesous Khristos theou hyios sooter*). Christ, seen occultly, had a fully organized Sampo or sun-body. We can also suggest that Sampo, as a relative of the word sammas, has the meaning of *pyramid*, the place where the secret wisdom was taught, because the sammas or boundary stone has a more or less pyramidal shape. However, this brings to mind speculations concerning the relationships between Finns and Egyptians which may be unwarranted.

29

The Boat Journey

VÄINÄMÖINEN INITIALLY CONSENTS to Ilmarinen's request that the journey to Pohjola be made by land. "Since you do not understand the matter, we will travel by shore. Let us search for a horse and bridle it with "a golden bridle" to cart "we two men along the shore" (39:127-146).

Naturally, Ilmarinen is distrustful of the sea and wants to travel to Pohjola by land. Earlier he traveled to Pohjola several times, to the secret world of his inner consciousness, by means of his sleep-consciousness, and experienced only worry and harm (most notably, in the rune concerning his proposal to the younger daughter of Pohjola). At any rate, he traveled "by land" in the sense that he was in the day-conscious I of his mundane physical body. Now he realizes that when Väinämöinen suggests they "travel by sea" that he must abandon his day-consciousness and rely on the dangerous sleep-consciousness. Therefore, it is no wonder that Ilmarinen starts off feeling that his courage will desert him.*

---

*Regarding the symbolic meanings of "horse" and "boat" we have the following example: When a Lapland sorcerer wanted to fall into a trance, he—in addition to other preparations—removed his cap, opened his belt, undid his shoelaces, hid his face in his hand, put his other hand on his hip, rocked forward and backward and cried out, "harness a draught reindeer!" or "push the boat out upon the waters!" Compare with J. Krohn, *Suomen suvun pakanallinen jumalanpalvelus* (*The Pagan Divine Service of the Finnish Family*), p. 114.

The two men did not travel far before they encountered "a vessel weeping, a boat bewailing." When Väinämöinen asks the reason for this sorrow, the boat answers:

"...Muut purret, pahatki purret,	"Other vessels, even bad ones,
Ne aina sotia käyvät...	Are always going off to war...
Minä veistämä venonen,	Here I am, a well-built vessel,
Satalauta laaittama	Hundred planker in construction,
Tässä lahon lastuillani,	Left to rot among my woodchips,
Venyn veistännäisilläni..."	Lying here where I was built..."[62]

Then Väinämöinen considers this to be a mirage of fate and says with comforting words:

"Elä itke, puinen pursi,	"Do not cry now, wooden boat,
Vene hankava havise,	Stop lamenting, oarlock vessel.
Kohta saat sotia käyä,	Soon enough you'll go to war,
Tappeloita tallustella!	Shuttling back and forth to battle.
Lienet pursi luojan luoma,	You, the product of the Maker,
Luojan luoma, tuojan tuoma..."	Creation of the great Creator..."[63]

And after hearing this, which makes it clear that this boat is no odder than other boats, Väinämöinen

Heitti hiekalle hevoisen,	Left the horse upon the sand.
Painoi puuhun marhaminnan,	Hitched the halter to a tree,
Ohjat oksalle ojenti,	Threw the reins across a branch;
Lykkäsi venon vesille,	Pushed the boat into the water,
Lauloi purren lainehille.	Sang it out upon the billows.[64]

In this episode the Kalevala wishes to describe an awakening that happens in Ilmarinen's consciousness, how his ideas about acquiring the Sampo change and become enhanced, and how the sleep-realm now appears to him in a new light.

The moaning boat is like the sound of a memory awakening in his soul. "Don't you trust me anymore, Ilmarinen? I am truly much older than your day-consciousness. You received your day-consciousness the last time you were born on earth but you received me during Pohjola's wedding. Don't you remember that you were initiated with Pohjola's delightful virgin? Don't you remember how you and your spouse were united in me? Don't you recall how your day-consciousness grew and expanded as if from the earth to heaven when you joined with the virgin of Pohjola? Where did your consciousness travel, and through what agency did this happen? Only with my aid! You stored in your brain the consciousness that you experienced in me; now you have a new brain and you have forgotten. But you will awaken your memories to life again! All those who have known the virgin of Pohjola and leave to battle for the Sampo, utilize such boats as I. I am no stranger than the others."

It begins to dawn within Ilmarinen that he does not need to rely on the resented and dangerous sleep-consciousness. The consciousness and the apparatus of this consciousness available to him do indeed have their origin in the sleep-world, but this in itself is not dangerous. The danger lay in moving his day-consciousness into the sleep-world when, in fact, the sleep-world's greater consciousness is meant to gradually awaken within his day-consciousness.

Ilmarinen begins to remember the grand spiritual experience he had in the past, and this now awakens within him like a new confidence in his own powers. He need not fear the unconscious when abandoning himself into the care of his own secret consciousness. An abyss does not loom beyond the day-consciousness; it is not an empty and bottomless void but a wider, greater, and deeper consciousness which is already familiar to him.

And Ilmarinen understands that one cannot reach the Sampo by other means. By itself, the day-consciousness cannot build it with its own powers. The sun-body must be built from inside and from above; its seed must already exist, it is the seed that develops and grows as if by itself. And this seed is given by life when a human being is created to be a human being. The human being becomes conscious of this seed during initiation.

Now Ilmarinen no longer resists his innermost sound through which the wisdom of Väinämöinen speaks. The boat is prepared for them to use and is pushed out on the waters. Then Lemminkäinen also joins the expedition.

Siitä vanha Väinämöinen
Lauloa hyrähtelevi;   Väinämöinen chants on softly.

Lauloi ensin laitapuolen	Conjured one side of the vessel
Sukapäitä sulhosia,	Full of lads with sleek brushed hair,
Sukapäitä, piipioja	Iron-fisted, leather-booted;
Saapasjalkoja jaloja;	
Lauloi toisen laitapuolen	Conjured on the other side
Tinapäitä tyttäriä	Troupes of tinsel-headed maidens,
Tinapäitä vaskivöitä,	Tinny trinkets in their hair,
	Tinsel-headed, copper-belted,
Kultasormia somia.	Graceful girls with gold-ringed fingers.
Lauloi vielä Väinämöinen	Väinämöinen went on singing;
Teljot täytehen väkeä,	Sang the benches full of people
Ne on vanhoa väkeä,	Of the older generation,
I'än kaiken istunutta,	Idle elders, long time sitters
Kuss' oli vähän sioa	Where a little room is left them
Nuorukaisilta esinnä.	By the younger generation.[65]

Here we can see what a miraculous boat they have and what a miraculous journey is underway. Väinämöinen sings the boat full of people. They are not ordinary human beings come from their homes, but beings chanted into view by magic power—and this is confirmed because they cannot get the boat to move. Väinämöinen sat down at the stern and

Pani sulhot soutamahan,	Then he set the youths to rowing
Neiet ilman istumahan;	With the maidens sitting idly.
Sulhot souti, airot notkui,	As they rowed, the oars
	were bending—
Eipä matka eistykänä.	But the boat did not move on.[66]

And the same thing happened with the maids, and the old people as well. The journey was not making any progress (39:303-310). When Ilmarinen finally sat down to row,

Jopa juoksi puinen pursi,	Blithely ran the wooden boat,
Pursi juoksi, matka joutui,	Sped the boat, the journey quickened.
Loitos kuului airon loiske,	Splash of oars was heard afar,
Kauas hankojen hamina.	Far the creaking of the oarlocks.[67]

And thus the Kalevala tells us how Ilmarinen became accustomed to using his new apparatus of consciousness—the first form of the Sampo or the so-called water-body. For the specialist, the rune's own words are witness to what is involved here. The word "boat" refers to the fact that this is a question of the emotion's sleep-world, which is usually symbolized by the term "water" (see Chapter 13 for an example). The water-body is shaped by emotions, created from the force of love. But why was a boat chosen as the symbol? Would not a living being that can swim (for example, a horse) be acceptable? When we discussed the works for wages, Hiisi's gelding (Tuonela's bear) corresponded to the foam of emotions. Also, Plato wrote that the human being of reason is a rider, and the feelings and passions in him are the mount that he leads. This is quite true, but the Kalevala's chosen symbol of the boat shows, in a subtle manner, that this is no more a question of the emotional character of an ordinary human being who may still, like an animal, be independently willful; instead, it is now a question of the cleansed emotional life of the initiate whose selfishness has died. Therefore, a "lifeless thing," a boat (which obeys and serves its owner absolutely), is more appropriate.

Above all, what proves that the Kalevala speaks about an occult apparatus for consciousness are the many human-like beings chanted into existence by Väinämöinen to sit in the boat. These beings represent the water-body's many faculties or senses which are used to study the emotional sleep-world. But on what foundation do we say this? This is based on the following two considerations:

First, the senses of the water-body are not spatial in the same way that those of the physical body are; rather, they "are everywhere." Some are in front, some in back, on the right and the left, at every side—it is as if the whole body is a sense organ—and the different senses are not distinct from one another but exist together. The same sense mediates the sensations of sight, hearing, touch, and so on. One may also say that a human being in the water-body sees, hears, feels, smells, and tastes with every part of the body, and this is vividly portrayed with the human-like beings placed on every side of the boat.

Second, in the emotion realm of the sleep-world, when we look at the subtle forms of things or, as is said, with the clairvoyant eye, a human being's usual feelings and passions are dressed with corresponding animal forms. One sees wolves, serpents, pigs, turtles, and so on, including every type of hybrid in which an exaggerated eye, mouth, or beak is especially frightening. This kind of vision usually occurs after death. The more a human being cleanses his emotions, the more the subtle forms of the thoughts and emotions look like flowers and plants, or geometrical objects and crystals and so on, as happens in the meditation of the "propositional excursionist." Only in rare cases does a thought of an uninitiated human being dress as a human; for example, this may happen if someone, with great love, wants to tell something to a relative. Consequently, the thinker's thought may appear before the relative in the form of the thinker.

It is different, on the other hand, for the seer who is advanced. His personal thoughts always dress—unless he wants it differently—in the human form. Why? The human form is a symbol. For example, if a seer wants to inform his student of something, he sends a thought to the sensitive student. The thought behaves like a living being, searching and looking like the seer, and fulfills the task like an envoy, returning afterward to its sender. If the seer wishes to know about some matter, he can just as easily send out a thought to find out, and the thought returns with the needed information.

In the sleep-image world of emotion, the form taken tends to correspond to the content; only they who master the laws and forces of that world can deceive. Human beings who happen to be there are like helpless children, and are recognizable only by their mere existence.

Since the faculties and senses of the water-body are portrayed as human-like beings looking around, this means they are autonomous— self-acting and self-conscious. It is as if the human being's day-conscious I is present within every faculty of the water-body! In this we can understand how versatile and expansive is the consciousness of this boat's activities in the sleep-world as compared to the brain-consciousness. One can study with those organized faculties and senses the side of the inner consciousness corresponding to the unseen cosmos, which is called "water." As such, he may in a vision be able to study the human soul's different emotional states, the fate of the deceased in Tuonela and in the heavens. However, the Kalevala's rune also reveals that those self-acting faculties simply cannot move the boat. Ilmarinen alone can use his vessel and be its master; Väinämöinen, the divine conscience of wisdom, has the stern.

We explained earlier why Lemminkäinen joins the company. The memories of Ilmarinen awaken and as a result he renews his connection to his higher emotional I, which is now represented by Lemminkäinen.

30

The Playing of the Kantele

T HE NEXT STAGE in the building of the sun-body is the organizing of the air-body or, as the Kalevala says, "the preparing of the kantele." Rather than being a new apparatus, this is "the rebirth" of the water-body, fitting it with new faculties, so that new vistas in the invisible world will be opened for the human being to study. The Sampoans go peacefully ahead. Their happiness affects the other beings of the invisible world. Steadfast old Väinämöinen

Laski laulellen vesiä,	Sailed on singing on the water,
Ilon lyöen lainehia.	Striking joyance on the billows.
Neiet niemien nenissä	Maidens on the tips of headlands
Katselevat, kuuntelevat:	Looked and listened wonderingly:
"Mi lienee ilo merellä,	"What's that joyance on the water,
Mikä laulu lainehilla,	What those songs out on the billows,
Ilo entistä parempi	Each one better than before,
Laulu muita laatuisampi?"	Tunes more moving than the others?"[68]

They journeyed "on the inland waters, through the marshland, and reached the rapids." The rapids were cleared without misfortune:

Itse vanha Väinämöinen	Then old Väinämöinen steered,
Laskea karahtelevi,	And the vessel rippled on,
Laski louhien lomitse	Sailed between the rocks and reefs,

174

Noita kuohuja kovia,	Over heaving swells and rollers,
Eikä puutu puinen pursi,	And the vessel was not halted,
Vene Tietäjän takellu.	The magician's boat not grounded.[69]

But suddenly trouble appeared and an insurmountable obstacle arose before the Sampoans:

Äsken tuonne tultuansa	But as soon as they were out,
Noille väljille vesille	Out upon the open water,
Puuttui pursi juoksemasta,	Suddenly the boat stopped moving
Venonen pakenemasta;	And the vessel stood stone still.
Pursi puuttuvi lujahan,	There the boat was firmly grounded,
Vene vieremättömäksi.	Vessel fixed and motionless.[70]

The obstacle was examined to see if it was a stone or a branch, and they discovered that the boat was stuck "on the shoulders of a pike." Now, before we continue we must discuss what this "pike" is.

The name itself brings to mind "the big and scaly pike" which Ilmarinen caught from Tuonela's river as his third work for wages, and we can expect that the Kalevala will here, as before, call the river "Tuonela's river." The "catching of the pike" meant that Ilmarinen had to purify the habits, faculties, and instincts which lived in his inner consciousness and at the same time in the physical body's invisible ethereal half. One wonders if now, on the Sampo-journey, it has the same meaning? It does, though Ilmarinen does not approach this cleansing from the perspective of the day-consciousness. Instead, it is done from the inner consciousness to bring about cleansing in the invisible world rather than the visible. The journey of the Sampoan progresses downward from the Self towards the body and not, as was the case with the propositional excursionist, the other way around. Therefore, without explicitly remarking so, the Kalevala indicates that this pike is also in Tuonela's river.*

---

*In Lönnrot's first compilation, Pohjola and Manala are mentioned in conjunction. See, for example, *Kalevalan esityöt* (*The Kalevala's Preliminary Works*), I. Väinämöinen: "across Pohjola's river, Manala's lowland" (pp. 230-231); "to those Pohjola waters, to Manala's lowlands" (pp. 550-551). Editor's note: See F. P. Magoun (1969) for English translation of *The Proto-Kalevala*.

Now the habits, faculties, and instincts of the invisible ethereal half of the physical body are in question. Moving freely within his water-body, a human being clings closely to the pike of the ethereal body. What is this? This simply means that he is as yet unable to shift his secret water-body's consciousness to the physical brain—the day-consciousness. His self-consciousness is not yet continuous and unbroken. In his day-consciousness he is Ilmarinen number 1, in his sleep-consciousness he is Ilmarinen number 2. This Ilmarinen number 2 is much more developed and skillful than number 1. The former is conscious of daily life—much smaller—and the day-conscious Ilmarinen has only a fraction of the memories that his nighttime twin brother does. The latter's greater faculties manifest to the day-consciousness only as transient magical events, as visions, revelations, passing inspirations, and so on. Tuonela's stream of oblivion continues to divide the day-consciousness from the secret consciousness. At any rate, the course of development ultimately demands that the reason for oblivion be eliminated; consciousness must be made unbroken and continuous. The water-body's faculties, instincts, and habits must be awakened within the physical brain.

How does this happen?

On their interrupted journey down the river, Väinämöinen first urges Lemminkäinen to remove the obstacle:

"Veä miekalla vetehen,	"Slash your sword through the water
Katkaise kala kaheksi!"	And just cut the fish in two."[71]

Lemminkäinen pulls the sword from his belt and

Veti miekalla meryttä,	Slashes with it through the water,
Alta laian laskettavi,	Reaching down beneath the vessel
Itse vierähti vetehen,	So that he himself fell in,
Kourin aaltoihin kohahti.	Plunging headfirst in the billows.[72]

When Lemminkäinen fared so badly, Ilmarinen interferes in the situation and

Tarttui tukkahan urosta,	Seized the fellow by the hair,
Nostatti merestä miehen,	Snatched him up out of the sea

Itse tuon sanoiksi virkki:	And remarked: "Everybody
"Kaikki on miheksi kyhätty..."	Is designed to be a man..."[73]

Then Ilmarinen himself pulls out his sword to cut the fish:

Miekka murskaksi mureni,	But the sword crashed into fragments,
Eipä hauki tiennytkänä.	Yet the pike paid no attention.[74]

Väinämöinen moves to help, and his own fiery sword of truth does away with the pike:

Siitä vanha Väinämöinen	Then old Väinämöinen lifted,
Nostalti kaloa tuota,	Heaved the fish up from the water,
Veti haukia ve'estä:	
Hauki katkesi kaheksi,	But the great pike broke in two,
Pursto pohjahan putosi,	Tail-part sinking in the sea,
Pää kavahti karpahasen.	Forepart landing on the vessel.[75]

Now the boat begins to move again, and Väinämöinen steers for shore, where the head-piece of the pike is boiled and eaten as a meal (40:173-204).

With this rather humorous description the Kalevala wishes to illustrate how difficult it is to take possession of the physical brain-consciousness and how imperturbable is the boundary of oblivion between the day-consciousness and the secret consciousness. It does not happen in the twinkling of an eye: Not at the moment of first enthusiasm (Lemminkäinen) nor with the aid of gallant self-esteem (Ilmarinen), but only with a thoroughly premeditated, calm, and forceful effort. What specifically is it that needs to be done so that the water-body, without hindrance, can affect the ethereal body and through it, the brain? The force-center corresponding to the brain must be awakened to full action within the physical body's invisible twin. Consciousness will then be able to pass through without hindrance; in its normal behavior it is like a whirlpool which swallows consciousness and, in effect, strikes it down into unconsciousness. The only thing entitled and skillful enough to awaken it is "the sword of the spirit"—i.e., a clear concept of the task to be performed, a firm faith in the unselfishness of ones motives, and patient, persistent effort. The sword is directed to the corresponding center of the brain, "the pike's head-part" is eaten, and the secret consciousness is opened to the physical brain. Now the human being will be able in broad daylight to use his water-body's full faculties and characteristics. What before was spontaneous and spurious, bursting forth unannounced, now becomes a permanent capacity. If the aspiring seeker has already somewhat developed his water-body's secret ability of perception, he will now become truly clairvoyant and clairaudient; he does not unknowingly attract the invisible world as a medium or natural psychic does, but moves within it as a free and masterful citizen. If he, on the other hand, in working on his water-body through the virtues of his previous character, has learned how to associate with the higher beings of the invisible world (gods, angels, faeries, seers) and has received from them inspiring impressions (manifesting perhaps as artistic creativity or a general ingenuity), he now has the chance to wander in continuous inspiration—and always feels like a king among people...

And yet only half of the work is done. The water-body still needs to be changed into the air-body. The Kalevala tells how Väinämöinen looks at the bones of the fish left on the rocks and ponders what he might build from them.

"Noista hau'in hampahista,	Fashioned from the pike's great teeth,
Leveästä leukaluusta,	Invented from its broad jawbone
Jos oisi sepon pajassa,	Somehow in a craftsman's workshop,
Luona taitavan takojan,	Workshop of a skillful artist,
Miehen mahtavan käsissä?"	In the hands of mighty talent."[76]

When Ilmarinen suggests that only emptiness comes from nothing, Väinämöinen responds that it will become a kantele, and immediately sets himself to work:

Laati soiton hau'inluisen,	Made the five-stringed harp of pikebone,
Suoritti ilon ikuisen.	Made a thing of joy forever.
Kust' on koppa kanteletta?	What's the body of it made of?
Hau'in suuren leukaluusta.	Of the jawbone of the pike.
Kust' on naulat kanteletta?	And the pegs, what are they made of?

Ne on hau'in hampahista.	Of the strong teeth of the pike.
Kusta kielet kanteletta?	And the strings, what are they made of?
Hivuksista Hiien ruunan.	From the mane of Hiisi's gelding.[77]

In a variant of the 44th rune, the body of the kantele is made of a weeping birch, which had grievingly complained of its sorrows to Väinämöinen. The pegs for his kantele are obtained in the following way:

Kasvoi tammi tanhualla,	In the barnyard grew an oak tree,
Puu pitkä pihan perällä,	Tall old oak tree at the yard end.
Tammessa tasaiset oksat,	On the oak are level branches,
Joka oksalla omena,	On each branch an acorn growing,
Omenalla kultapyörä,	On each acorn a golden wheel,
Kultapyörällä käkönen.	On each golden wheel a cuckoo.
Kun käki kukahtelevi,	When the cuckoo there is calling,
Sanoin viisin virkkelevi,	His five-noted song is singing,
Kulta suusta kumpuavi,	From his throat bright gold is welling,
Hopea valahtelevi	From his beak the silver pouring,
Kultaiselle kunnahalle,	Pouring on a golden hillock,
Hope'iselle mäelle;	Down upon a hill of silver.
Siitä naulat kantelehen,	From this oak will come the harp-pegs,
Vääntimet visaperähän	Screws to fit the curly-birch frame.[78]

And finally, as Väinämöinen leaves to seek strings for the kantele, he sees a maiden sitting in a clearing, singing away the evening while waiting for her beloved. Väinämöinen asks her for some of her hair to use as strings:

Antoi impi hapsiansa,	And she gave him of her tresses,
Hienoja hivuksiansa,	Of her long, luxuriant tresses,
Antoi hasta viisi, kuusi	
Sekä seitsemän hivusta;	Five, six, even seven strands,
Siit' on kielet kanteleessa,	And they made the joyful harpstrings,
Ääntimet iki-ilossa.	Tongues of gladness everlasting.[79]

And then the wonderful and familiar description of the playing of the kantele follows in both variants. First, the other heroes try to handle the new music machine without any success. Eventually Väinämöinen places the kantele on his knee and charms all of living nature with his playing (Runo 40:241-342; also Runos 41 and 44).

Here the Kalevala conveys an impression of the manner in which the water-body is changed into the air-body; in other words, how the kantele is brought into the boat. This kantele is made from the noblest and most artistic faculties of the ethereal body. Most notably, the weeping birch which went into making the kantele represents the finest forces of poetry and love. The head of the kantele is the brain and its strings go through the heart. Everything within the human being which is holy and beautiful, profound and magnificent, is gathered together to form a playing machine through which all living and deceased beings rejoice, are consoled, and made happy.

And who can play it? Only Väinämöinen. The human self cannot, and neither can the initiated self. Only the eternal loveliness of the great wisdom can, the sound of which is heard in the divine spirit of the initiate.

Here the Kalevala describes a profound and remarkable thing in the mystical-psychological development of the initiate: He finally achieves for a moment his longed for ideal, just once his yearning is fulfilled, finally his lengthy absence ends with a mergeance in his personal consciousness with God.

While playing the kantele he feels he has become a self-conscious medium of the force and influence of God—Logos. God's force, divine life and consciousness fill the entire solar system. "In Him we live, move and are." Without the sun-energy of our Logos there can be no life on earth; without His sunny consciousness there is no consciousness in the cosmos. When the kantele is formed between the heart and the brain of an initiate, he receives an immediate connection with life's force of Logos; he becomes a son of God who has for his use his father's forces. This is his ascent to the mountain of enlightenment, his crowning with the crown of immortality.

How beautifully did the seers of the Finnish people conceptualize this point! They loved to think of nature as a worker, an artist, a visionary. And when they wanted to show a human seer immersed in his enlightenment and honor, they put him "on the joystone, upon the songrock, high upon a silvery hill, upon a golden knob" (Runo 41:5-8). In his hands the kantele sends out in tonal waves the Creator's happiness and exuberant life-force to penetrate the hearts of His created ones.

When the water-body is changed into the air-body, the initiate becomes filled with "the Holy Spirit." His face shines and, in addition, human beings are charmed by him and are moved to worship him. Naturally, this is not permanent. It is "a gift from above." It will occur when the Logos desires and needs it to. "The wind blows where it wishes and you hear the sound of it, but do not know where it comes from and where it is going; so is everyone who is born of the Spirit" (John 3:8). But it is great to be a servant of the Master and one who fulfills God's will, always remembering how great it is to be a mouthpiece of Logos or God's finger on earth though it may not happen more than once in life. The affects are preserved in Väinämöinen's tears, even though they (the tears) "have changed into something else":

Helmiksi heristynehet,	Swollen, rounded into pearls,
Simpukoiksi siintynehet,	Into blue fresh-water pearls
Kuningatarten kunnioiksi,	That would honor any queen[80]
Valtojen iki-iloksi.	And delight the great forever.[81]

And that honor is only given to the one who has found himself, one whose higher self has emerged victorious and then, as Ilmarinen-Väinämöinen, steps onto the songrock.

Human beings influence each other continuously at all times whether they know it or not, or consciously will it. The effects are sometimes good and sometimes bad. But this is perishable and vanishes away until the time when God manifests His influence through them, and death is unmasked to reveal its immortal face.

The Theft of the Sampo

EFORE THE SAMPO—the sun-body—is completely ready, the air-body must be transformed into the "fire-body." In addition, the human being's physical apparatus must be fashioned into "God's shape" so that the initiate can feel the gloomiest forces of Hell and can agree with the prophet: "And if I found myself in the deepest Hell, even there, you would be with me, oh God."

As you know, the deepest secrets of magic, knowledge, and power are hidden in the physical body and in its ethereal twin. Until the truth seeker has won these, the ancient Finnish wisdom does not consider him to be a perfect seer. Because some of these forces can be awakened for selfish purposes, through energetic self-torture devoid of true mental development, they are also called the forces of (black) witchcraft or black magic.

We can understand this if we remember that a human being is a microcosm or a miniature reflection of the solar system, of which he is a member. Consequently, his physical body corresponds to the larger body of the cosmos. We can equally say that a human being's intellect is a miniature reflection of the intellect of Logos; as an organ, the human brain corresponds to the world's brain and God's pure reason can use it. In addition, as a human being's love is part of God's love, a miniature form of it, the human heart corresponds to the world's heart and, moreover, God's unlimited compassion can manifest through it. But in a human being's body there are organs which, in a manner of speaking, are stronger than the head and the heart; for example, the genitals. The stomach says, "I need nourishment," and the head must serve it. The genitals say, "We want to make a family," and the heart hurries to serve them. One who aspires to become a black magician merely needs to command himself to not serve the stomach. And to the heart he commands: You will not serve the genitals, you will serve only me, for I am your master. In comparison, one who aspires to become a seer satisfies his stomach's needs in the same way that he pleases his head, and sets his genitals in the service of the heart right away. He does not pretend that he himself is the master of his head or heart, but instead seeks the truth which his head can serve, and the love of God in which his heart can bathe. Ultimately, the seer must study both the stomach and the genitals and win them in a new way, in order to connect with the cosmic forces corresponding to them. And the same is true for the other physical organs and their corresponding forces. One must not think that they are "lower" than the head and the heart, one is not allowed to despise them and brand them "animalistic." There is no lower or higher in nature, nor better or worse; in its great economy everything is good, everything is in its own place, serving its own purpose. And if we wish to classify them into rank and file, we might just as well call the "lower" forces the "highest" because they are deeper and more difficult to attain. Therefore it is said that the forces of black magic or sorcery are the last which a white seer might employ...

In the 42nd rune the Kalevala describes with great drama the formation of the fire-body, the final taking of the Sampo as ones own. In terms of white magic this takes place from within, from inside the unseen world.

After having traveled on the wide open sea, the seers' boat arrives in Pohjola. The three men step into the hut and Pohjola's mistress asks what message the men bring. Väinämöinen answers plainly:

"Sammosta sanomat miesten,	"All our news is of the Sampo
Kirjokannesta urosten;	And concerns the ciphered cover.
Saimme sampuen jaolle,	We are here to share the Sampo
Kirjokannen katselulle."	And to view the ciphered cover."[82]

The mistress of Pohjola hurries to exclaim that the Sampo is not to be shared:

There is never enough, good fellows,
"Ei pyyssä kahen jakoa,   In one grouse for two to share,
Oravassa miehen kolmen."   Nor for three men in a squirrel."[83]

Väinämöinen makes up his mind: "If you will not share it with us, give us just the other half, then we'll take the whole mill with us!" And Louhi, greatly offended, calls her warriors to take up arms.

But then, Väinämöinen sits down to play the kantele and with his playing enchants Pohjola's people into a deep sleep. Then the men move to seize the Sampo,

Pohjolan kivimäestä,   In dark Pohjola's stone fortress,
Vaaren vaskisen sisästä,   There inside a copper mountain,
Yheksän lukon takoa,   Well secured behind nine locks,
Takasalvan kymmenennen.   And an inner bolt the tenth.[84]

Väinämöinen chants softly while Ilmarinen oils the locks and hinges and soon the heavy doors swing open.

"Oi sie lieto Lemmin poika,   "Now, you wayward son of Lempi,
Ylimmäinen ystäväni,   My great friend, go get the Sampo,
Mene sampo ottamahan,   Heave the ciphered cover up!"[85]
Kirjokansi kiskomahan!"

Väinämöinen urges, "Heave the ciphered cover up!" and Lemminkäinen tries to yank the Sampo from the earth but it is rooted down to a depth of nine fathoms. Lemminkäinen is not able to loosen it until he uses Pohjola's strong-bodied ox to plow up the Sampo's roots, the fastenings of the multi-colored (ciphered) cover.

When the Sampo is happily brought to the vessel, the three men begin to journey homeward, rejoicing with good humor. Lemminkäinen has a mind to sing but Väinämöinen explains that it is not good to sing until they are home. There are still dangers in the offing (42:123-268)...

If we say that a human being's heart is given to God at Pohjola's wedding, and especially in the formulation of the water-body, we should also say that in creating the air-body the head is given to God. For a human being to entirely and thoroughly be "the temple of the Holy Spirit," the other organs of the body must be subdued and offered to God.

As can be seen from the Kalevala's description, this is not an easy task. The Sampo or the sun-body is hidden within the physical body to a depth of nine fathoms, behind nine, even ten locks. In reality two of the Sampo's roots have already been dug up: the head and the heart. Although the rune doesn't mention this for aesthetic reasons, there remain the roots of: the sacrum, the navel, the spleen, and so on. These are the ethereal force-centers and their corresponding ganglionic nerve-bundles of the parasympathetic nervous system within the physical body. The nine or ten gates are the body's nine (or ten) "aperatures" (in the Indian books it is said that the human body is "the town of nine gates"): the ears, the eyes, the nostrils, the mouth, the rectum, and the genitals (the female sex has two openings).

Väinämöinen's playing enchants the people of Pohjola into a deep sleep. Likewise, with Ilmarinen's help, his song opens the nine gates. This means that mastery of the physical senses has been achieved. The body has its own consciousness and an aspiring truth-seeker cannot master anything unless he treats it like a living being. It is good to get ones senses under control so that they can be closed and opened at will. Then one will not see unless one wants to, will not hear unless one wants to, and so on. If one lets the vision of God in, one eclipses the human sight; likewise, if one lends his ears to the Creator, the human hearing is erased.

When Lemminkäinen is given the task of bringing the Sampo out of the stone hill and into the daylight, this means that love, at this moment, must enliven all the force-centers and nerve bundles of the body. This takes place with the help of the so-called "serpent-fire," which the Kalevala calls "Pohjola's good ox." This name indicates the mighty power which is hidden in the serpent fire, because when this physical serpent fire awakens within a human being the feeling may initially be so overwhelming that he literally realizes the words of Jesus: "I have won the world." This is equally expressed in a Roman poet's words: "Si illabatur orbis ille, impavidum ferient ruinae"—he feels so invincible, so unshakable, and so strong within himself. Soon he learns to analyze the experience and distinguish which aspects of these feelings are illusions.*

---

*Although the Kalevala does not mention it, this serpent fire has, in fact, already been on the scene. Pohjola's "big ox," present at the wedding of Pohjola, possibly refers to the serpent fire. The development of the psychic forces generally occurs in connection with the serpent fire. The serpent fire is described in the Sanskrit literature under the name *kundalini*; in Greek it is *speireema*.

Only love (Lemminkäinen) is qualified to awaken this force within the body, otherwise the power irresistably pulls one into black sorcery, which is to say, using the supernatural faculties for selfish purposes.

Immediately thereafter, when the Sampo is obtained and Väinä-möinen orders it homeward,

"Nenähän utuisen niemen,	To that misty point of land
Päähän saaren terhenisen,	At the head of Foggy Island,
Siellä onnen ollaksensa,	There to keep it for good fortune,
Ainiain asuaksensa..."	To abide thereon forever..."[86]

the meaning is that the Sampo (the fully formed sun-body) is not owned by the physical day-consciousness but vice versa. The Sampo is in the invisible world, in the inner consciousness, even though it was collected from the hiding places within the physical body. Though it was created in all its different forms with the aid of the physical body and from its materials, the physical day-consciousness is its humble servant.

The great work has been fulfilled and who should rejoice more than the human being who has accomplished it?

Siitä vanha Väinämöinen	Väinämöinen sailed away,
Läksi poies Pohjolasta,	Steering with a cheerful mind,
Läksi mielellä hyvällä,	Happy to be going homeward.[87]
Iloten omille maille.	

32

Final Doubts

V ÄINÄMÖINEN'S PRESENTIMENT OF DANGER hit the nail on the head: Lemminkäinen should not have sung out until "our own home doors appear, and their hinges creak out greetings" (42:267-268). The worst of dangers and the most difficult trial still awaits the Sampo-voyagers. Until now all had gone well. The journey to Pohjola was accomplished merrily, Louhi and the people of Pohjola were chanted into a hypnotic trance, and the Sampo was seized and taken from the stone hill. But now Pohjola awakens from its deep sleep and Louhi, the mistress of Pohjola, prepares herself to retake the Sampo because when she noticed the Sampo was missing,

Louhi Pohjolan emäntä	Louhi, matriarch of Northland,
Tuo tuosta pahoin pahastui,	Was disturbed, enraged by this:
Katsoi valtansa vajuvan,	Saw in it a loss of power
Alenevan arvionsa...	And a loss of reputation.[88]

It is a general rule of nature, you see, that if someone obtains power over a certain element, he arouses those who have guarded that force and they become his enemies. In forming the sun-body, a human being finally seizes the Sampo from its hiding places within his physical body, but it is not enough to say that he has achieved power over his own physical body. The fact remains that his body's organs correspond to specific forces and states in the cosmos, and these forces—the inhabitants of these states—rise up to oppose him, this daring one. And because at this point it is now a question of selfish forces, in a last hopeless attempt all the "forces of darkness" rise up against the truth-seeker. Here the Kalevala makes a clear distinction between Kalevala and Pohjola: Kalevala wants the Sampo for the reason that it will benefit and provide happiness for all humanity, while the "secret group" of Pohjola keep it closed within the stone hill so that nobody even knows about it. As an exponent of the forces of darkness, Louhi prepares herself to chase down the Sampoans and, invoking her ability to conjure, she calls up a fog, Iku-Turso, and a storm to torment the voyagers out on the sea.

These three oppressive hazards are: the fog of suspicion and despair, the Iku-Turso of selfishness and passion (the "old dragon"), and the storm of indiscreet activity and influence. These are not personal weaknesses but collective forces within humanity which attack an initiate.

Ututyttö, neiti terhen,	Then the Mistmaid, fog dispenser,
U'un huokuvi merelle,	Breathes a vapor on the sea,
Sumun ilmahan sukesi,	And the air is filled with fog
Piti vanhan Väinämöisen	Which delays old Väinämöinen,
Kokonaista kolme yötä	Holds him there for
	three whole nights,
Sisässä meren sinisen	Halted on the blue sea surface,
Pääsemättä perille,	Keeps him from his destination
Kulkematta kunnekana.	Or from traveling anywhere.[89]

It is humanity's great suspicion, despair, and exhaustion that surrounds a sailor and mockingly seduces his soul. "What, are you delirious? Are you better than we are? A moment ago you boasted of your strength, you won the world, you were at the level of the gods, and now you are the most tired of the tired! Where is that force which you felt in your limbs? Where is the God whom you trusted? It was an illusion, vanishing and perishable as everything under the sun. You were abandoned, as were we. Emptiness and darkness laugh at you, as it does us. Do you think that someone can become a god? Deceit and lies are everywhere. Not a single human being has attained what you seek because darkness is always stronger than the light." The human soul experiences a dark night of distress and may end in destruction unless he remembers the sword of the spirit on his belt, and raises the truth up high from the depths of his own depressed human state. He has lived for the truth and fought for it:

Yön kolmen levättyänsä	After standing for three nights,
Sisässä meren sinisen,	Moveless on the blue sea surface,
Virkki vanha Väinämöinen,	Väinämöinen spoke out firmly:
Itse lausui, noin nimesi:	
"Ei ole mies pahempikana,	"There is not a man so feeble,
Uros untelompikana	Not the most incompetent,
U'ulla upottaminen,	Who must yield to cloudy weather
Terhenellä voittaminen."	Or be overcome by fog."
Veti vettä kalvallansa	With his sword he struck the water,
Merta miekalla sivalti,	Slashed the blue sea with his iron;
Sima siuhkui kalvan tiestä,	There a jet of mead rose gushing
Mesi miekan roiskehesta,	And a flow of honey followed.
Nousi talma taivahalle,	Then the mist rose up to heaven,
Utu ilmoille yleni,	And the fog dissolved in air.
Selvisi meri sumusta,	So the sea was clear of mist
Meren aalto auteresta,	And the billows free of fog.
Meri suureksi sukeutui	There the sea lay widely open
Maailma isoksi täytyi.	And the world was big again.[90]

When this first danger passed, another appeared:

Oli aikoa vähäinen,	After a bit of time had passed
Pirahteli pikkarainen,	Like a tiny rash of rain,
Jo kuului kova kohina	Then they heard a wild commotion
Vieraltä veno punaisen,	Down beside the red boat's planking.
Nousi kuohu korkeaksi	Foaming waves were roaring high,
Vasten purtta Väinämöisen.	Rolling in on Väinö's vessel.[91]

Ilmarinen was so terribly frightened that "the blood drained from his features," while Väinämöinen looked down at the side of the boat and saw something odd:

Iku-Turso Äijön poika	Eternal Turso, son of Ancient,
Vieressä veno punaisen	In the sea beside the red boat,
Nosti päätänsä merestä,	Raised his head above the water,
Lakkoansa lainehesta.	Pushed his crown up through the billow.[92]

This is humanity's millennial egoism and bestiality, which in the form of an old dragon raises its head up from the depths of the cosmic consciousness. "How far do you think you will get with your unselfishness? How do you suppose the world will benefit from it? Don't you know me? Don't you know that I keep human beings tightly wrapped in my fists? Everyone serves me, I am the god of humans. What can you do with your knowledge? Who cares? And what knowledge can you have without me? I am the truth that humans seek. I present them with the only real happiness and blessing, something they continuously long for: The satisfaction of their passions. You, now, serve me also, and abandon your fanciful ideas about raising up humanity!"

A human being will be as frightened as Ilmarinen to see this monster of Mammon which commands all humanity on their knees. But Väinämöinen does not hesitate:

Vaka vanha Väinämöinen	Old reliable Väinämöinen
Saipa korvat kourihinsa,	Caught the creature by the ears,
Korvista kohottelevi,	Heaved him up and questioned him:
Kysytteli lausutteli,	
Sanan virkkoi, noin nimesi:	
"Iku-Turso Äijön poika!	"Eternal Turso, son of Ancient,
Miksi sie merestä nousit,	Why do you rise up from the sea,
Kuksi aallosta ylenit	Lift yourself above the billow
Etehen imehniselle,	And reveal yourself to humans,
Saanikka Kalevan poian?"	Even to a Kalevalander?"[93]

Sternly and seriously he questions this monster of egoism. Why has he cared to show himself to a son of God? Overwhelmed by fear, Iku-Turso confesses that he thought he would "kill the family of Kaleva, and get the Sampo back to Northland," promising at the same that he will no longer consider this if he is allowed to return into the depths of the sea. What else could be done? Egoism cringes in the face of righteousness and its soundless prayer is, "save me, let me live, I will leave you in peace!" And righteousness spares egoism because the generosity of a single human being does not eliminate evil from the world. Väinämöinen throws Iku-Turso back into the billows and commands him never again to rise from the waves.

Senpä päivyen perästä	Never has he risen since,
Ei Turso merestä nouse	Nor will he rise up from the water,
Etehen imehniselle,	Never in the sight of humans,
Kuni kuuta, aurinkoa,	Not as long as sun and moon
Kuni päiveä hyveä,	And the cheerful daylight brighten
Ilman ihailtavata.	Or the sight of sky delight us.[94]

This second hazard is survived, and now comes the third. After a little time has passed, Ukko, the highest god, raises a storm the likes of which Ilmarinen has never before witnessed:

Nousi tuulet tuulemahan,	Then the winds began to blow,
Säät rajut rajuamahan;	Vehement storms to rage with fury.
Kovin läikkyt länsituuli,	High the west wind lashed the water,
Luoetuuli tuikutteli,	And the southwest with more fury;
Enemmän etelä tuuli,	Even stronger blew the south wind,
Itä inkui ilkeästi,	While the east wind whistled madly;
Kauheasti kaakko karjui,	Awesomely the southeast howling,
Pohjoinen kovin porasi.	And the north wind weirdly wailing.
Tuuli puut lehettömiksi,	Trees were stripped of all their foliage,
Havupuut havuttomiksi,	Firs denuded of their needles;
Kanervat kukattomiksi,	Heather bared of all its blossoms
Heinät helpehettömiksi;	And the grasses of their sheaths.
Nosti mustia muria	Black ooze from the bottom rose
Päälle selvien vesien.	To ensoil the lucid waters.[95]

This represents humanity's weaknesses of independence and mind-less activity, which pulls people into its whirlpool without helping anyone. "Don't you, who want to be wise, see the blindness underlying human life? Don't you see that a human being is just a trembling poplar leaf in the storm of evolution and fate? What new careers do you imagine, what can you teach humans? What?—you want to make humans inde-pendent and free? The same human beings who scream for help as soon as I appear will give up just to be allowed to breathe calm air for a moment and think! And they do not even know me in my full fury: They call my silence a storm and dread it, but in my rage they become transfixed! The less they need to think and strive, the happier they are. They love to float along with the wind. What can you do for them by yourself? You will just awaken their hate and contempt!"

Ilmarinen goes out of his mind for awhile, but Väinämöinen reproaches him, saying that weeping will not ward off evil nor crying cancel evil days. Together with Lemminkäinen, Väinämöinen calms the storm and the churning billows of the ocean with a chant and they repair the boat to protect it from the waves.

In this way the initiate conquers this last distressing trial so that he no longer worries about what he has seen or heard. "Let the fist of fate be however tight, and let the whirlwind of development be however austere. The task of a human being is to ascend to be the master of ones own fate because only then can one be admitted as a son of God. Spiritual development exists for this reason and fate will serve those who pursue it.

33

The Last Battle

THE LAST BATTLE against the dark powers of Pohjola, against the angels of evil and darkness, takes place in the invisible world. However, a shadow from "the divine battle" is projected into mundane life, giving rise to hate, persecution, contempt and oppression.

It begins with the great conflict at Gethsemane. A human being anticipates the final offer but struggles within his soul and is frightened by it. "Take this chalice away from me," he prays with a tormented bloody sweat on his forehead. But soon the decision comes: "I only want what you want, Father."

The Kalevala describes this anxiety so dramatically and so effectively, yet with such a peaceful intention, that we must refer here to the entire episode in Runo 43 (verses 23-101):

Vaka vanha Väinämöinen	In the meantime Väinämöinen,
Laskevi sinistä merta,	Sailing over the blue sea surface,
Itse tuon sanoiksi virkki,	Is addressing Lemminkäinen:
Puhui purtensa perästä:	
"Oi sie lieto Lemmin poika,	"O you lively son of Lempi,
Ylimmäinen ystäväni,	You, most precious friend and comrade!
Nouse purjepuun nenähän,	Climb up there now to the masthead,
Vaatevarpahan ravaha,	Scamper nimbly up the mainmast;
Katsaise etinen ilma,	See what weather looms before us,
Tarkkoa takainen taivas,	Keenly scan the sky behind us:

Onko selvät ilman rannat,	Do the horizons show up clear,
Onko selvät vai sekavat!"	Are they clear or unsettled?"[96]

Lemminkäinen ascends the mast and observes the sky. "It's all clear," he calls, "just a tiny cloud to the north."

Sanoi vanha Väinämöinen:	Said old Väinämöinen slyly:
"Jo vainen valehteletki;	"Now you may be simply fibbing;
Ei se pilvi ollekana,	There may be no cloud at all
Pilven lonka lienekänä,	Nor a little cloudlet either,
Se on pursi purjehinen;	But a sailing boat behind us.
Katso toiste tarkemmasti!"	Look again, and look out sharply."[97]

Lemminkäinen looks again and informs him that he sees an island far away, with aspens full of falcons and birch trees full of speckled wood grouse.

Sanoi vanha Väinämöinen:	"That can't be," said Väinämöinen,
"Jo vainen valehteletki;	
Havukoita ei ne olle,	"Surely falcons they are not,
Eikä kirjokoppeloita,	Nor can they be speckled wood grouse:
Ne on Pohjan poikasia;	They're the boys of Pohjola.
Katso tarkoin kolmannesti!"	Look out carefully the third time."[98]

When Lemminkäinen looks for the third time, he recognizes his mistake and yells down that Pohjola's vessel is coming, "a hundred men on benches rowing, a thousand more just sitting."

Silloin vanha Väinämöinen	Väinämöinen saw the truth,
Jo tunsi toet totiset...	Recognized the situation...[99]

And without pondering the situation any more he orders the rowers to do their best so that Pohjola's vessel does not overtake them.

Souti seppo Ilmarinen,	Rowed the craftsman Ilmarinen,
Souti lieto Lemminkäinen,	Rowed the wayward Lemminkäinen,
Souti kansa kaikenlainen;	Everybody rowed and rowed.

Lyllyivät melat lylyiset,	Straining bent the piny oars
Hangat piukkui pihkaiset,	With the rowan rowlocks whining
Vene honkainen vapisi,	And the pinewood vessel rocking.
Nenä hyrskyi hylkehenä,	Like a seal the prow surged forward
Perä koskena kohisi,	As the stern-wake roared like rapids,
Vesi kiehui kelloloissa,	While the sea boiled up in bubbles
Vaahti palloissa pakeni.	And the foam in balls was flying.[100]

However, the sailing ship from Pohjola is faster than the Kalevala's rowboat, and old Väinämöinen

Jo tunsi tuhon tulevan,	Felt his ruin coming on him,
Hätäpäivän päälle saavan...	Saw the day of doom before him...[101]

Väinämöinen foresees that the battle against Pohjola will be disastrous for his own people, but before he abandons hope, he tries his mighty powers one more time. Turning to his faculty for magic, he conjures a huge rock underneath the sea into which the vessel of Pohjola might sail. And so it happened:

Tulla puikki Pohjan pursi,	Rushing came the Northland vessel,
Halki aallon hakkoavi,	Cutting straight across the rollers.
Jopa joutuvi karille,	On the unseen reef it grounded,
Puuttui luottohon lujasti;	Held fast by the hidden island.
Lenti poikki puinen pursi,	There the wooden boat was sundered,
Satakaari katkieli,	And the hundred-ribber broken;
Mastot maiskahti merehen	Into the sea the masts went splashing,
Purjehet putoelivat	Down with them the sails fell flapping
Noiksi tuulen vietäviksi,	For the wind to blow away,
Ahavan ajeltaviksi.	By cold Ahava far driven.[102]

Louhi, mistress of Pohjola, leaps into the water to lift up the vessel but sees that it is broken up and badly damaged. After thinking for a moment, she changes herself into an enormous eagle, one wing "grazing the clouds, the other touching the water." She loads all her armed warriors onto her tail and under her wings and flies onward to assault the heroes of Kaleva.

Jo tulevi Pohjan eukko,	There the dame of Northland's coming—
Lintu kumma liitelevi,	A peculiar bird approaching,
Harte'ista kuin havukka,	From its shoulders up a hawk
Vaakalintu vartalolta.	But in body like a griffin.
Yllättävi Väinämöisen,	Overtaking Väinämöinen,
Lenti purjepuun nenähän,	She alighted on the masthead,
Vaatevarpahan rapasi,	Moving quickly to the yardarm,
Päähän pielen seisotaikse;	Overbalancing the vessel
Oli pursi päin puota,	So the boat was near to sinking,
Laiva laioin kallistua.	Vessel almost keeling over.[103]

Ilmarinen prays to his god for protection in the impending battle, but Väinämöinen asks, half mockingly, if the mistress of Pohjola has decided to share the Sampo. In answer she cries out, "I do not intend to divide the Sampo with you, you wretch," and tries to grab hold of the Sampo in the boat.

Now begins a most difficult battle. Lemminkäinen pulls out his sword, strikes out and cries:

"Maahan miehet,	"Down, you men, and down,
maahan miekat	you swords!
Maahan untelot urohot,	Down, you worthless warriors!
Sa'at miehet siiven alta,	From beneath the wings by hundreds,
Kymmenet kynän nenästä!"	From each feather tip by tens!"[104]

Väinämöinen sees the end approaching:

Vaka vanha Väinämöinen,	Väinämöinen, knower eternal
Tietäjä iän-ikuinen	
Arvasi ajan olevan,	Judged now that his hour had come,
Tunsi hetken tulleheksi...	Felt the moment had arrived...[105]

He takes a paddle and strikes at the eagle's claws, one after another, as they dig into the Sampo, until all that remains is one "weak little finger."

Pojat siiviltä putosi,	From her wings the lads
	came dropping,
Melskahti merehen miehet,	In the sea the men were splashing,
Sata miestä siiven alta,	From beneath her wings a hundred,
Tuhat purstolta urosta;	From her tail a thousand plunging;
Itse kokko kopsahtihe,	Then the eagle too came crashing,
Kapsahutti kaaripuulle,	Down upon the boat ribs tumbling
Kuni puusta koppeloinen,	As a wood grouse drops from a tree top,
Kuusen oksalta orava.	As a squirrel from a fir branch.[106]

But oh! With her remaining "ring finger" Louhi flails out for the Sampo and

Sammon vuoalti vetehen,	Hooked it with her nameless finger,
Kaatoi kaiken kirjokannen	Hurled it with its ciphered cover
Punapurren laitimelta	Over the side and into the sea,
Keskelle meren sinisen;	Over the side of that red boat
Siinä sai muruiksi sampo,	Into the depths of the deep blue sea,
Kirjokansi kappaleiksi.	Where the Sampo crashed to pieces
	And the ciphered cover crumbled.[107]

The people of Pohjola were defeated, but at the same moment the Sampo was destroyed!

How are we to understand the symbolism of this? Why was the Sampo lost again?

We do not need to explain the symbolism of the battle against Pohjola because it is a vividly colorful description of a real battle in the unseen world; the psychological battle that is realistically described here holds true for the symbolic meaning. But the question remains why the Sampo, the sun-body, which was attained (or created) with much struggle and hard work, enduring many difficulties and dangers, has once again been lost, shattered in fact, broken into smithereens? Our mind becomes dejected in thinking about the Kalevala's heroes, remembering that it was Ilmarinen who originally forged the Sampo, and we must ask, with sadness: Was that clear-cut victory really a big defeat?

In this point the Kalevala—when opened with the mystic-psychological key—again reveals the vast amount of deeply profound wisdom and life-experience hidden within its runes. If the Kalevala allowed the Sampo to remain whole, won by the people of Kaleva, then wouldn't Pohjola be left without? The Kalevala would then have had to emphasize a dualism, the eternal polarity between good and evil which does not, in fact, exist in the divine wisdom. The Kalevala would represent the good—of course—and we would then judge Pohjola as being, so to say, an eternally dark and damned place. On behalf of the Kalevala heroes, we would then believe that goodness got its proper payoff and evil received its due punishment.

When the Kalevala lets the Sampo be shattered, it highlights its highest ethical teaching. The Sampo—the origin of wisdom and the bringer of happiness—is not for the individual to possess. Though Ilmarinen or Väinämöinen be just and good, the Sampo does not exist only for them as long as they battle the forces of darkness. In battling the forces of darkness they released themselves from their grip. In attacking the Kalevala heroes, the forces of darkness drew themselves out and away from God.[108] But is this possible? Can anything exist outside of God, outside of His being? Can evil exist independently, untouched by God's love? Can an ignorance so black exist that can never be reached by God's penetrating light?

No, we answer, such a thing does not exist. No devil exists that God's unlimited compassion cannot save. As such it would be a psychological and, morever, an occult error to let the Sampo stay unbroken for the Kalevala's people. The Sampo had to be shattered and broken into splinters so that everyone gets a part; in addition, Louhi brought the Sampo's cover back to Pohjola. Thus the initiate was taught about the Kalevala's last great lesson: total self-sacrifice! Only he who can completely and finally abandon himself can be totally useful as a messenger of Logos or God on earth. Truly, in a similar way, Christ also went this way at Golgotha and finally died on the cross for humanity's benefit.

The Kalevala's description of Väinämöinen's relief and humble gratitude when he saw the wind and waves carrying the fragments of the Sampo to land is deep and humane:

Vaka vanha Väinämöinen	Väinämöinen saw those pieces,
Näki tyrskyn työntelevän,	Those small fragments of the Sampo,
Hyrskyn maalle hylkeävän,	Splinters of the ciphered cover;

Aallon rannalle ajavan
Noita sampuen muruja,
Kirjokannen kappaleita.
Hän tuosta toki ihastui,
Sanan virkkoi, noin nimesi:
"Tuost' on siemenen sikiö,
Tuosta kyntö, tuosta kylvö,
Tuosta kasvu kaikenlainen,
Tuosta kuu kumottamahan,
Onnen päivä paistamahan,
Suomen suurille tiloille,
Suomen maille mairehille!"

Saw the sea swells lifting them,
Herded landward by the combers,
Driven shoreward by the breakers.

Heartened by the sight he said:
"There's a seed of future fortune,
Germ of everlasting thriving
For our plowing and our planting
And for crops of every kind
That will make the moon to glimmer
And the sun of fortune shine
On the wide farmlands of Finland,
On the lovely land of Suomi."[109]

And Väinämöinen's prayer for his nation when he himself had lost everything, illustrates how he has completely abandoned himself:

"Anna luoja, suo Jumala,
Anna onni ollaksemme,
Hyvin ain' eleäksemme
Kunnialla kuollaksemme
Suloisessa Suomen maassa,
Kaunihissa Karjalassa!"

"Give, Creator, grant, O God,
Grant us good life and good fortune

And at last to die with honor
In the lovely land of Suomi
And in beautiful Karelia."[110]

Thus ends the Kalevala's story of the Sampo and its revealing description of the great drama of initiation. The runes thereafter return to the continuing adventures of the heroes and portray the shrunken and devalued power of Louhi, even though her vengeance caused more problems for the people of Kaleva (Runos 45 and 46). It is not until the 49th rune that peace prevails. But the war for the Sampo is over and the Sampo is never encountered again unbroken.

Now the reader is entitled to question: Does all this mean that the initiate is not allowed to keep his own sun-body? How then can his connection to his eternal magic body be understood? Is the Sampo lost forever? What happened to the initiate's immortality? Isn't there a greater mystery hiding in this?

And we answer: Yes, it hides. Behind the Sampo's loss hides its future regaining. This is the law of life. All that is mentally lost, will be regained. "He who loses his life, will gain eternal life."

The Sampo-body will indeed one day become the initiate's own. The Kalevala clearly refers to this with Väinämöinen's words:

"Annapas ajan kulua,	"Let the rope of time run out—
Päivän mennä, toisen tulla,	One day go, another come—
Taas minua tarvitahan,	And again I will be needed.
Katsotahan, kaivatahan	They'll be waiting, yearning for me
Uuen Sammon saattajaksi..."	To bring back another Sampo..."[111]

And if we ask ourselves when this will happen in the initiate's life, we find the answer in the battle for the Sampo related above. Of course, answers the Kalevala, when an initiate is through fighting, when he no longer divides himself in two to battle evil, setting God against the devil, he offers himself to evil as a ransom, saying: "I no longer battle the forces of evil. Instead, now I can love them and gather them into me. Let all evil come over me and into me, for I will change it all into goodness and send it away better. Let all curses fall upon me to be transformed into blessings!"

This teaching is hidden within the rune as a delightful hope for the future and as the promise of resurrection.

We are familiar with another drama about initiation, in which the resurrection is described as a literal reality. The New Testament tells how Christ, in his immortal sun-body, breaks up the power of Tuoni (the Devil) and is resurrected. He truly died as humbly as a sacrificial lamb without resisting anyone involved, even forbidding Peter to defend him when Peter reached for his sword. But what he lost in this greatest human agony on the cross, is regained in the greatest divine delight of his resurrection. And this eventuality, referred to and anticipated in the Kalevala, will become true in the brightest, most miraculous events of another Holy Book (the New Testament).

PART IV

The Kalevala's Magic

The Occult-Historical Key

34

What Is Meant Here
by Magic

MAGIC IS USUALLY UNDERSTOOD to mean a sorcery or witchcraft used to increase material benefits in a way more expedient than conventional methods. It is said to be "good" or "white" magic if one has beneficial aspirations for oneself and friends. On the other hand, it is considered to be bad or black magic if it is used to damage others.

Allan Menzies writes in his book *World Religions* (1910), available in Finnish, "In every savage religion there is some amount of magic, and this magic is used, it is thought, to affect future events or to gain foreknowledge of them. The undeveloped human being does not have a proper knowledge of nature's laws nor does he understand the nature of causality, thus his imagination is unrestrained and he believes himself capable of influencing the course of nature in many ways. He imitates things he thinks will cause something to happen, and then waits for the affect he seemingly produces. He uses the power he believes he has over spirits, forcing them to fulfill his desires. He also uses objects which he believes to contain some hidden secret force in such a way that a desired result is expected. These superstitions thus relate to both the belief in spirits and the worshipping of objects, that is to say, to animism and fetishism. Among any tribe there is usually a specialist who knows these techniques and is capable of performing them" (pp. 56-57).

It almost feels like professor Menzies calls into question the Revival of Learning (the Renaissance) regarding magic and mysticism, and would brand all of it as being mere superstition and belief in illusion. On a more cautious and correct scientific foundation there is professor Heinrich Schurtz, who says in his book *The Original History of Culture* (1915): "The scientist of modern times has encountered many difficult problems in his search for answers. A more in-depth exploration of hypnotism has shown that negativity and arguments inciting skepticism are insufficient as explanations, and that many facts found among tribal cultures that appear to be mysticism, actually have a scientifically provable foundation. Nevertheless, for example, the convenient position that all shamans and medicine men were simply skilled jesters and conjurers has to be abandoned" (p. 757).

In the minds of their neighbors, the Finns and Lapps were always considered to be powerful magicians and sorcerers, and of course they had their reasons for believing this. No other Christian nation has preserved as many magic formulas and incantations than our nation. C. A. Gottlund writes in his study *Vanhoin Suomalaisten viisaus ja opin-keinot* (*The Wisdom and Teaching Methods of the Old Finns*): "They (the Finnish nation) is first mentioned for the fact that no other nation in the world is more famous for their Magic and Witchcraft than this Finnish nation. These traditions have risen to a uniform Doctrine or Knowledge, which appears to the outside world via brutal and curious icons, and through odd events, *none of which have been studied*. This Doctrine expresses some vanity but also much *great knowledge and wisdom*, which explain how, although the Finns may have lived mostly in mental darkness, they had a natural but odd *Wisdom*—quite magnificent though it turned unnatural—which expressed itself in a peculiar manner. With their wisdom and vanity they frightened other nations, and they were considered more powerful and knowledgeable than other human beings. Indeed, it has been said that they were in union with the Devil, that they received both their wisdom and power from him. Humans have always been quick to explain incomprehensible events as unnatural; and if the practicing of magic betrayed the Finns as unenlightened, those who believed this could not be any wiser than those who practiced and trusted in it."[1]

A long time ago, in 1782, K. S. Lencqvist's study of the old Finn's theoretical and practical superstitions (*Dissertatio de superstitione veterum Fennorum theoretica et practica*), written in Latin, was published in Turku.

Because it listed and classified magical phenomena more thoroughly than works that came later, as we have seen, we wish to repeat here Porthan-Lencqvist's classification.[2]

"Beneficial skills of incantation" or white magic were of the following kinds:

1) *Prophesying*, performed with a) a bowl or goblet filled with water (later with alcohol or coffee), b) a patient's garment, c) presentiments or precognition, d) lottery (on a sieve or a magician's drum), and e) choosing days.

"Presentiments were omens of future events and were seen in many kinds of occurrences and accidental events. A buzzing in the ears augured that some kind of news would be heard. Meeting an old woman, stumbling against a threshold, and falling from a horse's back were supposedly bad omens. A jackdaw's cawing, a cat's mewing, and an itching in the cheeks and chin meant the arrival of guests. Omens of death were of many kinds. For example, a knocking made against a wall was death's clock (Thermes Pulsatorum), as were the howl of dogs and the eagle-owl's cry, or pieces of straw or wood chips seen lying in the shape of a cross in front of a door" and so on.

The choosing of days was apparently based upon astrological knowledge. "They had their happy and unhappy days." For example, the final days of a waning moon and the first days of a waxing moon were "empty days" because the moon is not visible during that time. As such, it was not good to sow or spread manure over a field during those days.

2) *Charms*, with which sorcerers fortified themselves against harm and accidents caused by other sorcerers; also used to deflect such attacks. a) Incantation techniques were used to make their bodies invincible to all kinds of weapons, to guard cattle against wild beasts, to protect their dwellings from fire and their transport wagons from thieves, and successfully defend legal disputes. b) By taking oathes they tried to prevent the forces of nature from causing damage, and dangerous animals from causing harm. c) With conjurings they tried to drive away bears, diseases and other evil from themselves and friends. d) By enlisting or "engaging" (using the cross's mark, turning socks inside out, making knots, bribes, and offerings) one was believed to be able to repel the intrigues and plans of bad people who try to injure others with their magic tricks. e) By "turning around" one could protect oneself from the dangers and injuries

raised by an enemy. In this way, the masters of this skill tried to throw back these evil things upon the sender. f) By reversing, sorcerers tried to heal injuries and return lost objects. Thus, for example, they forced thieves to return stolen objects and could compel a divorced woman to love her husband again.

3) *Catching or bringing happiness.* This was done with many kinds of secret tricks, partly with the aid of some kind of home-spirit (Lencqvist says *spiritus familiaris*; we would say a brownie or gnome) who provides his friends with riches, money, and other goods.

"Incantation-skills for evil deeds," or black magic, were of the following kinds:

1) *Conjuration.* "With their spells magicians can confuse the abilities of other human beings to the extent that they lose control and seem to hear, see, and feel things that the magician wants them to, and thereby injure themselves." Lencqvist lists that the eyes, ears, tongue, and imagination can be betrayed, tells how someone can be made to go out of their mind, how mobility is reduced or stopped entirely, and how one can determine another person's feelings as much as one desires. Nowadays, all of these phenomena are called hypnotism.

2) *Bewitching* in the limited sense that "by wicked tricks they watch over another person's life, successes, and property with criminal intent, and do not consider such activities to be shameful as long as they are done secretly and safely." For this purpose a special lumbago or "hernia" was used, described as a ball, which caused severe pain in the internal organs of the body such that death would certainly follow. They could also trouble their enemies with diseases or make them melancholic, paralyzed, blind, or lame. They sought to disturb other peoples' marriages and make them unhappy, infertile, quarrelsome, or in some other way miserable. They even tried to deprave an enemy's character by compelling him to become a thief, an adulterer, a drinker, a spendthrift, or make him a profligate by similar means.

3) *Buttings and curses.* With these, "a mouthful of abuse was heaped upon the enemy or opponent whom had wished for evil things, and ruin was wished upon the enemy's whole tribe as well as the enemy himself. These were accomplished with specific ceremonies and magic formulas, in addition to all kinds of other wicked techniques."

Regarding the devices and techniques employed in the ceremonies of both black and white sorcerers, Lencqvist mentions:

1) *Magic signs*, being letters, numbers, and other kinds of signs. Also, we can include here

2) *Magic objects* such as sieves, magic drums, and so on.

3) *Words*, which is to say, words and short sentences with which diseases were removed, serpents were charmed, and so on.

4) *Spells*, that is, words of origins, the essential spells.

5) *Ceremonies and tricks.* "He must, before sunrise, go around visiting cemeteries and bury human bones here and there, never looking around or throwing anything behind himself. Hang a magic object around the neck or on the breast, without blinking an eye... one must run a specified distance holding ones breath..." and so on.

6) *Miraculous enthusiastic emotions and pranks.* "If one needs to chase away evil spirits one sets about this task with tremendous emotion, raging with pranks, rumbling around, contorting the body in and out."

7) *Unions with devils.* "There is no doubt that the kind of people who have gone so long in ungodliness and stupidity, initiating themselves with the enemy of God and humanity, seeks to receive eternal help for their wicked plans. It is true that the seed of ungodliness originates in paganism. This is true because we have shown above that our ancestors believed one could enlist the help of evil gnomes and spirits."

In this broad summary we see a satisfactory overview of the secret techniques—as far as they are understood—which are usually referred to as magic or witchcraft. The Kalevala is full of this magic. All of its heroes are skilled in incantations, including Lemminkäinen, Ilmarinen, Joukahainen, and above all Väinämöinen, whose mighty words and songs were not merely charming, but carried with them a creative and miracle-making force. As an example of a magical object, there is Lemminkäinen's hairbrush, which his mother and wife saw bleeding at the moment he met his death. At one point, when the moon and sun ceased to shine (49:75-110), Väinämöinen turns to divination by lottery.[3] It is also said that he cured sick people with ointments and magnetic gazes, as well as with prayers and spells (45:313-362). At any rate, ones attention never becomes fixed on these magical details because they appear to be wholly natural and minor points. The clue, however, is their lofty content and their aesthetic unity, which awakens a deep and permanent interest. But the question that every attentive reader must ask is: "What foundation and basis is there for such stories?!" And many a reader answers without doubt: "Certainly none!"

Caution is needed here. Reactionary denials are too easy and quick. As professor Schurtz remarked in the quotation given above, the modern investigator is no longer in the same position as the scientist during the Revival of Learning (the Renaissance). Currently, we officially know enough about the secret faculties of the human mind that we mark ourselves as ignorant, scientific fuddyduddies if we just shrug our shoulders at "fairy tales" and "miraculous stories."

Regarding the writer of this book, he has no reason to deny the reality of magic and magical phenomena. On the contrary, he—based on his own experiences—must confess that several of the phenomena given above are real, and he could even mention a few that are not listed. However, this does not mean that he would morally approve of them.

It does not surprise us that common opinion and the many critics who condemn witchcraft and magic adhere to a philosophy of life that does not reach beyond the concerns of everyday mundane life. Perpetual worrying about the benefits and needs of material life, its success, security, and well being, is really vile and overly concerned with details. Certainly, honest work and sincere behavior are no doubt much better magic in the long run than any spells and tricks. Education, civilization, and the Christian outlook have an undeniably elevating affect on nations. But common opinion and critique depends upon the understanding of magic that ultimately prevails. If the comprehension changes, so must the critical analysis.

We do not in the least wish to change common opinion about magic. We only want to publicly express our own opinion, which may already be clear to the reader, that essentially, and in truth, magic is quite different from the picture of tricks and spells presented above. In reality, magic involves activity in the unseen world and thus knowledge of the unseen world. A seer is just a human being who controls some of the forces in the unseen world, and therefore his actions as a seer seem magical. Far removed from the idea that this activity can impinge upon the realm of material and physical life, its aims are in fact superphysical, mental, and moral in quality. True magic only touches physical being indirectly; it only promotes a spiritual civilization. The magic of the other kind, when it truly appropriates the secret forces, is like prostituting the divine faculty.

With his magical abilities a seer expresses his contribution to the surrounding world and humanity. One part of his activities is simply education. His task is to educate humanity, to have an affect on them, perhaps even to acquire some of them as pupils. Thus we can say that magic, in this more limited meaning, is the psychic method which a seer uses when helping human beings to grow and when seeking to enlist students.

In the following we want to explain a few features regarding these educational methods of the Kalevala's seers, and then it may become clear why we generally refer to them as magical.

35

Then and Now:
Two Human Types

OR US TO CORRECTLY UNDERSTAND the education in magic offered by the Kalevala's seers, we must first review the essentials, the human quite environment where they first found themselves and had influence. That environment cannot be found in the era in which the modern form of the Kalevala runes were composed and sung, but must be sought in a much older period—the time of which the Kalevala's runes, at least certain fragments of them, truly speak. We do not wish to define how far back we need to go with a specific number of years; the Kalevala, as we will see, sings of so many periods and eras that we are accessing a span of tens of thousands of years. We must go so far back that we meet with a psychological environment markedly different from modern humanity, and this is the first era which was influenced by the seer-heroes of the Kalevala. Despite the suspicions of our scientific investigators, the Kalevala takes us, if we can see and feel the magical ambiance, to very ancient eras "beyond history," to a time when the modern Finnish nation did not yet exist although our ancestors—and why shouldn't we call them Finns?—were alive and making their mark. The origins and past history of the Finnish people are hidden in dim antiquity, but occultly seen this is a known quantity: Our Kalevalan spirit and culture are of Atlantean origin.* As to its form and its expressive style, the Kalevala is naturally an Aryan product but when one ventures into its spirit, Atlantean images and impressions arise. And therefore we must correctly understand the Kalevala's magic to begin to comprehend the psyche and soul of the Atlantean human.

We spoke earlier about humanity's Fourth Root Race and mentioned that these Atlanteans were more emotional human beings than those in the modern Fifth Aryan Root Race. (See Chapter 10, "The Lemminkäinen-Forces".) However, this short definition is insufficient. To get some kind of image of the Atlantean human it will be useful to compare with the modern European.

How can we psychologically define the modern human being? His innermost secret essence is emotion but he more or less uses his intellect to control himself and his actions. Officially, he admits that reason is supreme and regrets that it doesn't always prevail in his private life. Besides, he has a dim feeling that the intellect is much more than simply concerned with resourcefully and egotistically calculating things for its own benefit. His day-consciousness is essentially the activity of thought (a human being who cannot use his reasoning intellect while in the day-

---

*In *The Secret Doctrine* Madame Blavatsky says that Chinese, Japanese, Mongolians, Finns, and Turks belong to the seventh (Mongolian) sub-race of the Atlantean Root Race. Scientists such as Yrjö Koskinen in his dissertation *Tiedot Suomensuvun muinaisuudesta* (*Knowledge Concerning the Antiquity of the Finnish Family*), speculate that the peoples of the Finnish family are of Turanian origin and the old Chaldeans and Sumerians of ancient Babylonia are related to them. According to Theosophical classification, these people were also Atlantean. Historically understood, Kaleva could have been, as Ganander believes, the name of some giant. According to the legend, he had twelve sons of which, as we mentioned earlier, the main heroes of the Kalevala are the best known. All of their names are not known. J. R. Aspelin was no doubt correct in presuming that when the identities and careers of all the sons of Kaleva become clear, new insights into the history of the Finnish people will be gained. And who knows to what extent bishop Daniel Juslenius was right, though in a sense inaccurately, in his belief that ancient Finland was a powerful realm, ruled by its own national kings? Those were the times of "Kalevala," those ancient times, when Kalevala was not located on the modern peninsula of Finland. Lönnrot also mentions that within common folklore, many considered the sons of Kaleva to be giants, and it is appropriate to compare this with the tradition and occult knowledge that the Atlanteans grew taller than modern Aryans.

consciousness is sick, and is considered to be a lunatic in relation to other human beings). The modern human being's thought-life is based upon his perceptions, which come through his senses. For him, sleep-consciousness is shadowy and dim, often confused and lacking in reason, and he makes a sharp distinction between his day- and sleep-consciousness.

The more he becomes European the more independent he tries to be. The psychological impulse of civilization is found in the fact that it impels him to become an individual and personal being. He is his own self, not merely "his father's son," or a member of this or that family or tribe. His motto is "individual freedom" and he wishes for free competition to prevail as much as possible in his society.

In their innermost beings all humans are unchanging but in their personalities they change according to times and conditions. How different was the Atlantean personality compared with the European!

The average Atlantean was not nearly as developed in his reasoning ability and use of thought; he was not at all as independent, not as individualized. He did not have his "own will." In all things he thought and perceived with the same eyes as his parents, his kin, and his tribe. It was as if he lived in them, and they in him—and the deceased were always present in his memory. He was almost completely feeling and fantasy. He was more a part of a group-soul than an isolated individual soul, and this reveals the original psychological background for the worshipping of the deceased.

In addition, his day-consciousness was organized differently than that of a modern human being. It consisted of very little thought and reason and instead the world appeared to him as being full of emotion. This means that a great deal of what we nowadays call sleep-consciousness then belonged to the day-consciousness. The Atlantean mind was full of "sleep images"; the emotions of other people entered the mind as images. Speech was not used in the same way as it is today, and the physical perceptions of human beings and animals were—especially in the earlier Atlantean ages—seen to be dimmer than the emotions. Nature spoke to Atlantean souls in its own language—flowers in the meadow, stones on the earth, trees in the forest, lakes, mountains, clouds, wind, thunder, sun, moon, and stars—all reflected specific sentimental images within their consciousness, so it is not difficult to understand why the ancient nations in their thinking were animists. Among the ancient cultures that we are familiar with, manism and animism were inherited straight from the ancient Atlantean era.

But there is another reason for Atlantean animism. Because an Atlantean's day-consciousness partially moved in the sleep-world, he not only perceived the emotions of nature, but also the invisible beings of nature, which are called "fairies." These are partly fantastical forms constantly vanishing away—having their source in the internal streaming of elemental life coming from the vegetable kingdom, the air, water and wind—and partly living beings, actual fairies and nature spirits which live within the elements and belong to a wholly other developmental system than human beings and animals. Today, when a clairvoyant occultist encounters this living realm, these fairies in the invisible world, he confidently controls them with his thoughts and will. The Atlantean could not manage to control in this way. Because his thought was not developed enough, he could not use his willpower self-consciously. He had to rely on his emotion to awaken his will. How was this possible? With spells. The Atlantean had an excellent memory. By early childhood he had already committed to memory many kinds of spells and "words of origin." He needed these in everyday activities and with their help he conversed with nature and its beings, sometimes praying for their help, sometimes controlling them with his conjuring and spells.

When an Atlantean slept, his consciousness moved to that part of his mind which we call the inner consciousness much easier than does the consciousness of the modern human being. Nowadays, when a sleeper has enjoyed dreamless sleep, he awakens and feels especially strong and invigorated. He descended from sleep-consciousness into the inner consciousness, and this distancing from his everyday worries, to rest in the bosom of his own inner being, naturally replenishes his physical and ethical reserves. An Atlantean experienced this every night, suggesting a reason why ancient people were usually more healthy than modern humans. (When they became ill, a person was cured by having them fall asleep in a holy place such as a temple; thus, interacting in the world of the inner consciousness with the good and pure fairy of the holy place made him well. Also, because the disease manifested in the consciousness as a mental image, a "physican"—that is, a healer or seer using spells and conjurations—could drive away the mental image and with it the disease.) Moreover, the sleep-state of the Atlantean differed in several essential respects from modern dreamless sleep. When a modern human being awakens from a deep, dreamless sleep, he does not remember anything; he thinks he spent the whole night in an unconscious state. It was different for the Atlanteans. For them, falling into the inner consciousness was similar to what happens when modern human beings shift to the sleep-consciousness; upon awakening, the Atlantean brought memories back. He visited another world, his soul moved in the realms of the deceased and the gods, associating with higher beings and participating in the world's cosmic life. Today, native people still believe that while they sleep the soul floats around in strange lands. Nowadays, however, if one wants to preserve the memories from the inner consciousness, one must learn the special mental training of "falling into a trance," which we mentioned earlier.*

Keeping in mind these psycho-physiological differences, or soul-body differences, between the ancient Atlantean and the modern European, we can understand without further ado that their methods of education regarding magic are also essentially different.

Let us imagine that a seer of our times wishes to turn the world's attention to the wisdom of the ages, to the existence of the secret knowledge, to the possibility of salvation from evil, and that he wishes to gather pupils around him. What means would he use?

There exists only one honest and efficacious method: To awaken the human being's thought and intellect to action, to appeal to their own sense of truth and justice, to urge them to seek the truth and to show them the way. This is best accomplished through the spoken and written word. The modern human being is so sensitive to any kind of influence and authority that he considers, for example, religious ceremonies in church and other festivities (which, in the Middle Ages, inspired the

---

*See Chapter 27, "The Younger Sister of Pohja's Maid." In his book *Suomen suvun pakanallinen jumalanpalvelus* (*The Pagan Divine Service of the Finnish Family*), J. Krohn tells of the muzhan or seer, the magician of the Cheremis people: "He must also be rigorously moral in his life. Above all, it is demanded of him that he be in the immediate presence of the gods. He must foresee future events, expose thieves, heal diseases, and so on. He sometimes receives his revelations while awake, but most often when sleeping. Dreaming does not happen only at night in a natural way, but the artificial imitation of sleep is also used... Falling asleep in this way is just a new form of achieving the unconscious state in which the soul, believed to be released from the affects of the visible environment, is free to ascend to the sphere of supernatural experience" (p. 105).

human mind to devotion and saintliness) as a downright sterile system devoid of reason and free thought. And if a white magician tries to acquire and educate pupils in the secret knowledge and wisdom, he should explain to them immediately, at the very start, the difference between blind faith and natural human trust, and show them that occult self-education is in no respect unreasonable, that, in fact, the development of reason is one of its essential trademarks.

To be brief: Reason exists in the modern day-consciousness as the accepted master, and one must petition it during the magic education of adult human beings. Not until the reasoning day-consciousness cooperates can a human being benefit from his faith in his divinely born I and be truly enthusiastic about seeking and approaching it.

Let us think about the human seer who lived thousands of years ago on Atlantis. He too wanted to educate human beings in how to live rightly. He too wanted to awaken in them the desire and feeling of God and the knowledge of truth. His duty was also to gather around him pupils, to show them how they could accelerate their development and be elevated to the feeling of the higher I, that which saves one from evil. Was he, that ancient seer, in the same situation as his brother of our times? Could he appeal to the same experiences of his pupils and, above all, to the same intellectual understanding?

Not at all. His position was quite different. The real I, to which he could appeal, was of another order completely; the minor faculty of reason that he might awaken was extremely weak and ineffectual. But, in contrast to this, there was a great emotional force and an expansive and sensitive imagination. In this situation, how could one overlook the psychic faculty, that side of consciousness which was clearly in the foreground and the most developed? Naturally, a seer of that era had to appeal to the imagination and emotional force of human beings. How could this be done?

It was done with the help of a method that today we would perhaps call suggestion, that is, suggestion but not hypnotism. Hypnotism, in a limited definition, means the chaining of another person's will and consciousness so that he loses his independent thought and self-control; it is like sinking into an artificial sleep. A white Atlantean seer did not use this to teach magic because with this approach there could be no benefits in that era, only damage. Occult development is based upon self-education, and it cannot begin by arresting learning. The suggestive state that the ancient seer induced involved liberating his pupil from the group-soul or the group-dream which he was subject to. And he had to use suggestion to awaken a will to freedom and independence within his student. This suggestion awakened experiences that were stronger than those in everyday emotional life, opening the imagination to wider and more interesting vistas.

This usually began when the seer awoke self-love in his pupil. In the earliest times, he did not need to use suggestion for this purpose. His very presence, the exuberant love emanating from his heart, spontaneously struck responsive chords in sensitive human beings. Undeniably, however, in later times a seer did rely on the power of his imagination to draw the pupil's heart and attention near. There was no danger unless the seer was inexperienced.

All emotion draws its expressive force from human sexuality, as we remarked earlier. (See Chapter 10, "The Lemminkäinen-Forces.") When love was thus kindled in the pupil's breast, a relationship developed between him and the teacher. This relationship was unavoidable and was good as long as it stayed pure and unselfish. It helped the pupil become free from the dream of the tribal-soul and allowed the teacher to educate his student in reason and independence. Gradually the student grew free from his teacher's influence.

On the other hand, things were different if the seer was inexperienced or egotistical. Then he would lapse into the personal vicissitudes of his own awakening love, and the relationship between teacher and student could turn selfish, even physical. We cannot deny that some teachers, whose reason and imagination were superior, used these forces wrongly and for selfish reasons, to gain power over their weaker students. Today, great intelligence and cunning could also be used wrongly, if not simply by appealing to the emotions then by seducing and arresting the comprehending intellect of others. The way of black magic is always open.

Regarding Atlantean magic, in general terms we can say that it was based on emotion and therefore on sexual power.

36

Atlantean Magic
in the Kalevala

HEN WE SPOKE of the Kalevala's internal ethic we tried to open the meaning of some runes with the psychological key of self-education. This is a general procedure, independent of time, which does not touch upon the Kalevala's historical content. Now our duty is quite different. Now we must understand the Kalevala as an occult-historical description of time and approach its heroes as if they were human types who lived on earth. We say "human types" because, as we already said in Chapter 5, the names of the Kalevala's heroes (Väinämöinen, Lemminkäinen, and so on) are generic or familial names, typical in the respect that they were given to many individuals. Also, in using the key of Atlantean magic we cannot yet approach our heroes as personalities who walked the earth. Why? Because the Kalevala's external poetry and format are not Atlantean, so its Atlantean contents must be sought within it. The Kalevala's runes are songs assembled during the Aryan age, for Aryan listeners, and its viewpoint is Aryan, however old some of its contents may be.

By using the historical key which unlocks for us the Atlantean side of the Kalevala's magic, we begin by assuming that the Kalevala's main heroes (Väinämöinen, Ilmarinen, Lemminkäinen, and Louhi) are Atlantean magicians, and the last one mentioned represents the so-called black magic.

217

Väinämöinen, Ilmarinen, and Lemminkäinen were white magicians who sought students to promote humanity's development. Their students are described as young maidens, and this is to show—besides the fact that students' souls are always receptive and thus "feminine" in relation to the teacher—that they are inexperienced and predisposed to innocent goodliness. This was relevant because the educational process appealed to the emotions and the imagination. We don't mean to suggest that students were always women and teachers were always men. Teachers are described as men because a teacher's position is one of outward giving.

Lemminkäinen is a typical Atlantean magician. When we understand him correctly with this in mind, he appears as great, strong, and lovable. He is full of knowledge, his emotions are invincible, and he is an untiring ally. His countless love-adventures record the many times that he helped human souls with his love. For he was a great lover and he trusted infinitely in his own personal charms:

"*Jos en ole koiltani korea,*   "Since my House is not so high
Su'ultani aivan suuri,   And my kinship not so great,
Mie valitsen varrellani   With my handsome frame I'll conquer,
Otan muilla muo'oillani."   Capture with my other features."[4]

He always appealed to the emotions, and with them he could easily awaken the emotions of others. However, although he was prone to hint at his own irresistability, he rarely appealed to the imagination. He was vigorously strong, faithful, and confident in himself. The one who pleased him, she who he chose to educate, could not resist. The "Island's" (Poseidon's) Kyllikki stubbornly tried to resist and stand firm, but when Lemminkäinen arrived and opened to her his burning heart, her strength broke and she was happy to surrender to Lemminkäinen's lead.

He went along on his way with the clarity of purpose and straightforwardness of a hurricane. He finally learned to see that his personal charm and power were not enough. When he did not meet within the Island's population souls whom he might teach in the way he wished, he made up his mind to journey to Pohjola where was said to exist a proud and beautiful nation familiar with the secret skills. After arriving he realizes that he must appeal to the imagination as well as the emotions. He thus set about singing and conjuring with such charisma that the best singers in the place felt inadequate and ineffective. Their reservoir of poetry and magic dried up and their imaginations wilted powerlessly under Lemminkäinen's will:

Tulta iski turkin helmat,	From his coat hem fire was streaming,
Valoi silmät valkeata	In his eyes a light was gleaming
Lemminkäisen laulaessa	As the son of Lempi sang,
Laulaessa, lausiessa,	As he sang and worked his magic.
Lauloi laulajat parahat	Sang the best of singers down,
Pahimmiksi laulajiksi,	Made of them the worst of singers,
Kivet suuhun syrjin syösti,	Fed their mouths with pebbles edgewise;
Paaet lappehin lateli	Boulder after boulder flatwise
Parahille laulajille,	Heaped upon the best of them,
Taitavimmille runoille.	Best magicians, best of singers.
Niin lauloi mokomat miehet	All such miserable men he scattered
Minkä minne, kunka kunne:	Hither and yon
Ahoille vesattomille,	to barren tundras,
Maille kyntämättömille,	Fields unplowed
Lampihin kalattomihin,	and fishless ponds
Aivan ahvenettomihin,	Without a single swimming perch;
Rutjan koskehen kovahan,	To the mighty falls of Finnmark,
Palavahan pyörtehesen,	Into the boiling, whirling maelstrom,
Virran alle vaahtipäiksi,	Into foam beneath the current,
Kosken keskelle kiviksi,	There as boulders in mid-rapids;
Tulena palelemahan,	Conjured them to flame like fire
Säkehinä säykkymähän.	And to flash like shooting sparks.[5]

One of the listeners—Wet-Hat the cow-herder—remained untouched, unaffected by Lemminkäinen's song and, wondering to himself, perhaps waiting for some compliment, he finally asked Lemminkäinen why he had been spared. In all sincerity, Lemminkäinen answered, "You are bad, a worthless human, you have not a drop of imagination's holy fire, thus even my own divine song had no affect on you." This was taken as an insult by all present, and the cow-herder decided to plan his revenge.

After demonstrating his power, Lemminkäinen made it known that he now desired students. Louhi responded that this would not be a problem, but first he had to prove his seer-knowledge before they would agree to fully believe in him. In accomplishing these works for wages Lemminkäinen shows that he is capable of many kinds of conjuring, but in completing his final task he collapses onto the earth, unconscious. The black forces of the cow-herder of Pohja were superior; Lemminkäinen could not protect himself against those magic arrows. Later, when Lemminkäinen makes his second journey to Pohjola, he cannot do anything among the cold-blooded people of Pohjola.

Väinämöinen, when understood as an Atlantean seer, is of a different type than Lemminkäinen. He does not appeal directly to the emotions when awakening the attention of human beings. He lets the fame of his wisdom set to motion their imaginations and then his personal presence and singing completely charms them. His basic approach differs from Lemminkäinen's, and it is not as effective when looked at from the Atlantean perspective. He did not, in fact, manage to acquire any students among human beings, only seers like Ilmarinen and Lemminkäinen could follow his lead.

Anyhow, Väinämöinen is so famous by the time he arrives in Pohjola that he is received with great respect and affection, is entertained and asked to stay. But Väinämöinen longs for his own country, and he does not trust the people of Pohjola. After awhile it becomes clear that they are an egotistical "secret group," for Louhi asks Väinämöinen:

"Niin mitä minulle annat   "So, what will you give me then
Kun saatan omille maille,   If I see you safely home,
Oman peltosi perille,   See you to your homeland meadows,
Kotisaunan saapuville?"   Even to your very sauna?"[6]

When Väinämöinen offers her helmutfuls of gold, Pohjola's mistress answers that gold is merely children's flowers and asks Väinämöinen if he can forge a Sampo. And if he agrees to do it:

"...Niin annan tytön sinulle,   "...Then I'll let you have my daughter,
Panen neien palkastasi,   Give the maiden as your payment,
Saatan sinut omille maille..."   And I'll see you safely home."[7]

Because he cannot forge the Sampo himself, Väinämöinen promises to send smith Ilmarinen to both forge the Sampo and "appease the maiden."

However, on his journey homeward, he spies Pohja's beautiful virgin, is charmed by her and asks her to follow him. Thus, there was at least one person in Pohjola who, in Väinämöinen's eyes, was worthy of educating as his own pupil. Pohja's maiden was not agreeable right away, for she wanted to confirm that Väinämöinen was truly a seer who could conjure. She makes Väinämöinen cleave a horsehair with a dull knife, tie an egg into a knot, scrape birch bark from a stone, and chop fence-posts of ice "without splitting off a splinter." Finally, when Väinämöinen must carve a boat from the "crumblets" of the virgin's spindle and push it into the water "without a hand upon it," he could not do it right away and succumbs to all kinds of problems. When Väinämöinen finally finishes the boat and brings it to Pohja's virgin, she is already engaged to another seer, Ilmarinen. Väinämöinen wisely resigns himself to his fate, for he himself had sent Ilmarinen to Pohjola and was thus responsible for the people of Pohjola being charmed by Ilmarinen and claiming him as their teacher.

Ilmarinen is a lesser type of Atlantean seer. If we imagine him seeking students, he would not appeal to their emotions at all, and in his personal presence he barely makes any impression on the imagination. The only way that he might awaken interest is to let his works and deeds speak for him. But, in fact, the Kalevala does not say that Ilmarinen, out of love for humanity, seeks students. Not until he goes to Pohjola at Väinämöinen's bidding does there awaken within his heart a desire to join with the people of Pohjola. But when those whom he desires to have as students create obstacles for him, he sadly returns to his own country.

Anyhow, he did forge the Sampo for the people of Pohjola, which is to say, he taught them many things that they did not or could not know and eventually, as fate would have it, those chosen by Ilmarinen do become his students.

As we already said, Louhi, the mistress of Pohjola, represents black magic. This is apparent because she has ambitions for power and knowledge. In connection with her, there are no words of love. She judges Lemminkäinen to be insignificant. When she desires Väinämöinen for her son-in-law, she secretly thinks of all the knowledge and power which she could draw from him. And although Väinämöinen is too wise to teach Louhi (to forge the Sampo), he falls into her coils to the extent that he must promise the task to Ilmarinen. And Louhi easily bends Ilmarinen to her will. Ilmarinen is too honest to expect evil, and he teaches all of his secret abilities to Louhi. He eventually gets his reward, and belatedly observes that he taught his skills to many people who would misuse them for their own well-being and power. Finally fate strips everything from Ilmarinen, which is fortunate because he then understands that his duty is to retrieve all the power and knowledge that he squandered in Pohjola. The Kalevala identifies Pohjola as the stronghold of black magic and sorcery.

Many a reader might say that Lemminkäinen, for his part, is much "blacker." His method of using his personal charms to awaken others is almost "detestable." And the Kalevala really describes him in no uncertain terms; it truly finds him at fault to be "always playing around with women."

And so it goes. That is the way things seem in Aryan eyes. And what better proof of this than the fact, which we already mentioned, that the Kalevala was composed from the Aryan viewpoint? But alas, "times change, and we along with them." What seems black today, could have been white yesterday, and vice versa. We see here that it is not enough to look at a dog's hair, we must examine the roots!

We must penetrate closer to the Kalevala's heroes.

At the Change of Ages

I N THE PREVIOUS CHAPTER we made a general overview of the lives of the Kalevala's main heroes from the vantage point of Atlantean magic, but did not exhaust the Kalevala's occult-historical content. You see, since the Kalevala was composed during the Aryan age, it does not speak only of Atlantean memories. When we examine the Kalevala's magical content more precisely, we will find that the Kalevala refers to at least three periods: The Atlantean, the Aryan, and the critical stage in between. If we can see that the ancestors of the Finnish nation once lived as an Atlantean tribe in the highlands of Central Asia,[8] afterward wandering into middle, southern, and eastern Europe and finally settling in the north, we understand how they became quite Aryan upon arriving in Europe—perhaps even earlier—and why the Kalevala preserves memories from different epochs.[9]

As a true remnant and memory of the Atlantean age, there is the description of Lemminkäinen. As we already mentioned, this Kalevala hero was a typical Atlantean magician, and Kyllikki represents the people of the Island, the place where he most enjoyed his sojourn and was most successful. We have already discussed Lemminkäinen in great detail, so here we only wish to add a few more observations which confirm that he was a genuine Atlantean. Lemminkäinen deeply loved and trusted his mother, and his insubordination only shows that he had become more independent than the ordinary Atlantean; with just cause one can certainly say that he loved no one as much as his mother. While traveling around outdoors, when facing all kinds of dangers, he always turns to using spells. For example, the brush that he leaves as an omen is filled with his own magnetic power. He has merged with it in such a way that if it starts bleeding, his mother and Kyllikki will know that things are going badly with him. Also, he is quite warlike and often draws his sword on living beings, especially human beings, when his spells do not work.

On the other hand, Ilmarinen belongs completely to the Aryan age, and Pohja's maid represents the human souls whom he managed best. Earlier we described Ilmarinen's intellectual and, appearance wise, somewhat cold character, so we will be satisfied here to mention only a few more things. In this way we will see that Ilmarinen's blood had hardly a trace of the Atlantean. He never turns to incantations but only to works and deeds. He is the eternal smith. When he utters a prayer or a wish, it is brief and terse, not at all like an incantation, but more like what might arise within the breast of one of us. For example, when he leaves for Pohjola and sits down in the sleigh, he prays:

"Laske ukko uutta lunta,	"O thou Ukko, send down new snow,
Visko hienoa vitiä,	New fine snow in powdery flakes
Lunta korjan liukutella,	For my sleigh to slide on swiftly,
Vitiä ve'en vilata!"	Slippery snow to speed my way."[10]

And adds a wish:

"Lähe nyt onni ohjilleni,	"May good fortune bless my reins,
Jumala rekoseheni,	God be with me in my sleigh;
Onni ei taita ohjaksia,	Good luck will not break the reins,
Jumala ei riko rekeä!"	Jumala never wreck a sleigh."[11]

While doing his works for wages it is said that he used a spell, namely, the words for removing snakes, but this can be historically understood as metachronical.* And the Birth of Fire rune, in which Ilmarinen reads the words about the soothing of burns, is so transparently mythological in

---

*Translator's note. Metachronical means "from a different age"; thus, the meaning is that the charm for removing snakes is from a different, earlier time. Editor's note. The word "anachronism" is close, but also has the connotation of "out of date"—a meaning not intended here.

content that it cannot be counted as historical. Ilmarinen has no hypnotic or suggestive abilities.

Another Aryan feature in his character is the ability to easily kindle an accurate intuition and presentiment of a thing's true nature, a trust in "the five senses" (the same was said of his sister Annikki). This occurs at the very beginning of Ilmarinen's first appearance in the Kalevala. Väinämöinen returns from his misadventure in Pohjola downcast, upset that he ransomed Ilmarinen "to release his own head." When he describes the delightful virgin of Pohja to Ilmarinen and urges him to immediately leave for Pohjola, Ilmarinen, seeing what really happened, cries out:

"*Ohoh, vanha Väinämöinen,*	"Oho, you old sly one, you!
Joko sie minun lupasit	So already you have pledged me
Pimeähän Pohjolahan	To that twilit Pohjola
Oman pääsi pääsitimeksi,	For the safety of your own head,
Itsesi lunastimeksi!..."	As a ransom for yourself?..."[12]

And when Väinämöinen weaves a story about the moon glimmering in the high branches of a spruce tree, Ilmarinen counters:

"*En usko toeksi tuota,*	"I do not believe that's true,
Kun en Käyne katsomahan,	Since I have not been to see it,
Nähne näillä silmilläni."	Have not seen it with these eyes."[13]

Väinämöinen truly must use his best magic skills, including the ability to transport physical objects from one place to another, to make Ilmarinen go to Pohjola.

The third piece of evidence regarding Ilmarinen's Aryan nature involves the forging of the Sampo. Though the Sampo is the perfect magical object, one cannot make it with magic spells. For example, Väinämöinen can build a boat with the power of song but he refuses to take on the task of forging the Sampo. This proves that the Sampo is something quite new, unheard of, something which cannot be brought about solely with the power of emotion and imagination. The forging of the Sampo requires ingenuity, reason, and thought. The Sampo thus involves higher scientific education and its achievements, all based on the faculty of intelligence and a complicated material culture, the distinctive features of the Fifth Root Race. Also, the "multi-colored cover" of the Sampo can, with good reason, be understood as something like a book, on which the original information and teachings of Ilmarinen were recorded with secret signs.*

It is no wonder that Louhi wanted to retain the Sampo as her most valuable treasure. It thus seems as if Ilmarinen, the forger of the Sampo, has stepped into the ranks of the educators and benefactors of our Aryan race as an ambassador of Finland's people.

And what about Väinämöinen? He is as far from Lemminkäinen as he is from Ilmarinen. He is an Atlantean magician and he is not. He is intellectually developed like an Aryan, but is not a child of the Fifth Root Race. He is the wisest of all, wiser than the white Ilmarinen, wiser than Lemminkäinen, wiser than black Louhi. But he is a tragic person, for his childlike personality is of the intermediary age, not belonging completely to either the old or the new. This is observed in his relationship with Aino, the only one of the Kalevala's women whom one may put on the same level with Väinämöinen in terms of the soul's secret magnificence and its tragic conflicts.

For the scientist, Aino's magnificent personality and the meaning of her fate is a most absorbing and rewarding topic of study. So let us try to understand Väinämöinen as a living, wise, but suffering human individual!

---

*It is appropriate to compare this with the very competent argument made by the Norwegian writer Fries that the Sampo was the magic drum of the Lapps, a thing highly valued and quite famous. Editor's note: The reference here is probably to the work of J. Friis, *Lappisk Mythologi, Eventyr og Folkesagn*, Christiania, 1871.

38

Väinämöinen and Aino

VÄINÄMÖINEN WAS OLD, old in his wisdom and old in age, but not old in his soul and mind. He had a long stretch of living behind him and when he glanced in that direction there arose in his memory several beautiful deeds done for his people's benefit. He did make mistakes—who hasn't?—but he sincerely tried to fulfill the mission which had fallen to him. So many human souls he had educated! Parents had entrusted him with their children. With poetry and singing, by telling fairy-tales and making miracles, he drew to himself their young hearts and thus helped them arise from the toils of tribalism and familial blood. He had washed them clean of original sin and awoke within them their I-consciousness, taught them the elements of thought and led their first groping steps on the way of independence and knowledge. Many people were thankful former students of his, he was always welcome in thousands of homes, he was famous overseas and in many lands...

However, his heart was empty. Because he, the old, wise, and famous Väinämöinen felt lonely and rejected.

The ancient wisemen always chose one of their students early on to be a close friend and relation. They married while young so that when age overtook them they would have no regrets. As for Väinämöinen, he had many opportunities in his youth to take one with unbroken vows to be his own. He remembered several parents who wished in their hearts that he might take their daughter to be his "hen under arm." He remembered many girls, many young maidens, virtuous and beautiful, who certainly would have blushed if he approached them as a suitor. But he always remained aloof—his heart never jumped so uncontrollably that he thought his day had come—and he could not follow the advice of others in those matters.

And so the years passed and Väinämöinen became an elder. And he continued to live alone.

Then fate put Joukahainen in his way. When he subdued the young fanatic with his conjuring skills and was promised the young Aino, Väinämöinen's heart stirred strangely. Where did this sudden joy come from? Was it an omen? Would he now have a friend for his old age? Would he now meet a soul whom he could adore, a student whom he would be allowed to give everything to?... How good he would be then, how gentle and considerate, holding hands with his best friend, the soul he would lead through gardens of knowledge, strolling down wide lanes of visions and dreams of the future. He would coax music from golden strings of emotion, make musical tones to clothe his alluring song. And he would teach his soul-companion to rise into the firmament and sit on the rainbow's rim so that he, in glory, could step forward and greet her. What then could possibly separate their hearts?

Steadfast old Väinämöinen, the eternal seer, had given himself to fantasies. It portended something...

It portended a great sorrow. Väinämöinen eventually met Aino in the forest, bending birch twigs for a sauna whisk, and she was very pretty in her dress decorated with trinkets. Happily and with confidence he approached the girl and said playfully:

"Eläpa muille, neiti nuori,	"Not for anyone else, young maiden,
Kun minulle, neiti nuori,	Not for anyone else but me,
Kanna kaulan helmilöitä,	Young maiden, wear that
	beaded necklace
Rinnan ristiä rakenna,	Or the crosslet on your bosom,
Pane päätä palmikolle,	Put your hair up in long braids
Sio silkillä hivusta!"	Tie them round with silken ribbons."[14]

At first the young lass blushed from ear to ear, shyly averting her eyes. But then the red quickly vanished, her cheeks went pale, and she turned her head slowly toward him. Her eyes met the old man's gentle and goodwilled gaze and she hesitated, as if feeling for a brief moment the unexplainable warmth and power of those eyes. Then suddenly she tore herself free from her indecision and cried out:

"*En sinulle, enkä muille*	"Not for you or anyone else
Kanna rinnan ristilöitä,	Will I wear this crosslet here
Päätä silkillä sitaise,	Or tie my hair in silken ribbons.
Huoli en haahen haljakoista,	I don't care for foreign fashions
Vehnän viploista valita,	Nor for wheat bread sliver-sliced;
Asun kaioissa sovissa,	I can go in plainer clothing
Kasvan leivän kannikoissa	And can live on heels and crusts
Tykönä hyvän isoni,	With my good and kindly father
Kanssa armahan emoni."	And my mild and tender mother."[15]

Bursting into tears she snatched her trinkets and pearls, all her rings, ribbons and adornments, and flung them onto the earth. And before Väinämöinen had time to recover, the girl had run away.

Reflecting upon this, falling into deep thought, Väinämöinen slowly returned home. He could not remove the vision of the young Aino from his eyes, and he could not erase all the nuances that had passed over her features. There was fright, beseeching, reproach, hate, and bitterness, and in it all there was still something else... The girl's emotions glittered brightly in his memory but there was something mysterious in the background, something he did not understand... He did not understand the girl's behavior at all. Did he in any way harm Aino, had he done something wrong? Was not Aino his own? Did not Joukahainen promise his sister to him as ransom for his life? Should not moderation and justice be obeyed here, as the fathers' holy traditions decree... But the girl's eyes, and her intense and erratic feelings! He had never before encountered that kind of sight. Why was the girl frightened, reproachful, and why did she hate him? Was she already...?

And Väinämöinen stopped dead in his tracks as if struck by a lightning bolt, so strange was the thought that entered his mind. What if the girl was no longer completely a member of his family and tribe, what if the soul's strings were already being cut! What if she was already a human being, thinking for herself, becoming independent!... But how could this be possible? No seer had taught the girl anything; consequently, where could she have learned to think? Were humans now beginning to be born free? Was a new age coming?... If this were so, then children were no longer the property of their parents, their family, or their tribe—they could be masters over themselves... Oh, if this were true, then he could understand Aino. Her human freedom had been hurt, and there was nothing to do but leave the girl alone...

The old man sighed deeply. Good-bye, my fantasy, good-bye, my fading dreams...

But as he thought of Aino's distress, pity welled up in his heart. Her brother had sold the poor girl to his own enemy, and she was not even consulted in the affair. What else could she do but be afraid of me and hate me?

With a tear in his eye, pity and sorrow in his heart, Väinämöinen sat down on a rock. Again he asked himself how this was all possible, how the girl could have been born with the soul of a seer. Human beings really had not changed. The new race did not yet exist in the world. Yes, it would truly come someday, but not for a long time...

Then his eyes opened and he saw beyond the veil of life and death. He saw a female child who went to school with a seer. The seer taught her to be an independently thinking and feeling human being, and she became attached to her teacher with the entire force of her young soul. But death suddenly came and swept the girl away just when her grateful heart was overflowing with the desire to reward her dear teacher. However, death could not stop the girl's heart. Her fantasy continued in Tuonela, dreaming and building castles in the air. And when the moment came, she reincarnated on the earth—and was born as Aino... And in the seer Väinämöinen saw himself.

Now the puzzle had been solved. Now it was clear that Aino was already a seer-soul when she was born, and so it was natural that such a fate as she experienced made her bitter. One was not allowed to treat such souls as average human beings; they already looked at things from a different viewpoint. Certainly, the girl hated him because she did not recognize who Väinämöinen was. She did not remember her own past. Now the information had to get to the girl and her parents soon, and Joukahainen must be released from his promise—for Aino's sake...

Väinämöinen thought he had made a good resolution, but he did not feel happy. There was still something mysterious about Aino that he did not understand...

This too became clear in time. But it became clear with a greater sorrow...

What strange things of the heart now unfold, what message has been brought? Joukahainen's young sister has drowned herself, Aino girl has sought solace from her peculiar sorrow in the seawaves!

At first, Väinämöinen did not believe his ears but when the ghastly truth fully dawned upon his consciousness he, the old steadfast seer, was close to perishing from grief:

Itki illat, itki aamut,	Wept at evening, wept at morning,
Yöhyet enemmän itki,	Nightly was his woe most grievous
Kun oli kaunis kaatununna,	For the fate of his own fair one,
Neitonen nukahtanunna,	For the maiden who was sleeping
Mennyt lietohon merehen,	Underneath the restless rollers,
Alle aaltoja syvien.	Down beneath the seawaves deep.[16]

And for my part in this, sighed Väinämöinen, oh for my mindless, stupid, indiscretions:

"Ohoh hullu hulhuuttani,	"Oh, a madman in my madness,
Vähämieli miehuuttani,	Dimwit with my vaunted manhood!
Olipa minulla mieltä,	Once I had some common sense,
Ajatusta annettuna,	Well-endowed with powers of thinking,
Syäntä suurta survottuna,	Gifted with a good heart also—
Oli ennen aikoinansa,	But that was once upon a time;
Vaanpa nyt tätä nykyä,	
Tällä inhalla iällä,	Now in evil days like these,
Puuttuvalla polveksella	In this miserable generation,
Kaikki on mieli melkeässä,	My mind is only mediocre
Ajatukset arvoisessa,	And my thoughts completely worthless,
Kaikki toimi toisialla!"	All my actions gone astray."[17]

Because now he understood Aino! Her death made it clear what was mysterious about the scene of her flight: Aino did recognize him, she knew who he was, and loved him.

"Kuta vuotin kuun ikäni,	"Thus the one I always wanted
Kuta puolen polveani	And awaited half a lifetime—

Ikuiseksi ystäväksi,	To become my friend forever
Polviseksi puolisoksi,	And to be my lifelong helpmate,
Se osasi onkeheni,	Found her way on to my angle
Vierähti venoseheni,	And she landed in my boat.
Minä en tuntenut piteä,	I had not the sense to keep her,
En kotihin korjaella,	Take her home upon my sleigh,
Laskin jälle lainehisin,	But I let her slip away,
	Slip away beneath a billow,
Alle aaltojen syvien!"	Underneath the seawaves deep."[18, 19]

So he could not keep his friend because he could not love himself. He did not understand the depth of love and now, through a death, this became clear to him. The child taught this to him. He, old and wise, did not understand the secret power of new love, the love that joins together two free, independent human souls. His own seer-vision had not gazed that far into the future. But when self-love finally appeared, it chose for its dwelling the young woman's heart; it unfolded within the child's pure mind and taught it something that was hidden from the wise. And now the child, by voluntarily dying, had also saved the wise one from continuing in ignorance! Oh, the miraculous workings of fate, the Creator's bottomless wisdom!

39

Marjatta

THERE EXISTS IN THE KALEVALA a rune that refers to a future time as clearly as the Aino legend. This rune is thought to have been born during the age of Christian influence and created by the Christian imagination. This is the Kalevala's final rune, the 50th, which tells of Marjatta and her son. Since the Marjatta episode also joins with the final scene in Väinämöinen's life history, describing how Väinämöinen withdraws to make way for the impending new age—and thus continuing the Aino story through these events—we will take a brief look.

Aino is born to an Atlantean family, into Atlantean conditions, but her soul belongs to the Aryan age and the Aryan race. She is already a thinking individual. But how fine and delicate are these new faculties within her! Her personal tendency is to retain a firm connection with her family; the love she has for her mother, father, brother and sister—her entire home—is quite moving. Her new-born Aryan individuality lives within her like a bird in a cage. It will awaken to highest consciousness only when it is deeply hurt. When she, a human being, is sold, her moral righteousness flares up and she comprehends her unhappy lot. But her awakening does not provoke her to positive action, only to passive opposition. The conflict reaches its apogee when she realizes that even Väinämöinen does not understand her. And when she simultaneously realizes her own soul's secret—her love for Väinämöinen—her fate turns tragic: "It would have been better had I not been born at all." Her entire being becomes determined that nobody will be allowed to know what

she, the poor girl, feels and thinks. This fixed idea finally takes her—
without her even really knowing it—to suicide. No one knew me, none
will grieve for me... In a sense, Aino is the apotheosis of virginity and
fruitlessness.

It is very different with Marjatta. Marjatta is truly Aino reincarnated.
The aspiring to independence and personal self-preservation, which in
Aino is groping and unsure, achieves full self-consciousness in Marjatta.
But Marjatta's fate will be different. She goes from infertile virginity to
fertile motherhood, but experiences much grief and distress in the
process!

Marjatta korea kuopus	Marjatta, the beautiful,
Se kauan kotona kasvoi	For a long time grew at home
Korkean ison kotona,	In her high-born father's house,
Emon tuttavan tuvilla...	In her loving mother's chambers.[20]

Thus the rune begins, and it tells us right away, somewhat derisively,
exactly how self-consciously proud Marjatta was of herself in her virgin
purity:

Marjatta korea kuopus,	Marjatta, the beautiful,
Tuo piika pikkarainen	She the little, dainty maiden,
Piti viikoista pyhyyttä,	Kept her virgin state untarnished
Ajan kaiken kainoutta;	And her beauty all unblemished.
Syöpi kaunista kaloa,	Always ate the nicest fish
Petäjätä pehmeätä,	And the softest pine bark bread;
Ei syönyt kanan munia,	Would not even taste of hen's eggs,
Kukerikun riehkatuita,	Hens that chanticleer had mounted;
Eipä lampahan lihoa,	Would not eat the flesh of ewes,
Ku oli ollut oinahilla.	Any ewe a ram had mounted.[21]

When her mother ordered her to milk the cows, she snobbishly
answered:

"Ei neiti minun näköinen	"No girl such as I would do it,
Koske sen lehmän nisähän,	Touch the teats of any cow,
Jok' on häilynyt härillä,	Any cow a bull had mounted—

| *Kun ei hiehoista herune,* | It can't be unless the calves |
| *Vasikkaisista valune."* | Or the heifers trickle milk."[22] |

When brother asked sister to sit down in a sleigh that was pulled by a mare, the proud beauty replied:

"En istu hevon rekehen,	"I won't hitch a horse,
Joka lie orilla ollut,	Any mare a stud has mounted—
Kun ei varsaset vetäne,	It can't be unless the foals
Kulettele kuutiaiset!"	Or the month-olds do the pulling."[23]

As a final result, "Marjatta, the youngest and most beautiful child, always living as a virgin," left to herd sheep. Now, if the rune wanted to mock the girl's virginity, it would have let the subsequent events unfold in a different manner. Instead, it emphasizes how Marjatta's imagination was truly innocent and pure. The rune first provides a little critique:

Marjatta korea kuopus	Marjatta, the beautiful,
Viikon viipyi paimenessa;	Stayed a shepherdess too long.
Paha on olla paimenessa;	It is hard to be a shepherdess,
Tyttölapsen liiatenki:	Overmuch for any girl-child.
Mato heinässä matavi,	Snakes are slithering in the grasses,
Sisiliskot siuottavi.	Lizards wriggling here and there.[24]

And then the rune begins to tell us a legend about Marjatta's miraculous red lingonberry, the berry that she ate and became pregnant by. We see how Marjatta, one summer day, fell into a deep sleep while lying on a little hill and had a beautiful dream in which "a berrykin on a hill, red whortleberry on a heath" yelled to her: "Come, maiden, pick me up!"

Marjatta korea kuopus	Marjatta, pretty youngest child,
Meni matkoa vähäisen,	Went a little distance,
Meni marjan katsantahan,	She went up to see the berry,
Punapuolan poimintahan,	Pick the reddish lingonberry,
Hyppysillähän hyyvillä,	Pluck it with her dainty fingers,
Kätösillä kaunihilla.	With her slender hands so lovely.

Keksi marjasen mäeltä,	She found the berry on the hill,
Punapuolan kankahalta;	Red lingonberry on the heath.
On marja näkemiänsä,	It's a berry in appearance,
Puola ilmoin luomiansa,	Lingonberry by the shape,
Ylähähkö maasta syöä,	On a tree too high for picking
Alahahko puuhun nousta.	Yet too low to climb up after.
Tempoi kartun kankahalta,	From the heath she snatched a stick,
Jolla marjan maahan sorti;	With it knocked the berry down.
Niinpä marja maasta nousi	Then the berry started climbing
Kaunoisille kautoloille,	Up onto her lovely shoe top,
Kaunoisilta kautoloilta	From her shoe top
Puhtahille polviloille,	to her knee,
Puhtahilta polviloilta	From her white knee
Heleville helmasille.	to her apron.
Nousi siitä vyö-rivoille,	Then it moved up to her waistband,
Vyö-rivoilta rinnoillensa,	From the waistband to her bosom,
Rinnoiltansa leuoillensa,	From her bosom to her chin,
Leuoiltansa huulillensa,	From her chin up to her lips.
Siitä suuhun suikahutti,	Then it slid into her mouth,
Keikahutti kielellensä,	Tumbled quickly to her tongue,
Kieleltänsä keruksisihin,	From her tongue into her throat,
Siitä vatsahan valahti.	From her throat into her stomach.[25]

And that was Marjatta's dream. But the dream had a very real consequence:

Marjatta korea kuopus,	After that she was contented,
Tuosta tyytyi, tuosta täytyi,	And she felt herself fulfilled.
Tuosta paksuksi panihe,	Then she put on weight,
Lihavaksi liittelihe.	grew stouter.[26]

Her dream of virgin purity had come to a bitter end. Soon, her mother began to suspect what was up, but hid her thoughts. When the day of distress finally arrived for Marjatta, she asked her mother to warm up the sauna for her, but her own mother heartlessly answered:

"Voi sinua hiien huora!	"Woe to you, you whore of Hiisi!
Kenen oot makaelema,	Tell me whose bed partner are you,

Ootko miehen naimattoman,	Married man
Eli nainehen urohon?"	or unmarried?"[27]

For Marjatta, the day of distress became a day of reckoning. All the mindless pride with which she had troubled her kin, now was thrown back at her as a cold, judgemental, and merciless humiliation. What did it help to try to explain to her mother that she had become pregnant by her own faith? Her father also called her a harlot and ordered her out to find a bear's stone dwelling to have her cubs in...

So indeed, she did go away, but she cried out while going, still proud in her despair:

"En minä portto ollekana,	"I'm no whore
Tulen lautta lienekänä,	fit for hellfire,
Olen miehen suuren saava,	I'm the bearer of the Great One,
Jalon synnyn synnyttävä,	Deliverer of the Sacred Birth,
Joll' on valta vallallenki,	Man-child who will rule the rulers,
Väki Väinämöisellenki."	Even rule old Väinämöinen."[28]

Poor Marjatta! A mother's holy feelings had awakened in her. Now the rune abandons any mocking tone and with the greatest sympathy and compassion tells of Marjatta's difficult destiny.

Not one human being would help her. Everyone fled from her. Alone and rejected, she went into the forest, "to the room, in the redwood forest, into the stable of Tapio's hill," and prayed for God to help her:

"Tule luoja turvakseni,	"Come, Creator, be my refuge,
Avukseni armollinen	Be my help, thou Merciful,
Näissä töissä työlähissä,	In these toils,
Ajoissa ani kovissa!..."	these times of sorrow..."[29]

And there she delivered her son, "on the hay, near a horse, in the manger of the long-mane."

Pesi pienen poikuensa,	Then she washed
Kääri kääreliinahansa;	and swaddled him,
Otti pojan polvillensa,	Took the man-child on her knees,
Laittoi lapsen helmahansa.	Held her son upon her lap.[30]

Oh, how she loved her little one, a child of sorrow and grief. Her virginal pride was forgotten, changed into a mother's pure humility:

Piiletteli poiuttansa,	But she hid him from the people,
Kasvatteli kaunoistansa,	Cared for him, her lovely one,
Kullaista omenuttansa,	Golden apple,
Hope'ista sauvoansa,	staff of silver.
Sylissänsä syöttelevi,	At her breast she suckled him,
Käsissänsä kääntelevi.	In caressing hands she held him.[31]

And when her son once got lost in a swamp, what distress and despair did she experience! Who could measure a mother's love, reflected in the bottomless abyss of worry? And who could draw lines around its joys? The child was found and brought home, but still there was one more worry:

Siitä meiän Marjatalle	He was growing up so handsome,
Kasvoi poika kaunokainen;	Beautiful son of Marjatta.
Ei tieä nimeä tuolle,	No one knew what name to give him,
Millä mainita nimellä,	Knew the proper name to call him.
Emo kutsui kukkaseksi,	Mother would call him Little Flower,
Vieras vennon joutioksi.	Others call him Good-for-nothing.[32]

Thus, the child had to be christened. Now Väinämöinen steps onto the stage.

40

Marjatta's Son
and Väinämöinen

U NDERSTOOD ALLEGORICALLY, the Marjatta legend quite dramatically describes the origin of the new race. The central events of the episode refer directly to it: A long period of intentional virginity, supernatural conception, social rejection, discrimination by the world, and difficult tribulations. When nature begins to create a new Root Race, it invigorates the inner souls of a few individuals of the old race with new dreams and longings, such that these individuals are set apart in their habits and understanding. Then its divine messengers and helpers arrive to impregnate the prepared souls with the ideals of the new human type. Ultimately, they are led to take up a separate place from the rest of humanity, where together they overcome their new troubles and obstacles and, through great sufferings and distress, all the while receiving divine aid, begin a new human race. This allegorical meaning of the Marjatta legend is confirmed in its final moment: The small child meets with Väinämöinen. Väinämöinen, symbol of the old race's magic and educational method, says farewell to the newborn race and its new magic and departs from the world, though promising at the same time to return whenever he may be needed again—after all, he is ancient, wise, and experienced and is really like the new race's father. And this allegorical meaning is not negated even if we believe that this rune was formally constructed during the period of Christian influence.

This symbolic spirit remains continuously in the background and must be kept in mind although we take the final event to also be the final chapter of Väinämöinen's personal life history. Väinämöinen truly was the seer and magician of the transitional age and after meeting Aino he understood that the old method of magical education would not apply to the human beings of the new age. But he considered Aino to be an exceptional being and he did not fully encounter the new race until fate brought him into connection with Marjatta...

Before a name could be given to Marjatta's son, the old man who was asked to christen the child* explained that the child should first be examined:

"En minä risti riivattua,	"I won't christen one possessed,
Katalata kastakana,	Will not baptize this poor wretch,
Kun ei ensin tutkittane,	Not until he's well-examined
Tutkittane, tuomittane."	And a judgement has been given."[33]

But what does it mean that he must be examined? Should the child be examined to determine if he was of divine birth and to see if he could handle the school of fate? Yes, and who else could do this deed but old Väinämöinen?

Kenpä tuohon tutkiaksi,	Who should be the one to judge him,
Tutkiaksi, tuomariksi?	To examine and to judge him?
Vaka vanha Väinämöinen,	Old reliable Väinämöinen,
Tietäjä iän-ikuinen,	Eternal knower,
Sepä tuohon tutkiaksi,	he was chosen
Tutkiaksi, tuomariksi.	To examine and to judge him.[34]

The old seer arrived, lost in deep thoughts. He arrived to give judgement over the child of the new age, but his steps were heavy and

---

*Allegorically understood, this old man, "Virokannas," is the new race's *Manu* or mental exemplar and leader. The name Virokannas means the same thing as the Indian *Vaivasvata* [Manu Vaivasvata]. Incredibly, there is a Sanskrit word which resembles Virokannas and etymologically means the same thing as Vaivasvata, though in the mythology it is a demon's name. Vaivasvata, you know, means "that which comes from the sun" and *vairoottshana* (derived from *virootsha*, the sun) means the same thing.

slow as if walking into a sacrificial grove, where the most precious treasure must be sacrificed, or like a judge who must give grave judgement upon himself, from his own mouth. In his passing, his thoughts descended from heaven seriously, watchfully, with their expansive wings just lightly touching the earth.

"Will you endure, you, son of Marjatta, whose father is unknown? Will you bear the vision of your father? Can you avoid the sweet charm in his eyes? Are you truly the descendant of Aino, of Marjatta, the new human race born on the earth, conscious of your deeds, free from the past—or will you, too, fall apart? Will you stagger, will you collapse, and will you pull your father down to doom? Have all your father's efforts been in vain? Is death the end of everything? Or will you be victorious, the divine hero? Has the new day truly dawned? Will you further the work of your father? Will you allow his wisdom to return after the alotted time, to make you happier?"

And Väinämöinen asks Marjatta: "How was this son born, where conceived, and from who?" And Marjatta told him.

Then Väinämöinen spoke solemnly and gloomily, his voice secretly broken with sorrow, and pronounced his sentence:

"Kun lie poika suolta saatu,	"Since the boy came from a fen,
Maalta marjasta siennyt,	Sired by a berry of the earth,
Poika maahan pantakohon,	Let him be put in the earth
Marhamättähän sivulle,	There beside the berry patch,
Tahi suolle vietäköhön,	Or then taken to the swamp,
Puulla päähän lyötäköhön!"	Hit on the head there with a club."[35]

The spectacle of the old seer was severely judgemental, gave a powerful impression, and it lingered in the eyes of the little child.

The moment became a deep silence, a silence of waiting, hopelessness, and increasing distress. Then the child opened his mouth, and the half-month old boy began to speak:

"Ohoh sinua ukko utra,	"O you miserable old man,
Ukko utra, unteloinen,	Miserable old man, you stupid,
Kun olet tuhmin tuominnunna,	What a muddle you have made
Väärin laskenna lakia!"	Of both judgement and the law..."[36]

Now even the seer's face brightened a little, then quickly became clouded with tears. But the severity disappeared.

The boy continued defiantly:

"Eipä syistä suuremmista,	"Not for greater crimes committed
Töistä tuhmemmistakana	Nor the stupidest wrongdoing
Itseäsi suolle viety,	Were you taken to a fen,
Eikä puulla päähän lyöty..."	Hit on the head there with a club..."[37]

Väinämöinen's face brightened more, and a supernatural joy flashed forth from it—while Marjatta's son continued speaking:

"Kun sa miesnä nuorempana	"When you yourself as a younger man
Lainasit emosi lapsen	Pledged the daughter of your mother
Oman pääsi päästimeksi	As a ransom for your own head
Itsesi lunastimeksi..."	Just to save yourself from danger..."[38]

At this point the spell was broken and his eyes smiled quietly as he recalled Ilmarinen's first journey to Pohjola.

But the boy continued without mercy:

"Ei sinua silloinkana,	"And again you were not punished,
Eip' on vielä suolle viety,	Were not taken to a fen
Kun sa miesnä nuorempana	When you as a younger man
Menettelit neiet nuoret	Drove those gentle girls distracted
Alle aaltojen syvien,	To their deaths beneath the waves
Päälle mustien mutien."	On the black ooze of the bottom."[39]

Then the last suspicion, the final uncertainty, disappeared from Väinämöinen's mind. A tear rolled down his wrinkled cheek and a burden fell from his shoulders. "Yes, my son, you are victorious," his heart whispered with joy, "and I am now free, free to leave without concerns, free to return joyfully. Thank and honor the Creator."

Ja ukko Virokannas	So the old man
...risti ripsahutti,	...baptized him,
Kasti lapsen kapsahutti	Gladly christened this good child,

Karjalan kuninkahaksi,	King and lord of all Karelia,
Kaiken vallan vartiaksi.	As the guardian over all.[40]

And Väinämöinen, with peace and joy in his heart, turned around solemnly and stepped away. It appeared to the others that he was embarrassed and might become angry. But he walked to the beach and sang one last time, chanting for himself a copper boat. He sat down at the stern and sailed out into the clear open sea. And as he sailed in his boat, "to the upper worldly regions, through the lower realms of heaven," he uttered the following spell:

"Annapas ajan kulua,	"Let the rope of time run out—
Päivän mennä toisen tulla,	One day go, another come—
Taas minua tarvitahan,	And again I will be needed.
Katsotahan, kaivatahan	They'll be waiting, yearning for me
Uuen sammon saattajaksi,	To bring back another Sampo,
Uuen soiton suorijaksi,	To invent another harp,
Uuen kuun kulettajaksi,	Set a new moon in the sky,
Uuen päivän päästäjäksi,	Free a new sun in the heavens
Kun ei kuuta, aurinkoa,	When there is no moon, no sun
Eikä ilmaista iloa."	And no gladness on the earth.[41]*

---

*In the national songs, Marjatta's son is Kullervo rather than Christ. Kullervo's life story represents the various phases of the life of the soul of the Aryan race, though we do not explore this in the present work.

PART V

Väinämöinen's Return

The National-Occult Key

41

Väinämöinen and the Nation of Finland

O F ALL THE KALEVALA'S HEROES, Väinämöinen is the first and most superior, the one closest to the heart of the rune-singer. Everyone loves and admires him, and feels that he evokes the deepest aspirations within the spirit of the nation of Finland. Personified in him one finds our family's love of knowledge and wisdom, song and poetry, and our faith in the power of words and music. Väinämöinen's indomitable firmness, steadiness in all decisions, his invincible moderation and calmness, represent in the Finn's eyes the ideal character.

This is no miracle because within Väinämöinen's personality is hidden the secret which, in a somewhat peculiar manner, makes him the father, the prototype, of our whole nation. The keys of interpretation we have used up until now have either generalized his personality or drew it into view as very human. In other words, we have seen him as a god or a human being but not first and foremost as a Finn. The key that we now intend to use leaves Väinämöinen half-way between heaven and earth but makes him that full-blooded Finn that every child of the Finnish nation feels close to.

This key is the occult-national key. Above all it means that the spirit and soul of Finland—our so-called national spirit—is symbolized by Väinämöinen. Our nation's deepest intention, deepest faith, and deepest love is personified by him. But it also means something else. It means that Väinämöinen, as a divine "pagan," is not dead but lives on, that as a

247

representative of Finland's national spirit he is not just a poetic image, but a living personal reality.

How should this be understood? Since here we touch upon secret aspects of the invisible world, we must offer an explanation.

National differences, those both external and internal, include language, geography, natural conditions, climate, and other knowable factors. Every nation forms a unified entity which in the invisible world takes the form of its overarching mental ambiance or *aura*. Specific and distinctive inner features are contained in a nation's aura, such as temperment, modes of thought, the capacity to feel, mental endeavors, artistic predispositions and so on, which together make up what we may call a nation's personal soul.

But a spiritual secret is hidden behind this collective national soul. In the same way that the human being has a higher I whose temporary expression is the personality, so also a nation has a collective spiritual entity holding things together like an autonomous, thinking being, and we can call this the national genius. This is an independent being who does not belong to the human developmental system, but to another order, the so-called angelic hierarchies, which in Sanskrit are called *devas*. He is a comparatively high being in his own system and has acquired—perhaps only to further his own development—the life long duty of caring for a nation's destiny and leading its spiritual growth. His chosen nation is precious and close to his heart, and there exists in its character something which corresponds to his own nature. And becoming the leader of a nation, moreover, its servant, is a difficult task requiring great responsibility. In a sense, the nation's aura becomes like his external body or dwelling place, and he absorbs the nation's soul-life into his own. Thus begins a continuous interplay between the nation's personal soul and the guardian angel's own consciousness. The angel tries to nurture the nation's soul and dispense throughout its aura his own sublime inspirations and feelings. He cannot immediately affect the entire incarnated population of the nation; only the individuals who, filled with love for their native country, hear his voice, will go forth to express his words and willpower through heroic deeds, literature, and the arts. Of course the guardian angel is not alone, but is surrounded by a mighty group of assistants—angels and genii in the lower levels. However, underlying the deepest spiritual love for the native country is this grandiose, loving, and divine being who awakens and responds to love within individuals. Is it surprising that some nations worship him as their only god?*

Since Väinämöinen represents Finland's national genius, this also means that he personifies the soul-life of Finland, and that Väinämöinen—the Väinämöinen of the runes and the old religion of the Kalevala—is the guardian angel given to the Finnish nation.

At what moment Väinämöinen joined his own fate with that of Finland, we cannot exactly say. It happened in an era beyond recorded history, in a Kalevalan epoch when the culture of our ancestors flourished. We examined the stories found in the Kalevala's runes regarding the phases of Väinämöinen's life, looking for references to the life-cycle and fate of our guardian angel. Long ago, Finland's family was large and powerful. It encompassed the ancestors of the modern Finns, as well as the ancestors of the Lapps and other tribes of the Finnish family. It reigned over a large part of Europe and it ruled more through the power of wisdom than by violence. Its civilization was by nature more mental than material in quality. Its people practiced agriculture, hunting, fishing, trade, pursued a variety of livelihoods, but they were also, at the same time, a sensitive, religious, and musical people. For them life would have no value without song and poetry, without a deeper knowledge of nature and the seer's skills. Their seers were initiated into a high and mysterious wisdom and were famous for their mighty faculty of incantation. It was the Kalevala's culture, and those were the ages of Väinämöinen.

Then changes took place and upheavals occurred. Other nations appeared on the stage of history.** Väinämöinen drew aside; his realm

---

*I explored the relationship between nations and their devas in greater detail in *Suomen kansallishaltija* (*Finland's National Genius*), Helsinki 1913, Teosofinen kirjakauppa ja Kustannusliike.

**In keeping with this idea there is the fact that the Germans arrived in Europe after our Finnish ancestors, and the Germanic poems, the *Eddas* (which are in many ways similar to the Kalevala), can just as easily be understood to have borrowed aspects of its mythology from Finland rather than the other way around. Compare this with what Yrjö Koskinen says: "When we find things in European languages reminding us of Finnish, elements which cannot be satisfactorily explained by geographical relationships between historical groups, this, in my mind, is the strongest proof that the ancient population of Europe, which was already retreating into the north before history even began, was of the Finnish family." *Tiedot Suomen-suvun muinaisuudesta* (*Knowledge Concerning the Antiquity of the Finnish Family*), pp. 25-26.

dissolved. But his people, in groups, and over long periods of time, moved to the north and into the peninsula of Finland. People came to the areas of Häme, Karelia, Kainuu, Pirkkala, and Perm, and are known by those names today. The ancient times were preserved in their memories; during the long winters they made poetry and sang about those ancient times. And miracle of miracles, they strongly believed that the ancient glory would someday return. The memory of Väinämöinen's promise to return became a tradition. Later, after Christianity arrived in Finland and the people were taught to reject their ancient gods, Väinämöinen's withdrawal was connected in the runes to the Christian invasion, but the prophecy was not forgotten. Up until our own times the prophecy echoed upon people's lips, the farewell words of the ancient Väinämöinen, the eternal sage:

"Annapas ajan kulua,	"Let the rope of time run out—
Päivän mennä toisen tulla,	One day go, another come—
Taas minua tarvitahan,	And again I will be needed.
Katsotahan, kaivatahan	They'll be waiting, yearning for me
Uuen sammon saattajaksi,	To bring back another Sampo,
Uuen soiton suorijaksi,	To invent another harp,
Uuen kuun kulettajaksi,	Set a new moon in the sky,
Uuen päivän päästäjäksi,	Free a new sun in the heavens
Kun ei kuuta, aurinkoa,	When there is no moon, no sun
Eikä ilmaista iloa."	And no gladness on the earth.[1]

How should we understand Väinämöinen's promise? Does it have true meaning? Does it contain a higher reality? Is it a real tradition or was it just created in the imaginations of rune-singers?

We already argued that it is not from that critical period of pagan and Christian transition, but is from a much older age. It refers to the beginning of the Kullervo period,* and we are convinced that it is a true promise, given by our national genius Väinämöinen through a human Väinämöinen inspired by him.

And so we can ask: If it is true that our national genius did not

---

*We do not discuss Kullervo in this book. Editor's note: The life of Kullervo, as mentioned in Chapter 40, represents the life of the Aryan Root Race.

completely withdraw forever, what guarantee do we have that he will return, and when might that take place?

Our answer is that things will not happen quite the way they did in the past. When Väinämöinen previously led the Finnish tribes he was in a sense the organizer of the group-soul; his realm was gathered together from different elements or, better said, from different possibilities within different groups. Since then, Europe has changed a great deal. When he returns, Väinämöinen must choose a special tribe of the Finnish family. He must have an elite nation, a "chosen nation." Where will he find this, and when will Väinämöinen return?

Väinämöinen has already returned and he has already chosen his nation. The nation is the nation of Finland and Väinämöinen's return took place after the Middle Ages came to a close and a new age dawned in Europe as a whole. In the words of the Kalevala we can trace how our national genius and guardian angel has gradually joined with our modern national spirit.

"And again I will be needed." Yes, he will be needed when the new age dawns and the nations of Europe move into a freer and more civilized future. This happened, as we said, at the end of the Middle Ages and the affect of Väinämöinen is evident in Mikael Agricola's work and in other places.

"They'll be waiting, yearning for me." And this happened when our nation's selfhood awoke and began to feel its own unique stature, at the same time wishing for freer political circumstances and living conditions. The first stirrings of this aspiration occurred a few hundred years ago and consequently we saw the inner (and outer) separation of Finland from Sweden and its joining with the realm of Russia, a monumental advance for the nation of Finland.

"To bring back another Sampo." This occurred when the nation of Finland was spiritually prepared enough to retrieve the memories of the ancient Finnish culture. And this took place in the last century when Elias Lönnrot, above all others, was chosen as Väinämöinen's tool. As a result, his Kalevala and all the other runes, spells, and proverbs which have been gathered together comprise the new Sampo,* given to us by Väinämöinen.

---

*Compare this with the definition of the Sampo in Chapter 37, "At the Change of Ages."

"To invent another harp." After we receive the new Sampo (the Kalevala) and the ancient memories are awakened within our national soul, we begin an independent cultural project in the sciences, arts, religion, philosophy, and so on. This began to occur in the last century too, after the Kalevala's publication, and since then Finland has truly made many original contributions in many cultural areas. The great civilized countries already hold Finnish music, literature, architecture, and other Finnish achievements in high regard. Väinämöinen was not deceitful; his words have come true.

"To set a new moon in the sky, free a new sun in the heavens, when there is no moon, no sun, and no gladness on the earth." This takes place when our nation, formed by hard won experiences, suffers pain and distress along with the rest of the world. Modern Europe really is suffering the birth-pains of a tremendous labor, and it is generally believed that a new and better era will dawn after we have passed through a modern purgatory. In this aspect, Väinämöinen's promise has not yet come true, but we trust that he was not wrong even in this. For Finland the day will come, the day of brotherhood among all nations, when every nation is allowed without contest to manifest its holiest, innermost being. Then our nation will have the opportunity and a duty to obey the call of its own genius and create an independent, genuine Finnish civilization in all aspects of life.*

Now the reader must not shout out: "Is the ancient Väinämöinen really our guardian angel? Has he returned, and will he step to the side of Christ!?" Väinämöinen is not "pagan" or "Christian" any more than Christ is. Väinämöinen, as the essence of our national genius, is a living though secret reality, and if by Christ we mean the Logos, then Väinämöinen is naturally his servant. If, however, by Christ we mean the great initiated seer who in the person of Jesus wandered over the earth a few thousand years ago, then he (Christ) is a being of a different type altogether compared to Väinämöinen, who we understand to be our national genius and not a member of humanity at all. As such, the work of Christ is by no means in conflict with the influence of Väinämöinen, expressing itself as it does in the independent development of the Finnish nation. In the reality of life, in the development of nations and individu-

---

*Compare this with the ideas in *Finland's National Genius*.

als, it is not a question of one or another type of "faith." All religions and worldviews are brothers, branches and leaves of the same tree of wisdom and life; it is merely a question of looking at the different types of individuals and the different activities of each nation.

But if a nation wants to create a spirited civilization with happy citizens, it is unavoidable that a deep connection with the secret world of wisdom must be maintained. As long as the ancient nations performed their mysteries of communion in the holy Sampo Temple of the Secret Brotherhood of wisdom, then their civilization continued to bear fruit. But when the connection broke, the different nations were forced to go their own misguided ways and culture degenerated. In the Christian age the church takes the place of the ancient mysteries, its function being part church, part university. Initially the church maintained its inner relationship with Jesus and the secret world in general, but over the centuries the connection loosened, until today very few Christians are the personal disciples of Jesus,* and even those are not from the church's inner circle. Whether it happens within the church or outside of it, the ancient mysteries must be revived from their deathly state and restored to their previous condition of union with Jesus and the Secret Brotherhood if modern Christianity wants to continue developing with spirit.

And this renaissance of the ancient mysteries can only take place when each nation finds its higher self. The past century prepared Christianity for this, and we Finns know it from our own history. For each nation, discovering its higher self means that out of the oblivion of night everything from its ancient past that was spirited, noble, and beautiful will be raised into the daylight. And mere recollecting is not enough here; the ancient spirit must be renewed and invigorated, reborn into national consciousness. Therefore Väinämöinen's return to the nation of Finland means the revivification of ancient memories, the forging of the new Sampo, and so on. Now the duty of the nation of Finland is to re-enliven the spirit and wisdom of Väinämöinen and fuse it with the consciousness that modern Christendom has already nurtured and educated. And the twentieth century will witness to what extent Finland—and the other nations as well—accomplish this grand work. We have Väinämöinen's

*This matter is discussed more deeply in my book *The Esoteric School of Jesus*.

promise that he, our dear national genius, will do for his part what duty requires, that we can be sure of...

Suuni jo sulkea pitäisi,	Now I ought to shut my mouth
Kiinni kieleni sitoa,	And tie up my tongue tightly,
Laata virren laulannasta,	Stop the singing of the song
Herätä heläjännästä:	And the echoing of my voice.
"Eipä koski vuolaskana	"Not even the swiftest rapids
Laske vettänsä loputen,	Ever runs out all its water,
Eikä laulaja hyväinen	Nor does any expert singer
Laula tyyni taitoansa;	Ever pour out all his wisdom.
Mieli on jäämähän parempi	To hold back a song is better
Kuin on kesken katkemahan."	Than to cut it short halfway."
Niin luonen, lopettanenki,	
Herennenki, heittänenki...	
Elkätte hyvät imeiset	Do not think it odd, good people,
Tuota ouoksi otelko,	
Jos ma lapsi liioin lauloin,	That a child should sing too much,
Pieni pilpatin pahasti!	Such a little one pipe badly.
En ole opissa ollut,	I have never been instructed
Käynyt mailla mahtimiesten,	Nor have learned in wizard lands,
Saanut ulkoa sanoja,	Borrowed charm-words from outsiders
Loitompata lausehia...	Nor my spells from far-off places...
Vaan kuitenki kaiketenki	But however that may be,
Laun hiihin laulajoille,	I have skied a trail for singers,
Laun hiihin, latvan taitoin,	Skied the trail, snapped the brush tips,
Oksat karsin, tien osoitin;	Broke the branches, showed the way.
Siitäpä nyt tie menevi	That way now will run the future,
Ura uusi urkenevi	On the new course, cleared and ready
Laajemmille laulajoille,	For new poets of greater power,
Runsahammille runoille	Singing songs of mightier magic
Nuorisossa nousevassa,	For the rising younger people,
Kansassa kasuavassa.	For the new and growing nation.[2]

Notes

Foreword

1. Friberg (1988) Runo 17:507-510.

I. The Kalevala as a Holy Book

1. Blavatsky, H. P. 1888. *The Secret Doctrine.* Book 1, p. 305.
2. *Suomalaisia kirjailijoita (Finnish Authors)*, Helsinki 1909, Otava p. 24.
3. Kaarle Krohn, *Suomalaisten runojen uskonto (The Religion of Finnish Runes)*. Helsinki 1915. Suom. Kirj. seura, p. 360.
4. Translator's note. The term *archetypes* was used to translate *mieli- ja ajatus-kuvat* (mind- and thought-images; Ervast 1916:28). The term was known when Swiss psychologist Carl Jung adopted it for use in his psychology of the collective unconscious. Ervast was probably unaware of Jung's work when he wrote *The Key to the Kalevala* in 1916. Afterward he did read appreciatively both Freud and Jung, saying that they had opened a little door to the secret world; their work was the beginning for modern psychology's understanding of human psychology, human mysteries. In general, many concepts related to the unconscious had been formulated by the late 1800s. It was topical to converse about the unconscious during the first half of the 1800s. Eduard v. Hartman's (1842-1906) book *Philosophie des Unbewusstes (The Philosophy of the Unconscious)*, published in 1869, provided a stimulus for the unconscious to be more commonly understood. Dostoyevsky's *The Idiot* (1868) shows a deep understanding of the human psyche. In Ervast's use of the term "mind- and thought-images" he anticipated the importance of the archetype concept, although he did not explicitly use the term. For the purposes of this translation, "archetype" can be considered a synonym for "mind- and thought-images."

5. Friberg (1988) Runo 3:1-14. Editor's note. In Eino Friberg's beautiful translation of the Kalevala, line numbers in the original Finnish Kalevala are given to the left of the verse, while sequential numbering is given on the right. There is frequently a difference between the two because Friberg often collapsed two lines from the original Kalevala into one line in his translation. The line numbers given in these end notes refer to the sequential numbering of Friberg's translation. The citation style is self-explanatory; e.g., Runo 3:1-14 refers to Runo 3, lines 1 through 14. The line numbers given in Ervast's text refer to the original Kalevala line numbering.

6. Translator's note. The question arose whether this phrase—*osviittoja tiedon tien suhteen* (Ervast, p. 33)—should be translated as "way-to-knowledge" or "wisdom path." In modern literary Finnish this phrase would be *viitteitä tiedon tien suhteen* which, rendered into English, is: "suggestions (hints) regarding the way-to-knowledge." *Tiedon tie* means "the way-to-knowledge" (or the way of knowledge). *Tieto* = knowledge, *tiedon* = knowledge's (possessive knowledge or "...of knowledge"). *Tie* = way, road. In comparison, "wisdom path" is *viisauden polku*; wisdom = *viisaus*, and path = *polku*. Thus, it is more appropriate to use the term "way-to-knowledge" rather than the less accurate gloss "wisdom path." Page references to Ervast's *Kalevalan Avain* are to the 1992 edition by Kristosofinen Kirjallisuusseura ry. (Tampere, Finland).

7. Translator's note. Pekka Ervast had a thorough understanding of Blavatsky's work. He was one of two translators of Blavatsky's *The Secret Doctrine* into Finnish.

8. "Suomen kansalliseepos" ("Finland's National Epic"). In *Tietäjä*, 1909, p. 79. [This is a journal that H. P. Blavatsky apparently contributed to.]'

II. The Mysterious Knowledge of the Kalevala

1. Kaarle Krohn. *Suomensuvun uskonnot* (*The Religion of the Finnish Family*). 1915 [2nd part to *The Religion of Finnish Runes*], p. iv.

2. Editor's note. This kind of developmental model as applied to social systems is known as Social Darwinism. It is currently considered regressive by some social commentators to the extent that it is used to justify transnational corporate feudalism. Apparently, Ervast also considered this model, as applied to the development of religions, to have dubious value.

3. Allan Menzies. *Maailman uskonnot* (*World Religions*), p. 5.

4. Editor's note. The *Proto-Kalevala* was published in 1835. The final 50-Runo version of the Kalevala was published in 1849. Kalevala Day is celebrated on February 28th.

5. Editor's note. This phrase was a common Theosophical way of expressing a spiritual hierarchy of intentional forces or beings.

6. Editor's note. "Name and idea" here refers to literal vs. symbolic or denotation vs. connotation.

7. That people today still retain a sense of Väinämöinen's divine nature and quasi-symbolic meaning is observed in the following excerpt from the journal *Kotiseutu* (March, 1909): "I received a striking definition of Väinämöinen last winter, totally coincidentally, in connection with other business in Niemelä, Juntusranta village in Suomussalmi. An old man, a crofter named Jaakko Heikkinen, said it—he was already 83 years old, was born in the region, and knew a number of old stories and some ancient knowledge. This is what he said: 'Väinämöinen does not have bones and muscles like us, but when wizards and rune-singers take power from the earth and water and the moon and sun and from everything, what gathers together is Väinämöinen.'"

8. Julius Krohn, *Suomen suvun pakanallinen jumalanpalvelus* (*The Divine Pagan Service of the Finnish Family*), Helsinki 1894, p. 80.

9. Editor's note. See Lönnrot's foreword to *The Old Kalevala*, p. XI.

10. John 1:1-3. Editor's note. In this passage, following Ervast's intention, "the Logos" was substituted for "the Word," "He," and "Him." All Bible quotes are from *The American Standard Bible, The Open Bible Edition*, Thomas Nelson Publishers, 1977.

11. Modern psychology denies *will* because its empirical-inductive stance is by nature predisposed to materialism and therefore is, from a philosophical viewpoint, deterministic. In this view, will doesn't exist because freedom doesn't exist. Expressions of a so-called "human will" are not expressions of a free will, rather, they are thought to be unavoidable results from pre-existing states, thoughts, or emotions. Will, at bottom, is just emotion or thought; "will" in itself is thus non-existent. This is modern determinism but one can immediately point out that some states of consciousness do not cause any reaction; a harmoniously pure and stable consciousness does not breed effects, and being in bliss is a thing onto itself. The modern world of conflict is the *conditio sine qua non* of determinism, and as such only gives an idea of mental life to a certain level of development. Thus, determinism does not reach deep enough nor rise high enough; no being with free will has yet come into its sphere of theorizing. The spiritualistic viewpoint is grounded in the knowledge that free being is possible.

12. Editor's note. These three human functions may be compared with Dios-Eros-Logos, for the following reason. "The Son" is "the loving *Eros* principle" and "discriminating reason" is equivalent to the *Logos* principle. These two are in essential respects antithetical. The willing function of "God the Father" may be called *Dios*; willpower emerges from a union of our emotional and intellectual aspects or, deity is the transcendent will emerging from said union. Ervast refers to the whole tripartite scheme as the Logos Trinity, an identification which derives from the first "Word" or "Logos" in the Bible, ultimately having three aspects.

13. R. Engleberg, *Kalevalan sisällys ja rakenne* (*The Content and Structure of the Kalevala*); Helsinki 1914, p. 106.

14. Friberg (1988) Runo 1:123-132.
15. Kaarle Krohn, *Kalevalan runojen historia* (*The History of the Kalevala's Runes*), Helsinki 1903, p. 357.
16. Friberg (1988) Runo 1:101-103.
17. Kaarle Krohn. *Kalevalan runojen historia* (*The History of the Kalevala's Runes*), Helsinki 1903, p. 357.
18. Friberg (1988) Runo 1:109-112.
19. Friberg (1988) Runo 1:113-118.
20. Friberg (1988) Runo 1:119-122.
21. Friberg (1988) Runo 1:139-147.
22. Friberg (1988) Runo 1:159-160.
23. Friberg (1988) Runo 1:176-179.
24. Friberg (1988) Runo 1:194-197.
25. Friberg (1988) Runo 1:206-209.
26. Friberg (1988) Runo 1:255-256; 259-264.
27. Friberg (1988) Runo 2:7-8.
28. Friberg (1988) Runo 2:16-19.
29. Julius Krohn, *Suomalaisen kirjallisuuden historia* (*The History of Finnish Literature*), I, pgs. 290-291.
30. Friberg (1988) Runo 2:216-219.
31. Friberg (1988) Runo 1:277-284.
32. Friberg (1988) Runo 1:305-310. Editor's note: This was Friberg's favorite quote; see the National Public Radio program produced by Alex van Oss (1994).
33. Friberg (1988) Runo 1:315-320.
34. From the Old Kalevala. See F. P. Magoun (1969).
35. Kaarle Krohn. *Kalevalan runojen historia* (*The History of the Kalevala's Runes*), Helsinki 1903, p. 507.
36. Friberg (1988) Runo 11:11-14.
37. Friberg (1988) Runo 11:17-20.
38. Friberg (1988) Runo 14:414-419.
39. Friberg (1988) Runo 15:571-574.
40. Friberg (1988) Runo 12:477-486.
41. Editor's note. Martti Haavio (1967) argued for the likely source of the rune of Lemminkäinen's death and resurrection. According to Haavio, the historical connection is to the story of Osiris and his resurrection, arguably the source of mythological ideas found in Christ's resurrection.
42. Compare this with the cynical or "realistic" perspective of Aunus: "Lemminkäinen was born out of wedlock. The same has been said about Jesus."
43. Kaarle Krohn. *Kalevalan runojen historia* (*The History of the Kalevala's Runes*), Helsinki 1903, pgs. 581-582.
44. F. P. Magoun, Jr. 1969. *The Old Kalevala and Certain Antecedents*, Harvard University Press, Runo 26:36-41.

45. K. Krohn. *Kalevalan runojen historia* (*The History of the Kalevala's Runes*), Helsinki 1903, p. 344.

46. Goethe. 1808. *Faust: A Tragedy*, Bayard Taylor translation (1964:36) part 1, scene II.

47. Editor's note. The use of "self" here is similar to Carl Jung's later use of the term Self. A definition of this term: the totality and center of the psyche which continuously exerts an urge toward wholeness.

48. Friberg (1988) Runo 47:76-80.

49. Friberg (1988) Runo 47:87-94.

50. Friberg (1988) Runo 48:131-132.

51. Friberg (1988) Runo 48:189-192.

52. Friberg (1988) Runo 9:27-30.

53. Friberg (1988) Runo 9:64-67.

54. Friberg (1988) Runo 9:104-109.

55. Passage from the Old (Proto-) Kalevala. See F. P. Magoun (1969). Translator's note. The verse translated "when he previously forged the sky" mistakenly uses the pronoun "he"; the forger may, in fact, be Luoja.

56. Friberg (1988) Runo 9:136-139.

57. Friberg (1988) Runo 9:141-149.

58. Friberg (1988) Runo 9:169-173.

59. Friberg (1988) Runo 9:198-203.

60. Friberg (1988) Runo 9:234-241.

61. Friberg (1988) Runo 9:256-262.

62. Krohn, J. *Kalevalan runojen historia* (*The History of the Kalevala's Runes*), p. 178. One could add to this the fact that the Indian *Bhavishja Purana* tells of an ancient sun temple, built by *Saamba*.

63. Translator's note. In Friberg's translation, the phrase "many ciphered cover" is sometimes used, derived from the Finnish term *kirjokansi*. The more accurate translation of this term is "multi- (or many) colored cover." The distinction is important for understanding Ervast's teaching about the Sampo (see Chapters 31-33). In modern Finnish, *kirjo* means spectrum, as in a spectrum of colors or a spectrum of viewpoints. In Theosophical thinking, the fully developed spiritual body is multi-colored. Though we will preserve Friberg's poetically-motivated use of "many ciphered cover," the reader should bear these considerations in mind. Editor's note: Elsewhere, Friberg translates *kirjokansi* as "many-colored cover" (e.g., Friberg (1988) Runo 38:271; 39:13).

64. Friberg (1988) Runo 10:250-257.

65. Friberg (1988) Runo 10:393-406.

66. Friberg (1988) Runo 14:444-447.

67. Friberg (1988) Runo 50:441-450.

68. Matti Varonen. *Vainajainpalvelus muinaisilla suomalaisilla* (*The Worship of the Deceased Among the Ancient Finns*). Helsinki 1895, p. 16.

69. Kaarle Krohn. *Suomalaisten runojen uskonto* (*The Religion of Finnish Runes*), p. 59.

70. One can read [in English] more deeply on this topic in Theosophical literature, some of which we will mention here: C. W. Leadbeater's *Life After Death*, Annie Besant's *The Wisdom of the Ages*, and H. P. Blavatsky's *The Key to Theosophy*.
71. Friberg (1988) Runo 16:390-401.
72. Friberg (1988) Runo 17:11-14.
73. Friberg (1988) Runo 17:100-104; 140-147.
74. Friberg (1988) Runo 17:511-523.
75. Friberg (1988) Runo 16:174-179.
76. Friberg (1988) Runo 16:186-192; 203-206; 216-219; 229-232.
77. Friberg (1988) Runo 16:264-267.
78. Kaarle Krohn. *Suomalaisten runojen uskonto* (*The Religion of Finnish Runes*), p. 12.
79. F. A. Hästesko. *Mielikuvitus ja todellisuus Kalevalassa* (*Imagination and Reality in the Kalevala*), p. 9.
80. Rafael Engelberg. *Kalevalan sisällys ja rakenne* (*The Contents and Structure of the Kalevala*), p. 247.
81. Friberg (1988) Runo 41:89-90.
82. Friberg (1988) Runo 41:29-35; 68-73; 113-118.
83. Friberg (1988) Runo 44:242-243.
84. Friberg (1988) Runo 44:296-307.
85. Friberg (1988) Runo 7:276-279.
86. Friberg (1988) Runo 44:238-241.
87. Friberg (1988) Runo 44:289-295.
88. Friberg (1988) Runo 41:55-67; 91-112; 129-133; 150-153; 156-157; 160-163.

III. The Kalevala's Inner Ethic

1. Rafael Engelberg. *Kalevalan sisällys ja rakenne* (*The Contents and Structure of the Kalevala*).
2. Friberg (1988) Runo 3:20-33.
3. Friberg (1988) Runo 3:112-121.
4. Friberg (1988) Runo 3:272-274.
5. Friberg (1988) Runo 3:322-325.
6. Friberg (1988) Runo 3:316-321.
7. Friberg (1988) Runo 3:331-336.
8. Friberg (1988) Runo 3:433-434; 440-443.
9. Friberg (1988) Runo 3:448-451.
10. Friberg (1988) Runo 3:466-468.
11. Friberg (1988) Runo 3:515-520.
12. Friberg (1988) Runo 4:15-20.
13. Friberg (1988) Runo 4:22-38
14. Friberg (1988) Runo 4:119-136.
15. Friberg (1988) Runo 4:191-208; 217-224.

16. Friberg (1988) Runo 11:306-311.
17. Friberg (1988) Runo 12:97-100.
18. Friberg (1988) Runo 12:105-112.
19. Friberg (1988) Runo 12:358-359.
20. Friberg (1988) Runo 12:374-378.
21. Friberg (1988) Runo 10:78-87.
22. Friberg (1988) Runo 10:92-95.
23. Friberg (1988) Runo 10:97-107.
24. Friberg (1988) Runo 10:109-114.
25. Friberg (1988) Runo 19:21-30.
26. Friberg (1988) Runo 19:51-56.
27. Friberg (1988) Runo 19:101-106.
28. Friberg (1988) Runo 19:117-124.
29. Friberg (1988) Runo 14:366-371.
30. Friberg (1988) Runo 19:150-157.
31. Editor's note. For an idea of what Ervast means here, see his book *H.P.B.: Four Episodes from the Life of the Sphinx of the XIXth Century*, translated into English and published in 1933 by the London Theosophical Publishing House. A copy is held at the Theosophical Library in Wheaton, Illinois.
32. Friberg (1988) Runo 19:170-177.
33. Friberg (1988) Runo 20:545-562.
34. Friberg (1988) Runo 21:355-362.
35. Friberg (1988) Runo 21:365-382; 394-398; 404-407.
36. Friberg (1988) Runo 37:1-11.
37. Friberg (1988) Runo 37:34-43.
38. Friberg (1988) Runo 37:44-59.
39. Friberg (1988) Runo 37:140-152.
40. Friberg (1988) Runo 37:174-187.
41. Friberg (1988) Runo 37:190-197.
42. Friberg (1988) Runo 37:209-211; 216-219.
43. Friberg (1988) Runo 37:234-235.
44. Friberg (1988) Runo 38:1-10.
45. Friberg (1988) Runo 38:77-85.
46. Friberg (1988) Runo 38:87-88; 93-99.
47. Friberg (1988) Runo 38:103-112.
48. Friberg (1988) Runo 38:226-227.
49. Friberg (1988) Runo 38:283-287.
50. Friberg (1988) Runo 38:263-267.
51. Friberg (1988) Runo 38:269-281.
52. Friberg (1988) Runo 39:3-6.
53. Friberg (1988) Runo 39:8-20.
54. Friberg (1988) Runo 39:51-54.
55. Friberg (1988) Runo 39:85-88.
56. Friberg (1988) Runo 39:96-103.

57. Friberg (1988) Runo 39:104-108.
58. First Corinthians 15:53-55.
59. First Corinthians 15:40-44.
60. First Corinthians 15:46-49.
61. First Corinthians 15:51.
62. Friberg (1988) Runo 39:176-177; 182-185.
63. Friberg (1988) Runo 39:199-204.
64. Friberg (1988) Runo 39:247-251.
65. Friberg (1988) Runo 39:263-277.
66. Friberg (1988) Runo 39:286-289.
67. Friberg (1988) Runo 39:300-303.
68. Friberg (1988) Runo 40:5-12.
69. Friberg (1988) Runo 40:83-88.
70. Friberg (1988) Runo 40:89-94.
71. Friberg (1988) Runo 40:122-123.
72. Friberg (1988) Runo 40:128-131.
73. Friberg (1988) Runo 40:133-136.
74. Friberg (1988) Runo 40:145-146.
75. Friberg (1988) Runo 40:162-166.
76. Friberg (1988) Runo 40:200-204.
77. Friberg (1988) Runo 40:222-229.
78. Friberg (1988) Runo 44:166-179.
79. Friberg (1988) Runo 44:207-211.
80. Editor's note. The Friberg translation gives "king" here, whereas the original Kalevala reads "queen."
81. Friberg (1988) Runo 41:252-255.
82. Friberg (1988) Runo 42:37-40.
83. Friberg (1988) Runo 42:42-44.
84. Friberg (1988) Runo 42:91-94.
85. Friberg (1988) Runo 42:110-112.
86. Friberg (1988) Runo 42:169-172.
87. Friberg (1988) Runo 42:177-179.
88. Friberg (1988) Runo 42:312-315.
89. Friberg (1988) Runo 42:346-353.
90. Friberg (1988) Runo 42:354-370.
91. Friberg (1988) Runo 42:371-376.
92. Friberg (1988) Runo 42:388-391.
93. Friberg (1988) Runo 42:392-399.
94. Friberg (1988) Runo 42:430-435.
95. Friberg (1988) Runo 42:444-457.
96. Friberg (1988) Runo 43:23-33.
97. Friberg (1988) Runo 43:48-53.
98. Friberg (1988) Runo 43:60-64.
99. Friberg (1988) Runo 43:71-72.

100. Friberg (1988) Runo 43:79-88.
101. Friberg (1988) Runo 43:96-97.
102. Friberg (1988) Runo 43:118-127.
103. Friberg (1988) Runo 43:166-175.
104. Friberg (1988) Runo 43:212-215.
105. Friberg (1988) Runo 43:226-228.
106. Friberg (1988) Runo 43:235-242.
107. Friberg (1988) Runo 43:244-250.
108. Translator's note. To understand these two sentences we must realize that Pekka deciphers symbolic meaning here and the interpretation is psychological. The meaning is as follows. When a human being battles against the evil that is within himself, he divides the original unity into two parts; he identifies with the good and expels the evil. In other words, when a human being places himself into the camp of God, it is as if he pushes evil out and away from God.
109. Friberg (1988) Runo 43:273-287.
110. Friberg (1988) Runo 43:377-381.
111. Friberg (1988) Runo 50:441-245.

IV. The Kalevala's Magic

1. *Otava eli Suomalaisia huvituksia* (*The Great Bear or Finnish Entertainment*) part I. Stockholm 1831, pgs. 26-27.
2. See the studies of Henrik Gabriel Porthan, Finnish translation by Edv. Rein. Suom. Kirjallisuuden seura [The Society of Finnish Literature]. Helsinki 1904, pgs. 173-207.
3. Editor's note. Regarding divining by lottery: "In divining by lot, a chip of wood was put into the center of what may be called a riddle box. The bottom of this was divided into squares, each of which was marked by a sign of something that would point to an answer such as wind, water, forest, witch. As the question was being asked, the box was shaken so that the chip moved about. The square on which the chip settled gave the answer" (Friberg 1988:397).
4. Friberg (1988) Runo 11:75-78.
5. Friberg (1988) Runo 12:441-460.
6. Friberg (1988) Runo 7:282-285.
7. Friberg (1988) Runo 7:308-310.
8. Our famous historian Yrjö Koskinen says: "At least it should be remembered that the name *Suomi, Same* does not belong only to the modern Finnish nation [Suomi means Finland in the Finnish language], but might have extended over all the Finnish families in ancient times. If we now wish to summarize what was said earlier, great advances have been made in our historical understanding: The ancient Turanians had great power in the area between Sind and the Euphrates. That the Turanians belong to the Finnish family is speculation, though imminently probable; linguistic

analysis points to it, and studies of ancient cuneiform scripts lean to that side... But as for a final judgement, it is notable that the Finnish language and Finland's ancient poetry, both of which seem to rest on some foundation of ancient culture, will determine much in this course of study." *Tiedot Suomensuvun muinaisuudesta*, (*Knowledge Concerning the Antiquity of the Finnish Family*), Helsinki. (Koskinen 1862:18-19).

9. In his study called *Hafva Lappar och Finnar på skilda tider invandrat till Norden?* (*Did the Lapps and the Finns Wander into the North at Different Times?*), Joh. Ad. Lindström concludes the following: "For the final conclusion of this study we hold the view that the Finns are the oldest people in Europe, and from time immemorial they have ruled its northern lands" (See *Suomi*, 1859, loc. sit., p. 40). It appears that former historians were more courageous in drawing their conclusions than modern ones. Does this depend solely on "the inferiority of their knowledge"? Doctor K. Meijer thought (as Wettenhovi-Aspa does in our days) that some of Europe's original Turanian population came from Africa. Compare this with a passage in the dissertation by Koskinen cited above, page 31. Modern science argues that the earliest inhabitants of Stone Age Scandinavia (about 10,000 years ago) were Lapps, but by the later Stone Age (roughly 6,000 years ago) the population was Germanic. See also C. Grimberg, *Svenska folkets underbara öden* (*The Wonderful Fate of the Swedish People*), I, Stockholm 1913, p. 20. That these later human beings had long skulls does not prove in our minds that they were Germanic, because the Finns—at least the Karelians and Kainuans—also have long skulls.

10. Friberg (1988) Runo 18:400-403.
11. Friberg (1988) Runo 18:411-414.
12. Friberg (1988) Runo 10:97-101.
13. Friberg (1988) Runo 10:116-118.
14. Friberg (1988) Runo 4:15-20.
15. Friberg (1988) Runo 4:22-30.
16. Friberg (1988) Runo 5:7-12.
17. Friberg (1988) Runo 5:158-168.
18. Friberg (1988) Runo 5:169-181.
19. These lines are extracted from the poem "Angling for Vellamo's Maiden" [Runo 5] but in content they belong to the Aino episode.
20. Friberg (1988) Runo 50:1-4.
21. Friberg (1988) Runo 50:16-25.
22. Friberg (1988) Runo 50:29-33.
23. Friberg (1988) Runo 50:38-41.
24. Friberg (1988) Runo 50:69-74.
25. Friberg (1988) Runo 50:89-112.
26. Friberg (1988) Runo 50:113-115.
27. Friberg (1988) Runo 50:148-150.
28. Friberg (1988) Runo 50:174-178.

29. Friberg (1988) Runo 50:270-272.
30. Friberg (1988) Runo 50:299-301.
31. Friberg (1988) Runo 50:302-306.
32. Friberg (1988) Runo 50:381-386.
33. Friberg (1988) Runo 50:392-395.
34. Friberg (1988) Runo 50:396-400.
35. Friberg (1988) Runo 50:402-407.
36. Friberg (1988) Runo 50:410-413.
37. Friberg (1988) Runo 50:414-417.
38. Friberg (1988) Runo 50:418-421.
39. Friberg (1988) Runo 50:422-427.
40. Friberg (1988) Runo 50:428-431.
41. Friberg (1988) Runo 50:441-450.

V. Väinämöinen's Return

1. Friberg (1988) Runo 50:441-450.
2. Friberg (1988) Runo 50:462-465; 480-485; 536-542; 553-562.

Bibliography

Agricola, Mikael. 1551. *Dauidin Psalttari* (*Psalter*). Mikael Agricola kootut teokset III. See Heininen (1994).

Alighieri, Dante. *La Divina commedia*. See Gennaro (1986).

Besant, Annie. 1994. *The Ancient Wisdom: An Outline of Theosophical Teaching*. Wheaton, IL: The Theosophical Publishing House.

The American Standard Bible, The Open Bible Edition (1977). New York: Thomas Nelson Publishers.

Blavatsky, H. P. 1888. *The Secret Doctrine*. Los Angeles, CA: Theosophy Company.

——1888. "Kalevala, the National Epic of the Finns." *Lucifer*, Vol. III.

——1889. *The Key to Theosophy*. London: Theosophy Company.

——1909. "Suomen kansalliseepos" ("Finland's National Epic"). In the journal *Tietäjä*.

Bosley, Keith (translator). 1989. *The Kalevala: An Epic after the Oral Tradition*. New York: Oxford University Press.

Castrén, M. A. 1839. *Kalevala* (Swedish translation). Helsinki.

——1852-1870. *Nordiska resor och forskningar I-VI*. Helsingfors.

Collan, Fabian. 1838. *Väinämöinen och Ilmarinen, näst Ukko Fornfinnarnas högsta gudar*. Helsingfors Morgonblad.

Comparetti, Domenico. 1898. *The Traditional Poetry of the Finns*. London & New York: Longmans, Green.

Crawford, John Martin (translator). 1888. *The Kalevala: The Epic Poem of Finland*, 2 volumes. New York: J. B. Alden.

Engelberg, Rafael. 1914. *Kalevalan sisällys ja rakenne* (*The Contents and Structure of the Kalevala*). Thesis, University of Helsinki.

Ervast, Pekka. 1913. *Suomen kansallishaltija* (*Finland's National Genius*). Helsinki: Teosofinen kirjakauppa ja Kustannusliike.

——1915. *Jeesuksen salakoulu* (*The Esoteric School of Jesus*). English translation in press, Blue Dolphin Publishing, Nevada City, CA.

———1933. H.P.B.: *Four Episodes from the life of the Sphinx of the XIXth Century*. London: The Theosophical Publishing House.

Friberg, Eino (translator). 1988. *The Kalevala: Epic of the Finnish People*. Otava Publishing Company, P.O. Box 134, SF-00121, Helsinki, Finland, in cooperation with The Finnish North American Literature Society, P.O. Box 4, SF-20541, Turku, Finland. Contact information: http://www.teleport. com/~johnv/

Friis, J. 1871. *Lappisk Mythologi, Eventyr og Folkesagn*. Christiania.

Gennaro, Angelo A. de. 1986. *The Reader's Companion to Dante's Divine Comedy*. New York: Philosophical Library.

Goethe, Johann Wolfgang von. 1808. *Faust: A Tragedy*. English translation by Bayard Taylor, the Washington Square Press paperback edition (1964).

Gottlund, C. A. [1828] 1831. *Vanjohen Suomalaisten viisaus ja opin-keinot* (*The Wisdom and Teaching Methods of the Old Finns*. Stockholm.

———[1828] 1831. *Otava eli Suomalaisia huvituksia* (*The Great Bear or Finnish Entertainment*), part I. Stockholm.

Grimberg, C. 1913. *Svenska folkets underbarra öden* (*The Wonderful Fate of the Swedish People*), I, Stockholm.

Haavio, Martti. 1967. *Studia Fennica*. Helsinki: Suomalaisen Kirjallisuuden Seura.

Hästesko, F. A. *Mielikuvitus ja todellisuus Kalevalassa* (*Imagination and Reality in the Kalevala*).

Heikkinen, Jaakko. 1909. Comments in the Finnish journal *Kotiseutu*.

Heininen, Simo. 1994. *Mikael Agricolan Psalttarin reunahuomautukset*. Helsinki: Suomalaisen Kirjallisuuden Seura.

Hellner, Herman. 1904. *Kalevala ett teosofisk diktvärk* (*Kalevala, A Theosophical Epic*). Teosofisk Tidskrift.

Humu, Martti. See M. Ramstedt.

Kirby, W. F. (translator). 1907. *Kalevala: The Land of the Heroes*. London: J. M. Dent & Sons.

Koskinen, Yrjö. 1862. *Tiedot Suomensuvun muinaisuudesta* (*Knowledge Concerning the Antiquity of the Finnish Family*). Helsinki.

Krohn. Julius. 1885. *Suomalaisen kirjallisuuden historia* (*The History of Finnish Literature*). Helsinki.

———1894. *Suomen suvun pakanallinen jumalanpalvelus*, I (*The Pagan Divine Service of the Finnish Family*). Helsinki: Suomalaisen Kirjallisuuden seuran kirjapainossa.

Krohn, Kaarle. [1904] 1903. *Kalevalan runojen historia* (*The History of the Kalevala's Runes*). Helsinki: Suomalaisen Kirjallis.

———1914. *Suomalaisten runojen uskonto* (*The Religion of Finnish Runes*). Helsinki: Suom. kirj. seura.

———1915. (*The Religion of the Finnish Family*). Helsinki: Suom. kirj. seura.

Leadbeater, C. W. 1912. *The Life After Death, and How Theosophy Unveils It*. Kila, MT: Kessinger Publishing.

Lehtinen, Ildikó (editor). 1986. *Traces of the Central Asian Culture in the North.* Finnish-Soviet Joint Scientific Symposium Held in Hanasaari, Espoo, 14-21 January 1985. Helsinki: Suomalais-Ugrilainen Seura.

Leino, Eino. 1909. *Suomalaisia kirjailijoita (Finnish Authors).* Helsinki: Otava.

Lencqvist, K. S. 1782. *Dissertatio de superstitione veterum Fennorum theoretica et practica (Dissertation on ancient Finnish superstitions in theory and practice).* Turku, Finland.

Lindström, Joh. Ad. *Hafva Lappar och Finnar på skilda tider invandrat till Norden? (Did the Lapps and the Finns Wander into the North at Different Times?).*

Lönnrot, Elias. *Kalevalan esityöt (Preliminary Works for the Kalevala, I. Väinämöinen).*

———1835. *The Proto-Kalevala.*

———1849. *The Kalevala.*

Magoun, Francis P., Jr. (translator). 1963. *The Kalevala; or, Poems of the Kaleva District.* Cambridge, MA: Harvard University Press.

———(translator). 1969. *The Old Kalevala, and Certain Antecedents.* Cambridge, MA: Harvard University Press.

Menzies, Allan. 1910. *Maailman uskonnot (World Religions).* Porvoossa: Werner Soderstrom Osakeyhtio.

Moyne, Ernest J. 1963. *Hiawatha and Kalevala: A Study of the Relationship Between Longfellow's "Indian Edda" and the Finnish Epic.* Folklore Fellows Communications, No. 192. Helsinki.

Porthan, Henrik Gabriel. 1904. Translation (into Finnish) by Edv. Rein. Helsinki: Suom. Kirjallisuuden seura (The Society of Finnish Literature).

Ramstedt, M. *Kalevalan sisäinen perintö (The Inner Testament of the Kalevala).*

Schurtz, Heinrich. 1915. *Kulttuurin alkuhistoria (The Original History of Culture).*

Steiner, Rudolf. 1912. "Das Wesen nationaler Epen mit speziellem Hinweis auf Kalevala" ("The Nature of National Epics with Special Emphasis on the Kalevala"). Helsinki lecture of April 9th, 1912, transcript available from the Rudolf Steiner Library, 211 Madison Avenue, New York 10016.

Suomi. 1859. (A Finnish journal.)

Varonen, Matti. 1895. *Vainajainpalvelus muinaisilla suomalaisilla (The Worship of the Deceased Among the Ancient Finns).* Helsinki.

Additional Reading

Ervast, Pekka. 1983. *Sermon on the Mount: Key to Christianity*. London: Theosophical Publishing House, Rosicrucian Literature Society.

Friberg, Eino. 1926. *Sparks*. Harvard University Press.

——(n.d.) *The Presence*. Manuscript in possession of the editor.

——(n.d.) Collected Poetry. Manuscript in possession of the editor.

Haavio, Martti. 1952. *Väinämöinen, Eternal Sage*. Folklore Fellows Communications, No. 144. Helsinki.

Harva, Uno. 1927. *Finno-Ugric and Siberian Mythology*. The Mythology of All Races Series, IV. Norwood, MA: The Plimpton Press.

Jenkins, John Major. 1996. *Readings from the Kalevala*. Selections from Eino Friberg's 1988 translation of the Kalevala. Louisville, CO: The Sampo Press. P.O. Box 635, Louisville, Co. 80027-0635.

Kennerley, Eija. 1966. Old Rune Singers of Finland. *Folklore* Vol. 77.

Kivi, Aleksis. 1959. *Seven Brothers*, translation by Alex Matson. Helsinki: Tammi Publishers.

Kivi, Aleksis. 1991. *Seven Brothers*, translation by Richard A. Impola. Finnish American Translator's Association. 20 DuBois Road. New Paltz, NY. 12561.

Kolehmainen, John I. 1973. *Epic of the North*. New York Mills: Northwestern Publishing Company.

Kuusi, Matti; Keith Bosley; and Michael Branch. 1977. *Finnish Folk Poetry, Epic*. Helsinki: Finnish Literature Society.

Oss, Alex van. 1994. The Kalevala. In *Legacies: Tales From America*. National Public Radio. Cassette copies available from The Radio Store: 1 (800) 747-7444.

Petaja, Emil. 1966a. *Saga of Lost Earths*. New York: Daw Books.

——1966b. *The Star Mill*. New York: Daw Books.

——1967a. *The Stolen Sun*. New York: Daw Books.

———1967b. *Tramontane*. New York: Daw Books.

Pentikäinen, Juha Y. 1986. The Background to the Finnish Creation Myth. In *Traces of the Central Asian Culture in the North*, edited by Ildikó Lehtinen, pp. 195-212. Finnish-Soviet Joint Scientific Symposium Held in Hanasaari, Espoo, 14-21 January 1985. Helsinki: Suomalais-Ugrilainen Seura.

———1989. *Kalevala Mythology*. Bloomington: Indiana University Press.

Penttilä, Ari. 1994. The Land of Heroes Revisited: A Comparison of Two Recent Translations of Kalevala. In *Finnish Literature in North America: Papers Presented at the First Two Symposia on Finnish Literature in North America, September 21st, 1991 and April 29th, 1992*, edited by Keijo Virtanen, Richard Impola, and Tapio Onnela. Turku, Finland: Institute of History, Cultural History.

Puhvel, Jaan. 1987. The Impact of the *Kalevala* on the Estonian Epic. In *The World of the Kalevala*, edited by Michael Owen Jones, pp. 56-65. Los Angeles: UCLA Folklore and Mythology Publications.

Raivaaja, Finnish American Weekly. Raivaaja Publishing Company. P.O. Box 600, Fitchburg, Mass. 01420-0600. Ph: (508) 343 3822.

Rank, Inkeri. 1987. The Mythology of the Ancient Finns as Reflected in the *Kalevala*. In *The World of the Kalevala*, edited by Michael Owen Jones, pp. 38-55. Los Angeles: UCLA Folklore and Mythology Publications.

Ross, Carl. 1988. The Utopian Vision of Finnish Immigrants: 1900-30. *Scandinavian Studies 60*, pp. 481-496.

Santillana, Giorgio de; and Hertha von Dechend. 1969. *Hamlet's Mill: An Essay on Myth and the Frame of Time*. Boston: Gambit.

Setälä, Emil N. 1932. *Sammon Arvoitus (The Riddle of the Sampo)*. Helsinki: Otava.

Siikala, Anna-Liisa. 1986. Shamanistic themes in Finnish Poetry. In *Traces of the Central Asian Culture in the North*, edited by Ildikó Lehtinen, pp. 223-234. Finnish-Soviet Joint Scientific Symposium Held in Hanasaari, Espoo, 14-21 January 1985. Helsinki: Suomalais-Ugrilainen Seura.

Smirnov, K. A. 1986. The Finns in eastern Europe in the 1st millennium B.C. In *Traces of the Central Asian Culture in the North*, edited by Ildikó Lehtinen, pp. 235-248. Finnish-Soviet Joint Scientific Symposium Held in Hanasaari, Espoo, 14-21 January 1985. Helsinki: Suomalais-Ugrilainen Seura.

Viherjuuri, H. J. 1965. *Sauna: The Finnish Bath*. Brattleboro, VT: The Stephen Greene Press.

About the Author

PEKKA ERVAST was a writer, occultist, and Christian mystic, born December 26, 1875, in Finland, the easternmost and sparsely populated country in the Fennos-Scandia region.

Since early childhood, Ervast searched honestly for truth, often beset by conflict between ideals and reality that prevailed in all walks of life. He sought the real purpose of our existence and how we should honestly live, but he found no answers within his own cultural circle of religion.

During his early university years, Ervast became acquainted with theosophy, and soon after, with the aid of the great Russian writer Lev Tolstoy, Ervast discovered esoteric Christianity.

Ervast has testified that when he followed Jesus' teachings to the best of his ability, he entered a mystical path where totally new worlds opened for him. There he knew the meaning of life and understood human beings not only from this life's view point, but as reincarnating spiritual beings, journeying through the school of this world in order to learn and evolve.

Pekka Ervast's life was not long—he died at 58—but his life's work was all the more significant. During the course of his Theosophical and Rosicrucian activities, he delivered over 800 public lectures, most of them freely without written notes, and often as if answering unuttered questions of his audience. The larger part of Ervast's literary works comprise over a hundred volumes, including his lecture series.

Ervast could speak clearly and intelligibly to the most profound questions related to philosophy, theosophy, and various religions. His message reached searchers of truth equally in all strata of population, and his works have spread to hundreds of thousands of Finnish homes. Through his life's work, he has been and still is a most important inspirer and instructor to his nation—its spiritual teacher.

It is unfortunate for all of humankind that Ervast lived and worked in such a restricted linguistic area and within such a small, isolated country, for he was well versed in all great religions and in several different cultures. As a universal humanist living in truth and love, in basic meditation, he should have been recognized world-wide, spreading light and blessing. This now is our intention and hope.

Printed in the United States
45877LVS00007B/16-21

9 781577 330219